ANSELM AND LUTHER ON THE ATONEMENT

Was It "Necessary"?

Burnell F. Eckardt, Jr.

Mellen Research University Press
San Francisco

Library of Congress Cataloging-in-Publication Data

Eckardt, Burnell F.
    Anselm and Luther on the atonement : was it "necessary"? / Burnell
F. Eckardt, Jr.
        p.   cm.
    Includes bibliographical references and indexes.
    ISBN 0-7734-9825-7
    1. Atonement--History of doctrines. 2. Anselm, Saint, Archbishop
of Canterbury, 1033-1109. 3. Luther, Martin, 1483-1546. I. Title.
BT265.2.E33   1992
234' .5--dc20   92-27796
                                                                      CIP

Editorial Inquiries:

Mellen Research University Press
534 Pacific Avenue
San Francisco
CA 94133

Order Fulfillment:

The Edwin Mellen Press
P.O. Box 450
Lewiston, NY 14092
USA

Printed in the United States of America

To Carol

Only a God-man can make the satisfaction by means of which man is saved.

Anselm of Canterbury, *Cur Deus Homo*

And the Gospel is nothing more than the story of the little son of God and of his humbling, as St. Paul says, 1 Cor. 2,2: I determined not to know anything among you, save Jesus Christ, and him crucified.

Martin Luther, *Church Postil*

Contents

Foreword

Burnell Eckardt's work is distinguished because he is able to treat Anselm and Luther within the framework of their respective historical-theological contexts without using one author to exalt or denigrate the other. So often treatments of a medieval figure are a disguised effort to attack the medieval theologian in order to praise Luther. In other words, an Anselm scholar will appreciate Eckardt's work as will a Luther specialist.

Much of the previous work on Anselm and Luther has been done to highlight Luther vis-à-vis medieval theology, to discover Luther's uniqueness, and/or to show Luther's recovery of biblical-patristic truths at the expense of scholastic distortions. Eckardt offers a critique of such work on the level of both method and content. Those who seek to discredit the adequacy of Anselm's theology from Luther's perspective are themselves seriously challenged in this work.

The style is invigorating, the argument engaging, the question commendably narrowed, the conclusions trustworthy.

The discipline of the study is the history of theology (outside of theology the approach would be considered the history of ideas). The reasons for the selection of authors and subject are amply offered. The study is based on the reading of the Latin texts and addresses the methods of Anselm and Luther as well as their respective understanding of the necessity of the atonement.

The purpose of medieval argument carried out on the level of fittingness (the *decuit* part of *potuit, decuit, fecit*) is clearly understood and presented by Eckardt. Anselm's work has often been misunderstood as philosophical apologetic, subject to epistemological and metaphysical critique; whereas Anselm, working within the given of the church's faith and seeking to understand and serve that faith, sought to show the beauty and suitability of a certain argument for the understanding of the trinity. The use of reason by both Anselm and Luther for the purpose of bolstering faith (*approbatio*) is quite different from modern philosophy.

The position of Luther on the necessity of the atonement is a hotly debated issue in modern Luther research precisely vis-à-vis Anselm. No one is in a better position to sort through the issues than Eckardt. His position has been strengthened by his doctoral training at Marquette University where confessional Luther research has been replaced by the study of Luther in Luther's own historical and catholic context.

Eckardt is able to appreciate and present Anselm and Luther within the framework of their theological agendas. He ably criticizes those who import theological presuppositions not derived from the historical authors themselves. The different approaches of Anselm and Luther are clearly presented. The resultant conclusions about the two historical authors must be read to be appreciated.

Professor Kenneth Hagen   Marquette University

Over the years there have been many books touching upon Anselm's and Luther's doctrine of the vicarious atonement, at times comparing the views of the two great theologians and often drawing the most unfounded and bizarre conclusions. Eckardt's study goes directly and objectively back to two major sources of the doctrine of the atonement as it has been taught in Western Christendom for the last thousand years. He too compares the two great theologians, finding clear differences between them in reference to theological method and doctrinal content, but teaching substantively the same doctrine of the atonement. Eckardt convincingly shows us two things. First, two theologians can treat an article of faith from different perspectives, using different methods, and arrive at a common conclusion. Anselm approached the atonement with a principle of *sola ratione*, fettered only by his tacit understanding of the bounds set by Scripture and the Church Fathers; Luther approached the atonement according to his principle of *sola scriptura*. They arrived at the same conclusion. This fact has bothered many scholars as they have tried to delineate and compare the two theologians' positions; but it is a fact, nevertheless, just as is often seen in the enterprize of engineering or accounting, etc. Second, Eckardt shows us that two theologians, both of whom consider theology as an organic whole, can have a radically different doctrine of man and of sin, and teach essentially the same doctrine of the atonement. One can call this a felicitous inconsistency, or whatever, but it is a fact, nevertheless. But Eckardt's greatest contribution is simply to offer the reader the position of two great theologians on the central article of the Christian faith.

Robert Preus

Concordia Theological Seminary
Fort Wayne, Indiana

Preface

There will never be a topic more worthy of research than the doctrine of the atonement, which we find at the heart of the mystery of the Christian faith. Many have, to be sure, argued that at the heart of the faith we ought rather place the incarnation of our Lord. But inasmuch as the atonement presupposes the incarnation, I believe the former to be more encompassing and at the same time focused, as a topic of study. This was doubtless the presupposition of Blessed Anselm of Canterbury, whose celebrated study on the atonement is named *Cur Deus Homo*, a name which, while emphasizing the incarnation, drives attention to the question of the incarnation's purpose, the *cur* of the *deus-homo*. Without the incarnation there can be no atonement, but without the atonement, any emphasis on the incarnation will be found wanting, bereft of its end. Indeed God became man in order that man may become divine, yet even this familiar patristic λόγιον presupposes the need for man to become divine, that the image of God in which he was once created was in need of restoration, due to the serpentine deception of Eve into thinking that she needed to become like God, an effectual renunciation of her creation in his image.

Such discussions sound perhaps a bit archaic for much of twentieth- or twenty-first century scholarship steeped as it so often is in the foundations of nineteenth-century thought. But theological scholarship aiming at a true catholicity in perspective will inevitably have to come to terms with that vast world of Christian thinkers of antiquity, to say nothing of the holy apostles and prophets themselves. Antiquity is something the nineteenth-century and its heirs have tended all too often to leave untouched, or to consider antiquated. It is refreshing to see an emerging trend in more recent years toward a recovery of what was lost, both in exegetical and in historical circles. The present study is offered in hopes of doing some small part toward encouraging that renaissance.

This study actually began with a consideration, not of St. Anselm, but of Martin Luther. I found in his *theologia crucis* a perspective which has proven to be an invaluable touchstone for the application of theological thought to Christian experience, the integration of faith and life. The cross of which Luther speaks is at once the cross of Jesus and the cross of one who follows him.

This integration can be seen as well in the method of Luther as in his message. His language is that of one held so captive to the Word of God that at times one is hard-pressed to distinguish his words from those he recites from the Sacred Scriptures. The use of quotation-marks around sections of Scripture he employs is an editorial addition by the Weimar editors; Luther himself was not as inclined to see the need for setting the words of the Bible apart from his own message. I was impressed by the sense of urgency which attaches itself to Luther's words, and I soon began to see a reason for this emerging: it appears that for Luther the necessity of the atonement itself appears somehow to be fully integrated with what Luther evidently saw as a necessity for the preaching of Christ to the people. This, I then determined, was truly worthy of further investigation.

But when I first determined to do this research, I was led soon to discover to my dismay that in order to do it full justice I would have to research at least the entire medieval era, and perhaps much more, surveying every major figure until Luther's day. What began as an attempt to learn Luther's position on the necessity for the atonement soon evolved into a discovery that Luther's entire approach to theology must be taken into account, and that his approach or method is at variance in some way with that of practically every medieval figure, regardless of theological orientation. Now it was no longer such a simple question that I wished to research. Now I had to ask questions not only of method, but of whether there can be a legitimate concern for faithfulness in method to the catholic tradition and the Sacred Scriptures, and if so, what does faithfulness in method mean, and whose method is faithful. Realizing (with the help of able advisors) that such a task would require much more effort than the scope of a doctoral dissertation was supposed to take, I became rather discouraged, until I came upon a recent article by Risto Saarinen of the University of Helsinki, in which he admits to having come upon the same problem. "Today," writes Saarinen, "it is practically impossible to present any aspect of Luther's theological output without a lengthy survey of its historical and philosophical background" (Saarinen 1990, 31). So, when I appreciated the fact that every student of Luther must cope with the same difficulty, I determined that this study would simply have to be incomplete in many respects.

The logical choice for a narrowing of scope presented itself rather quickly, since it was St. Anselm of Canterbury who had first given celebrated status to the question of the necessity for the atonement, in his *Cur Deus Homo*. The question of the incarnation (*cur deus homo*), which for Anselm is really a close corollary to the question of the necessity for the atonement, was quickly repeated, in the *De Sacramentis* of Hugh of St. Victor and the *Sentences* of Peter Lombard, and thereafter by those who took it upon themselves to comment on the *Sentences*, as was popular for the next several centuries. But in centuries to come, varying shadows would be cast upon the question itself, as well as upon the method of addressing oneself to the question, due to such matters as the re-discovery of Aristotle in the thirteenth century, the condemnations of Aristotelian logic in 1270, differences between the Augustinians and the Thomists, differences between the Thomists and the Scotists, the distinction between *potentia absoluta Dei* and *potentia ordinata Dei*, the razor of Ockham, and the age of the late Nominalists. But I determined that all these considerations must be ignored, if I were to complete this project within a reasonable time-frame and length of manuscript. Thus the present study has taken only the first name on the lengthy list of medieval schoolmen and monks who might shed light on Luther's position on the question of the atonement's necessity. It is, after all, Anselm who was first to deal substantially with the subject, and it is also Anselm in whom the primordial evidence of scholastic method is seen. If one name must be chosen, there is none more fit than Anselm. Therefore the scope of this study was limited to a comparison between his view alone and that of Luther. Perhaps the rest can come later.

Indeed the completion of this project already has me looking toward the next. Narrowing one's scope is sometimes a painful process, for it forces one to leave some very tempting stones unturned. The question I must ask myself now, at the completion of the present study, is which of those to return to. The answer will not come easily, for each is enticing. There are, besides the several considerations I ignored in the narrowing of this study, some new questions the study itself has raised. In giving attention to a comparison of Anselm to Luther, I have found some compelling reasons for taking one or the other separately. Anselm was a man of prayer and contemplation, while Luther was a man of proclamation. Much more could be said, on the one hand, about the profound reverence for the incarnation seen in Anselm's meditations and prayers, about which I was forced to say only a brief word in what follows herein. Many of Anselm's *orationes* might at first sound offensive to readers whose traditions do not include the invocation of saints, but one wonders just what was his purpose in praying to the Blessed Virgin, or to St. John the Baptist, or to St. John the Evangelist, or to St. Stephen, when discovering at length his prayer to the wood of the cross, for Anselm was surely not *literally* invoking something inanimate. There was a prevailing vein of thought in Anselm's day which considered all things to be in some way alive to God, even including stones and wood, and thus fit for communing with. The question of the obediential potency of all things created would have to be researched and understood in order to grasp Anselm's prayer to the wood of the cross. Prayers in this perspective tend more toward being meditations than actual invocations. Indeed the whole question of what is or ought to be meant by meditation is one toward which Anselm's perspective could contribute much. One discovers in his prayers and meditations a rather uncanny sense of proximity to the sacred history, a penetrating grasp of the historicity of Jesus Christ. With this must come at least as it were a mental genuflexion, with the realization that when Anselm spoke of the *deus-homo*, he meant what he said. Delving into a more detailed study of this, I would surely find myself also giving careful attention to the Psalms, as Anselm quite clearly followed the catholic tradition of employing the Psalms in meditation and prayer, as well as in the language of his discourses. I have already done a considerable amount of study on the Psalms and their Christological nature, so I shall be eager at some point to continue the study. The Psalter is that special place in the Sacred Scriptures where theology and doxology are most inextricably wedded.

In Luther's sermons, on the other hand, there is evidence of an equally profound grasp of the need for delivering the words of the faith in the mode of proclamation. This has been given some treatment herein, but much more could be said, especially in terms of application to the realm of preaching in the churches of the present day. It is not enough, I have learned from Luther, to be correct in what one says from the pulpit; one must also give careful attention to *how*, in what sort of words and language, it is said. Some very practical homiletical lessons can be learned from a study of Luther's sermons. By referring often, for example, to the congregation in the second-person plural, rather than exclusively employing the first-person plural, gives the message an air of authority, an implicit encouragement to hold the preaching of the Word sacred. Or again, Luther's frequent practice of doubling a word for special emphasis, as when Christ says, *I, I am the Resurrection*, serves well as an attention-riveting device. But such devices are not gimmicks akin to what has become so common in churches of our day; rather, they are patterns learned from the Sacred Scriptures. The prophets, Christ himself, and the apostolic epistles referred with regularity to the addressees in the second-person. So also, Jesus' words *truly, truly* provide evidence of the method of repetition Luther learned to employ with other words as well. Luther's method, his "how" of preaching, while never itself a topic of his own discourse, would be well worth analysis, as well as sorely needed in a day in which we who are called upon to preach the Gospel still seem to find ourselves methodologically so ill-equipped, in spite of all that has been written about preaching.

It is that "how" which has to some degree also tempered the form of this manuscript. The careful reader will note an instance of this in seeing that there is no effort made herein to use "correct" gender-neutral language. No doubt some will regard this choice as "sexist", though it is certainly not my intention to denigrate women. It is, rather, in keeping with my premises which have me looking rather askance at perspectives which have arisen in the nineteenth-century or afterwards, that I have frequently employed the masculine pronoun generically, as did the entire English-speaking world until only very recently. Here is one instance in which language has not evolved of its own course; rather, contemporary American ideology has forced it rather consciously into this mode. Scholarly writing has thus been forced into some quite unnatural grammatical contortions, all for the worry of offending the politically sensitive.

I wish to express my sincere thanks to Professors Kenneth Hagen and Wanda Cizewski for their guidance, assistance, and at some critical junctures in the course of my research, much needed encouragement. I credit Dr. Hagen's grasp of Luther's thought and Dr. Cizewski's expertise in medieval studies for providing me with the rich soil needed for this fruit of my labors, which might well otherwise have been quite futile.

In addition, I wish to acknowledge the valuable assistance of Dr. Franz Posset in the tedious task of proofreading, especially of the German of the Weimar edition which because of its faithfulness in reproducing the exact spelling of the autographs is often quite inconsistent. It is, furthermore, a great advantage to have a proofreader whose mother tongue is the object of the proofreading.

My thanks also for the encouragement given by compeers, my colleague here in Berlin, the Reverend Pastor David Meyer, without whose support I most likely could not have begun, much less completed, this research; also the Reverend Chaplain Jonathan Shaw, who first directed me to the sermons of Martin Luther which have proved to be my most valuable source material; the Reverend Pastor Karl Fabrizius, fellow candidate at Marquette, whose perpetual prompting kept me at task until its completion; and the Reverend Pastor Paul Grime, also a doctoral candidate at Marquette, who has provided much needed technical assistance to me in the preparation of the final copy. The encouragement of good friends is so easily taken for granted; I have found inestimable the value of having such as these.

For financial support I am most grateful to Mr. John Wiebe and the trustees of the Wiebe Mission Fund, especially the Reverend Doctor Robert Preus, who recommended me for assistance. To Dr. Preus I am doubly indebted, since his support of my work has been so avid as to have resulted also in the sponsorship of the Luther Academy, of which he is chairman, and to which I am also grateful. I can scarcely hope that this modest offering will measure up to such high expectations as his, and I find myself humbled by the thought.

Above all these acknowledgements I wish to thank my dear wife Carol, who in the raising of our five young boys has taken well the additional share of the burden, resulting from and corresponding to those many hours I spent poring over books and manuscript pages. She more than anyone has borne my burdens and so fulfilled the law of Christ.

Soli Deo Gloria!

Berlin, Wisconsin   BURNELL F. ECKARDT, JR.
The Vigil of Pentecost
Anno Domini 1992

Abbreviations

Luther's works

AE   American edition of *Luther's Works* (Philadelphia and St. Louis, 1955-).

AP   *Sermons of Martin Luther*. [American Postil] (Reprint ed., Grand Rapids, Michigan, 1988).

DBD   *Day by Day We Magnify Thee: Daily Readings for the Church Year Selected from the writings of Martin Luther* (Philadelphia, 1982).

LC   Luther's *Large Catechism*

StL   *Martin Luthers sämmtliche Schriften.* St. Louis, 1880-1910).

Trigl.   *Concordia Triglotta: Die symbolischen Bücher der evangelisch-lutherischen Kirche* (St. Louis, 1921).

WA   *D. Martin Luthers Werke.* Kritische Gesamtausgabe (Weimar, 1883-).

WA, Br   *D. Martin Luthers Werke.* Briefwechsel (Weimar, 1930-1948).

WA, TR	*D. Martin Luthers Werke.* Tischreden (Weimar, 1912-1921).
WA, DB	*D. Martin Luthers Werke.* Deutsche Bibel (Weimar, 1906-).

Anselm's Works

S	*Sancti Anselmi Opera Omnia.* Schmitt edition (Edinburgh, 1946).
CDH	*Cur Deus Homo* (Why God Became Man)
DC	*De Concordia Praescientia et Praedestinationis et Gratia Dei cum Libero Arbitrio* (The Harmony of the Foreknowledge, Predestination, and Grace of God with Free Choice)
DCV	*De Conceptu Virginali et de Originali Peccato* (The Virgin Conception and Original Sin)
DG	*De Grammatico* (The Grammarian)
DLA	*De Libertate Arbitrii* (The Freedom of Choice)
DIV	*Epistola de Incarnatione Verbi* (The Incarnation of the Word)
DPSS	*De Processione Spiritus Sancti* (The Procession of the Holy Spirit)
M	*Monologion* (A Soliloquy)
P	*Proslogion* (An Address)

Other works

Migne J. P. Migne, *Patrologia latina.* ˙Paris, 1886.

A note on the references:

In the notes, I have provided in most cases the original from which I have translated. In my referencing of the works of Luther, if the Weimar or St. Louis edition appears first, before the translation I have referenced, it means that I have given my own translation and merely provided the reader with the translation for easy referencing. If the American translation appears first, and the original second, it means that I have used that translation in my manuscript, rather than my own. I have found the translation of Luther's Church Postil by John Nicholas Lenker et al. (reprint, 1988) to be particularly acceptable, and have employed it often. In the case of Anselm, I have provided only the original, from the Schmitt edition. There are two reasons for this. The first is that I was not entirely satisfied with the translations available, and the second is that in some cases the Hopkins translation has been conveniently paginated in a way which corresponds nearly exactly to the pages of the Schmitt edition. For the *De Incarnatione Verbi*, the *Cur Deus Homo*, the *De Conceptu Virginali et de Originali Peccato*, the *De Processione Spiritus Sancti*, the *Epistolae*, and the *De Concordia Praescientiae et Praedestinationis et Gratiae Dei cum Libero Arbitrio*, the pages of Hopkins, volume 3, correspond, generally within a page or two, to the pages of Schmitt, volume 2. For the *Monologion* and the *Proslogion*, the pages of Hopkins, volume 1, correspond, more roughly, to the pages of Schmitt, volume 1. Scriptural references include parenthetically the Vulgate reference where it differs from the English, for example, Psalm 27 (26).

Chapter I

Introduction

One of the reasons a comparison between St. Anselm of Canterbury (1033-1109) and Martin Luther (1483-1546) is intriguing is that Anselm can be in some ways as captivating a figure as Luther, although the canon of his works is considerably smaller. Anselm was the monk of Bec, thrust against his will into the archbishopric at Canterbury; Anselm was the protagonist on behalf of his poor subjects against a king whose displeasure drove him at length into exile; Anselm was the ascetic, whose disciplined life commanded the undying respect of his students for all that he wrote; Anselm was a man ever desirous of serenity and peace. Contrast Luther, the Augustinian Friar, forced by conviction to oppose what he eventually saw as the prevailing abominations of the ecclesiastical authorities against the Gospel of Christ; Luther was the protagonist therefore on behalf of Christ, his Gospel, and his Church; Luther was a man of robust spirit, of a remarkable energy and drive, who earned respect by the conviction and compulsion with which he taught; Luther was the man of battle, ever seeing the need for the proclamation of the Gospel, and ever aware that this proclamation will bring out the devil against whom battle must be expected. In this contrast between these two figures alone is enough reason for embarking upon the project of comparing them.

But there remains another compelling reason for this study, which provides it with an even better justification. It so happens that among twentieth century scholars who wish to regard the thought of Martin Luther as being in some sense akin to their own, there is a clear tendency to pass negative criticism on Anselm. In particular his presentation of the atonement as vicarious satisfaction has come under fire, and in general his thought has been panned, with a few notable exceptions. Anselm is generally caricatured as a legalist, emphasizing justice over love. McIntyre (1954) laments that "no major Christian thinker has suffered quite so much as St. Anselm from the hit-and-run tactics of historians of theism and soteriology" (2). At the same time, particularly those Luther scholars rejecting the "Anselmic" vicarious satisfaction have shown a tendency to portray Luther as one whose views were likewise irreconcilable with those of Anselm. This is of course understandable, being preferable to an admission by a Luther scholar that his own thinking might be at odds with Luther's, which is what one would have to do were he to admit that Luther and Anselm show substantial correspondence in their respective views on the atonement. So it has been, ever since the nineteenth century, that certain influential scholars could always be found who have wrenched Luther and the vicarious satisfaction apart, condemning Anselm, whom they call the father of the vicarious satisfaction, and praising Luther as their own father.

The debate appears to have begun in earnest in the nineteenth century, when Johann Christian Konrad von Hofmann (1810-1877) opposed the "orthodox doctrine of vicarious satisfaction" as biblicism in the name of a *heilsgeschichtliche* theology (see Forde 1969, 3). Hofmann (1959, 76) declared that "the saving truth which the Scripture proclaims authoritatively to the Church does not consist in a series of doctrinal propositions," by which he meant doctrinal formulations having to do with the vicarious satisfaction, "but rather in the fact that Jesus has mediated a connection between God and mankind." For Hofmann, the Bible is not "a text book teaching conceptual truths but rather a document of an historical process," that is, *Heilsgeschichte* (204).

Hofmann was attacked by a number of his "orthodox" colleagues, among them Theodosius Harnack (1886, 339-350), who brought Luther into the debate, attempting to show the latter's adherence to the vicarious satisfaction. This Forde (1969) calls "a fateful step," to which Hofmann responded by working to demonstrate that Luther cannot be associated unambiguously with the doctrine of vicarious satisfaction (57f). Hofmann quoted Luther at great length, in an attempt to embarrass the orthodox (63). He was supported by Albrecht Ritschl (1822-1889), whose approach was not only to debate Harnack over Luther (Forde 1969, 81), but also to attack Anselm (Ritschl 1966, 4-7). Ritschl made a distinction between the glory and the justice of God in Anselm, saying these are incompatible: the glory of God puts him above man, while the justice of God makes him man's equal; but satisfaction holds only for equals (263f).[1] Therefore, said Ritschl, either Anselm should adhere to the notion of the glory of God and insist that God punish all sinners and allow no satisfaction, or lay emphasis only upon the possibility of satisfaction, thus forcing Anselm's disjunction *aut poena aut satisfactio* upon the author himself (McIntyre 1954, 90).

The twentieth century saw a continuation of the dispute, and although it may be said to have continued in the more muted terms characteristic of twentieth-century debate, it has by no means reached a stalemate (contra Forde 1969, 68, but see Forde 1984, 6f). Chief among the Anselm critics was the Swedish Lutheran Gustaf Aulén, who revived the debate when his *Christus Victor* was published in English, in 1931. Aulén's division of the Christian views on the

---

[1]Actually, Ritschl does include here a like criticism of Luther as well, indicating that his misrepresentation of Luther is not as gross as Forde's, for which see further on p. 5.

atonement according to their imagery in interpretation of it has gained considerable renown, enough to suggest that his work may be considered a twentieth-century classic.[2] At one end of Aulén's spectrum is what he calls the Latin view, characterized especially by Anselm, and at the other end is the so-called "classical" view, for which Aulén claims the support of Irenaeus and Martin Luther.[3] The division of atonement theories along these lines labels the Latin view as the "legal satisfaction" view.

> The Latin idea of penance provides the sufficient explanations of the Latin doctrine of the Atonement. Its root idea is that man must make an offering or payment to satisfy God's justice; this is the idea that is used to explain the work of Christ.(Aulén 1969, 82)

Aulén contrasts this against his understanding of the classical view, which interprets the atonement in terms of a cosmic battle in which the forces of good win victory over the forces of evil.[4] The success of this monograph has given new life to the older attempts of Hofmann, Ritschl, and company to contend for a fundamental and irreconcilable separation of Luther from Anselm. Indeed one wonders, upon reading more recent uncritical repetitions of this contention, whether *Christus Victor* may have served virtually as a source document supporting these claims.

---

[2]In his introduction to the paperback edition (Aulén, xi), Jaroslav Pelikan makes reference to the work as "a modern classic."

[3]Without debating whether Aulén has overstated his case, let it be acknowledged that the making of distinctions in atonement theories along the lines he has put forward is certainly a valid exercise, even if one does not wish to make these distinctions in as sharp and mutually exclusive terms as he has.

[4]"The Word of God, who is God Himself, has entered in under the conditions of sin and death, to take up the conflict with the powers of evil and carry it through to decisive victory. This has brought to pass a new relation between God and the world; atonement has been made. The mercy of God has delivered men from the doom which rested upon them" (Aulén 1969, 32).

Among the more recent critics is Jürgen Moltmann, who rejects traditional Christological formulations altogether in favor of his radical kenotic Christology (see Scaer 1976, 213; Eckardt 1985, 22-25). Yet Moltmann, while dismissing Anselm's terms as radical (Moltmann 1974, 260, 261) makes bold to contend for the support of Luther (70f et passim). Some of Moltmann's favorite terms--crucified God, theology of the cross--have been borrowed from Luther. Although Moltmann is not entirely uncritical of the Reformer (72f), it is nonetheless beyond dispute that he wishes to be seen as one building his own 'theology of hope' from Luther's ideas.

The 1984 re-publication of F. W. Dillistone's 1968 study on the atonement likewise cast aspersions on Anselm's view while praising Luther. Echoing the earlier contentions of Sir Richard Southern, Dillistone sees the *Cur Deus Homo* as the product of a cultural milieu characterized by feudalism and monasticism, giving Anselm no credit for the ability to take from his images without being subject to them. The *Cur Deus Homo*, he contends, is impressive "if set in the midst of medieval feudalistic conceptions of authority, of sanctions and of reparation" (1984, 193). Martin Luther, on the other hand, though also seen as a child of his times, is likened nonetheless to none other than St. Paul himself (370-376). Luther's struggles are praised as a reaffirmation of his identity "within the pattern of the Cross" (376).

Among others who have made references to the supposed incompatibility of Luther and Anselm is Joseph Burgess (1985), who claims that the "satisfaction" theory of atonement, though not originating with Anselm, is nonetheless not compatible with justification by faith (98).

But most mischievous of all is Gerhard Forde, who in the new ELCA dogmatics text (1984) clearly shows his own bias, taking great pains to demonstrate Anselm's great deficiency when compared to Luther, on the basis of the claim that the vicarious satisfaction is more unique to Anselm. To Forde,

who claims to be opposed to any attempt to capture the significance of the
atonement in theories (leading us to wonder how he can be left with anything at
all to say about it), Anselm has erred in pitting justice against mercy, a complaint
coming near to Ritschl's contention. When Anselm insists that the demands of
justice must be fulfilled before God can be merciful, Forde claims that he
removes from God any opportunity to be merciful. "If God has been satisfied,
where is God's mercy?" (23) On the other hand Luther, as Forde reads him, has
set the matter straight.

> Luther's treatment points the way to overcome the old antitheses in
> atonement doctrine: satisfaction versus victory, objective versus
> subjective. . . .
> Luther's achievement points us in the proper direction. Its abiding
> merit is the great reversal: Atonement occurs when God succeeds, at the
> cost of the death of the Son, in getting through to us who live under
> wrath. (59)

Perhaps Forde's treatment is the most annoying because it is most clearly an
effort to put words into Luther's mouth, words which are in fact more convincing
of Forde's antagonism towards the Anselmian view than of his accuracy in
representing Luther here.

I believe that most of this criticism is misguided and uninformed. Anselm
needs to be defended against it. Further, notwithstanding the "Lutheran"
approach many of them claim, it is evident to me that these scholars have
seriously misread Luther as well as Anselm on some crucial points. In particular,
Luther's teaching on the "Anselmic" vicarious satisfaction needs to be reiterated-
-and this can easily be done--in response to more recent misinterpretations of him.
Aulén's denial of Luther's agreement with the *satisfactio vicaria* is simply
incorrect, and must be confronted. So also is his refusal to see how high is the
christology of Anselm. In terms of theological substance, the positions Luther
takes on isolated subjects tend by and large to agree with those which Anselm had
taken some four hundred years earlier, at the start of the scholastic era. If

stylistic and methodological matters can be temporarily discounted, the general agreement of Luther and Anselm on traditional christological issues is not difficult to demonstrate. Anselm's answer, *per se*, to the question of the incarnation's necessity, together with his expressed christological thought in general, may in most aspects be said to appear indistinguishable from the position, *per se*, which Luther would take over four centuries later. It is not here that most of the major differences between Anselm and Luther are to be found.

There is one exception, and it is significant, so should be noted briefly here. On the question of the essence or precise definition of sin, Anselm and Luther are fundamentally at variance with one another. Anselm's definition of sin as privation of justice forces him to deny that concupiscence is sin, thus indicating a definitive incompatibility here with Luther. This does figure largely into what more conspicuous differences they do have, as we shall see.

But Aulén's contrast of Luther against Anselm was really made at altogether the wrong level. The most prominent points of contrast between Luther and Anselm are found in the realm of prolegomena, and specifically in the areas of method, approach, and intention; the predominating differences between them are not to be found by considering doctrinal substance alone. The reason Anselm and Luther appear to some to bear contrasting views, in areas where it is really misleading to say they disagree, is their respective differences in approach. Here, where Anselm appears to be the forerunner of the entire scholastic era, it can quickly be seen that he and Luther are very dissimilar. This is not accidental. Luther's method does not differ simply because of something as insignificant as his unusual personality. Rather, it is because one cannot consistently adhere to Luther's thought while operating with the scholastic frame of mind whose first fruits were budding in the works of Anselm. Put another way, Luther and Anselm may be seen to have great similarities if we match in isolation position against position, but Luther's thought as a whole cannot be pushed into an Anselmian mind. Luther's approach, or the structure of his thought, is generally quite different from that of Anselm, whose *sola ratione* principle lay at the root of his well known *fides quaerens intellectum*--faith seeking understanding. This method is not seen in Luther, who was not so optimistic about the results of the inquiry of reason, due to his different understanding of sin's essence. A major portion of this study is devoted to understanding the *sola ratione* methodology, according to which, simply put, all arguments in support of a point are made from reasoned or logical premises, entirely without recourse to any authoritative statements, whether from Scripture or from ecclesiastical tradition.

Anselm's method intentionally fostered a robust exercise of reason. The primary characteristic of this method was a chain-of-reasoning progression of thought, according to which point is built on previous point, ascending a ladder of logical reasoning leading finally to the conclusion which Anselm had set out to prove. Anselm generally determines to lay out his argument *sola ratione* (by reason alone), known in the *Cur Deus Homo* by the term *remoto Christo* (Christ being removed), to wit, that what is already known of Christ or of his work from Scripture or ecclesiastical tradition is considered off-limits entirely. Once Anselm has done this, he must resort to his only remaining raw material, namely reason. Using reason alone, then, he must construct his case by using one conclusion to lead to another, in a chain-of-arguments form of reasoning. In the course of this method's employment, Anselm posed certain questions to which his own answers were radically different from the answers of many of the later scholastics; yet in the introduction of the method by which these questions were raised and addressed, he was himself partly responsible for their positions so diametrically opposed to his own.[5] Anselm can in this way be seen as the first of the scholastics, because his method in itself suggested the extent to which dialectics may be taken and indeed was taken not only by his irascible adversary Roscelin of Compiègne, but also by the later scholastics. Anselm's *sola ratione* approach was not born of any desire on his part to discredit the authority of Scripture, as anyone at all familiar with Anselm can testify (so Southern 1983). Yet Anselm's approach does appear to belie a lack of the confidence Luther would later manifest in the power and purpose of the Word of God. The apparent differences between Anselm and Luther on the question of the atonement and its necessity can be understood more clearly as differences of method and intentions. In turn, a consideration of Anselm's purpose and method in writing demonstrates a fundamental disagreement with Luther's thought about the power and purpose of the Word of God.

My observations are based in part on a presupposition that purpose is strongly linked to theological orientation, inasmuch as one's theological thought will inevitably have a bearing on his conception of the theological task. If the Word of God is perceived to have internal capability of accomplishing its own ends, then the student of that Word will believe that the Word itself can set the agenda for the theological task, and will even prefer that the agenda be gleaned from the Word; such was Luther's approach. But if this capability is not granted to the Sacred Scriptures, then it must be assumed that the agenda will have to be set by another entity, such as reason.

Both Anselm and Luther need to be examined more carefully, in order to provide a more honest comparison. McIntyre's lament of hit-and-run tactics rings

---

[5]Evans (1989, x) is right, however, in setting Anselm apart from the later scholastics on this score: "Although he loved the unravelling of puzzles, not all of which seem as urgent or central today as they did to his contemporaries, he is never guilty of the trivialization of which Luther and others complained in the work of later mediaeval scholasticism. There is always an issue of perennial concern at the heart of any matter he considers."

true especially once a straight comparison of primary materials is made. There are, to be sure, some significant differences between Anselm and Luther, but these can only be appreciated when their areas of greater agreement are first established. This is why my own treatment shall move from correspondence to contrast.

Luther's Acquaintance with Anselm

Luther was well acquainted with the works of Anselm, as is clear from his marginal notes of 1513-1516(?). Notes from Luther's hand in the edition of Anselm with which he was working indicate that he was quite familiar with the entire corpus of major treatises, as well as a number of letters. Luther includes a brief and tidy summary of the *Cur Deus Homo*, as well as several student's notes on the pages, indicative of a careful study (WA 9, 104-114). The main trouble with these notes is their early date, belonging as they do to a period generally taken to be well before the perceptible onset Luther's formation as the Luther we know. Still, we may be certain that Luther had a well-informed awareness of Anselm. Further, although Luther's references to Anselm in his own works are rare, they are helpful in that they tend to support nicely what this research purports to demonstrate independently of those references, for the most part.

According to the Weimar index, works of Luther containing references to Anselm include a 1518 sermon on penitence, the 1527 preface to the First Epistle of John, a 1536 disputation on justification, a 1542 *pro licentia* Disputation at which Luther presided, the preface to Genesis, written between 1535 and 1545, and commentaries on Psalm 15 and 90, from 1540 and 1541, respectively. Here follows a brief discussion of each.

A Sermon on Penitence (1518)

This sermon is interesting because Luther refers in terms sounding quite like Anselm to a most beautiful kind of uprightness (*speciosissima iusticia*) which can be obtained by intuition and contemplation, which begins to become the love of wisdom, whose beauty is apparent (*cuius pulchritudinem viderat*). This love, he says, is true penitence, which is worthy of absolution. Luther is careful to distinguish an abstract or carnal virtue from a concrete virtue, the latter of which is predicated on the Word of God.[6] Thus it is only as a concrete virtue that Luther refers to love, and thereupon he cites Anselm with approval: "So therefore Blessed Anselm teaches of the ascent to the love of God from the love of good men" (WA 1, 319f).

Lectures on the First Epistle of John (1527)

Here Luther, speaking on I John 2.2 ("He himself is the propitiation for our sins") refers to some teachers who have misunderstood the atonement, supposing that sins can be atoned by works. "Even the most saintly martyr Cyprian" is mentioned among these, as well as Bernard and Anselm. These he numbers among the elect, who have notwithstanding lapsed into some errors (WA 20, 637f).

Disputation on Justification (1536?)

In this disputation Luther is found arguing with and rejecting the scholastic definition of sin, and in so doing, he mentions Anselm by name (WA 39/I,

---

[6]For Luther, this term refers to the Scriptures, whereas Anselm's use corresponds to the Johannine *Logos*. See my discussion in chapter five on the difference between Luther and Anselm on "Word of God."

116:19).[7] This is a key document for a comparison between Luther and Anselm on sin; I will therefore take it up in detail in chapter four, when delineating the points of difference between Luther and Anselm, for it sets forth in no uncertain terms their disagreement on the nature of original sin.

The *Pro Licentia* Disputation of Heinrich Schmedenstede, at which Luther Presided (1542)

This *Promotionsdisputation* of a student of Luther, Heinrich Schmedenstede from Lüneburg, follows the scholastic pattern of point and counter-point, as did the 1536 disputation on justification. In this document is found Luther's reply to the contention that justification cannot be by faith because nobody can say whether the first fathers had the promises of the same word of Christ. Here Luther declares that everywhere in the Scriptures God is seen as one who speaks. The patriarchs did not believe in a God who was mute (*non haberunt Deum mutum*) or who merely does works, but who spoke with them abundantly and daily (*plenum et quotidianum*). Luther goes on from here, citing Anselm[8] in support.

> Now therefore in this way I argue: whenever the Word of God is heard, men are found believing, because, as Anselm has clearly said, Where God has spoken, what is spoken is not without effect; and we see it in the life of the fathers or of the saints. Therefore it is not their life, but the Word of God, which sounded forth from heaven. To add a minor point, Adam, Eve, and Abraham heard the Word of God. Therefore they believed. So also do we hold to the Word of God. It is spoken to us daily through his ministers of his Word and through his sacraments. Truly the papists and

---

[7]Anselm's name appears only in the Hamburg codex.

[8]Actually, the reference is to Isaiah 55.11, but Luther is evidently thinking primarily of Anselm's use of this text.

the Turks have a silent God; therefore they do not believe (WA 39/II, 199:6-14).[9]

Not only does Luther refer here to Anselm, but he also employs some rather Anselmian reasoning not normally characteristic of Luther. Luther's stress upon the patriarchs' trust in God's Word leaves to the reader's assumption the link between the Word of God and the Word which is God, i.e., the Christ. This link is clearly stated in Anselm's *Monologion*, to which Luther is evidently referring here. Anselm there attempts to show *sola ratione* the triune nature of God by reference to the fact that God speaks, and that this self-expression of God is actually another person of the Trinity, viz., the Word.[10]

Preface to Genesis (1535-1545)

Luther here declares that external obedience must follow internal obedience; but the monks (*Monachi*) have inverted this, and have held only to the external, in their monastic way of life. Anselm is mentioned in this connection:

> As Anselm says, they live in a factitious religion (*factitia religione*), which is instituted without a word, by human will. Then they suppose that this external change is to be effected, so that the heart and the whole man is changed. From this hypocrisy necessarily follows. For if the heart is impure, righteousness is a dream (WA 42, 454:22-25).[11]

---

[9]"Nunc igitur ita argumentor: Ubicunque auditur verbum Dei, fiunt homines credentes, quia, sicut et Anshelmus praeclare dixit: Quando Deus loquitur, non frustra loquitur, vide in vita patrum aut sanctorum. Non tam vita eorum, quam verbum Dei, quod eis de celo sonavit, considerandum est. Addam igitur minorem: Adam, Eva, Abraham audiverunt loquentem Deum. Ergo fuerunt credentes. Talem Deum verbosum nos quoque habemus. Loquitur nobiscum quotidie per ministros sui verbi et sacramenta sua. Papistae vero et Turcae mutum habent Deum; ergo non credunt."

[10]This actually appears to me as something of a *Fremdkörper* in Luther, a rather remarkable instance of his use of a bit of Anselmian logic.

[11]"Sicut Anselmus vocat, vivunt in factitia religione, quae sine verbo, humano arbitrio est instituta. Deinde statuunt hanc externam mutationem hoc effecturam, ut mutetur cor et totus homo, hinc necesse est sequi hypocrisin. Cum enim corda impura sint, somniant iustitiam."

What Luther sees in Anselm as a disapproval of the monastic silence here gains his approval, in spite of Anselm's own penchant for asceticism and monastic solicitude.[12]

Commentary on Psalm 15 (1540)

Here again Luther cites with approval Anselm's rejection of the *factitia religio*. God, says Luther, acts without respect to merit (*sine respectu ullorum meritorum*), whether religious merit or anything like it. Confidence in merit condemns, being self-appointed (as it has no sanction of Scripture). So therefore, "as Anselm says, the practice of religions (*factitiae religiones*) pertains to the theology of the devil" (WA 40/III, 439).[13]

Commentary on Psalm 90 (1534-5)

Here Luther simply cites with approval Anselm's declaration that Adam and Eve were Christians, and that after the Fall they were recalled to life (WA 40/III, 507:3-4; AE 13, 90).[14]

---

[12]I have not located a reference anywhere in the works of Anselm to this *factitia religio*, nor is there a reference in Evans' concordance to Anselm's works. See note 13, below.

[13]"ut Anshelmus vocat, factitiae religiones pertinent ad theologiam Diaboli."

Although I have not found this *factitia religio* anywhere in Anselm, there is a vaguely related reference in Anselm's Epistle 177, which does not appear, however, among the works to which Luther is known to have had access (WA 9, 105-6). This is a letter to a Bishop Osmund, of Salisbury, in which he instructs him to compel the daughter of the king of Scotland to return to the religious order which she left. In the letter he dares to call her a daughter of perdition, and says that the devil (*diabolus*) has made her lay the clothing of religion (*velamen religionis*) aside and shamelessly makes her to remain in a secular habit (Letter 177, S III, 60-61). The trouble with this reference is that it seems to portray in Anselm nearly the opposite perspective from that which Luther attributes to him in his "Preface to Genesis" reference. Possibly Luther was mistaken in attributing comment on the *factitia religio* to Anselm.

[14]"Anshelmus colligit alibi, quod Adam et Eva fuerint Christiani et quod post lapsum statim revocari ad vitam." Cf. CDH II:16.

These references, which may be said to exhaust the index to the Weimar edition,[15] may be summarized in some brief observations.

First, Luther's general attitude toward Anselm can be gleaned from these references. His approval of Anselm in six of these eight references suggests clearly that it is not in keeping with the facts to contend for a fundamental doctrinal chasm between them; on the other hand his disapproval of Anselm in two instances indicates that he was certainly not as enamored with him as was, say, Karl Barth. His reference, in his lectures on First John, to Anselm as one who erred but who is considered nonetheless elect, demonstrates a certain respect for him within limits. In the first two references above, Anselm is referred to as "Blessed," whereas the title is dropped subsequently, but the scantiness of references precludes the assignment of significance to this.

Secondly, the fundamental disagreement between Luther and Anselm on original sin is shown beyond doubt in the Disputation on Justification, to be taken up in detail in chapter four.

Thirdly, Luther's reference to Anselm in his sermon on penitence shows his awareness of a key to understanding Anselm, namely the latter's recognition of the value of beauty. He approves of this concept in this sermon, though it would certainly not be considered a common theme in Luther.

Fourth, the Anselmian argument rather uncharacteristic of Luther in the disputation of 1542 demonstrates not only a continued respect for Anselm even in Luther's later years, but a continued understanding of him as well.

---

[15]There is an additional, rather obscure reference in WA 4, 140 (AE 11, 294), where Luther refers to a Blessed Anselm's fable of the puppy and the hound (*similitudo catuli et molossi*), which reference I have not located in Anselm, though he was well known for his storytelling. It is probably a reference to the anonymous proverb, "The puppy is whipped so that the hound may be afraid." See AE 18, 145; WA 13, 171:30-31. AE 18, 145 makes an erroneous reference to Juvenal, *Satires*, VI, 122.

Fifth, Luther's two references in his commentaries to the *factitia religio*, to which, he contends, Anselm is opposed, indicates a willingness in Luther to derive aid from Anselm the monk in his own rejection of the monastic distortions of Christian life.[16]

Having made these observations, I wish now for the most part to lay them aside, for the following comparison of Luther to Anselm is one of substantial agreement or disagreement, which in order to be fair might do better to consider each on his own terms, rather than on the terms of each other.

---

[16]Whether or not Luther is in error in attributing to Anselm a discussion of the *factitia religio* (see note 12, above) is irrelevant, since we are not dealing at this point with Anselm himself, but with Luther's perception of Anselm.

Chapter II
Points of Correspondence

Correspondence, Looking from Anselm to Luther

While attempting to deal with general correspondence between these two figures, I discovered that some areas of correspondence are easier to track when looking from Anselm to Luther, that is, examining Anselm first, and thereupon to note Luther's general agreement, while other areas of correspondence are easier to track conversely, looking from Luther back to Anselm. Whether an issue is easier to consider looking from Anselm to Luther or vice-versa depends, of course, on which of the two considered the issue in itself a more central concern. For Anselm, sin's reality and universality are of central importance as foundation-blocks for his argument for the vicarious satisfaction. So also is the justice of God, i.e., that attribute of God which requires that he always act in accord with what is right and proper, as the Supreme Judge that he is, and never otherwise. While these are, to be sure, issues on which Luther can compromise no less, they are nonetheless for him not linch-pins, not focal points. Necessary and indispensable ancillaries might be a more appropriate label for them in Luther's thought.   For Luther, what is more of a guiding motif—Aulén's Lundensian approach to research has some merit, within limits—is his doctrine of Christ.   Luther stresses his high Christology with regularity and vigor; it is as it were a fortress from which some of his heaviest ordnance is deployed.   So also is faith, to which Luther's words continually encourage the reader.   Luther employs a variety of means of doing this, which he generally derives directly from his exegesis.   Not least among these, for example, is the *fröhliche Wechsel* —the happy exchange—which he employs in several creative ways, for the chief purpose of instilling in the reader/hearer a robust faith.   So it is easier to treat sin's reality and universality, as well as the conviction that God is just, from the Anselm-to-Luther angle, while Christology and faith can best be examined looking from Luther-to-Anselm.   Recognition of this is an aid to comprehending what is at the root of the differences between Anselm and Luther, when we reach that point of consideration, which is why it has been necessary to point to it here. The difference in critical stress points will correlate with the more significant differences to be discussed.

Further, what Anselm has to say on the atonement is generally better understood than what Luther has to say, by those scholars who compare the two; the stretching of matters to fit into the mold of their supposed antithetical views generally happens more on the Luther end.   Misunderstandings of Anselm usually spring from a failure either to take his method into account or to understand it. But there is no major disagreement among scholars about what Anselm meant by vicarious satisfaction.   This is no doubt primarily because of the neatness of Anselm's method when compared to that of Luther.   There is also a reason for this comparative neatness, which should become more readily apparent within the confines of our discussion of methodological differences.

Anselm generally argues from certain premises to his conclusions, and puts forth every effort to make the argument air-tight, as is most evidently the case in the *Cur Deus Homo*, his major treatise on the vicarious satisfaction and its necessity. Evans (1978) rightly asserts that "it is only by querying Anselm's first principles that it is possible seriously to question his conclusions" (10).

The premises, in order, of Anselm's argument in the *Cur Deus Homo* can well be listed and summarized simply as 1) sin, 2) God's justice, and, 3) the vicarious satisfaction. In looking from Anselm to Luther, I have therefore chosen this order.

(~1) Sin

Sin, as Ritschl (1966, 327) puts it, "is the negative presupposition of reconciliation." Both Anselm and Luther emphasized the seriousness of sin, and although they bear fundamental disagreement over the precise nature of sin, Anselm calling it a privation of original rightousness and Luther in general agreement with the Augustinian expression of sin as the vice of concupiscence, a morbid quality of the soul, nonetheless they agreed in seeing sin as necessitating the redemptive work of Christ. For Anselm, death has been sin's consequence since the fall of Adam (CDH I:3; S II, 51:5-6).[1] Indeed, if man had not sinned, God ought not to have required him to die (CDH I:9; S II, 62:3-4).[2] The human race is consequently called *massa peccatrix*—a sinning mass (e.g., CDH I:5, S II, 52:17; DCV 1, S II, 140:4). The reality of sin is assumed and emphasized especially in response to the suggestion of Boso, Anselm's interlocutor in the *Cur Deus Homo*, that perhaps a single act of remorse could

---

[1] "Per hominis inoboedientiam mors in humanum genus intraverat—Through the disobedience of man death entered the human race."

[2] "Patet quia, si non peccasset homo, non deberet ab eo deus mortem exigere—It is clear that if man had not sinned, God ought not to have exacted death from him."

blot it out. Following comes Anselm's famous reply, *"nondum considerasti, quanti ponderis sit peccatum*—you have not yet considered how weighty a matter is sin" (CDH I:21, S II, 88:18). Sin, moreover, covers the entire human race, including even the Blessed Virgin, who was born with original sin "because she sinned in Adam, in whom all have sinned" (CDH II:16; S II, 116:21-24).[3] In his *De Libertate Arbitrii* Anselm upheld Augustine's anti-Pelagian *non potest non peccare*: "Certainly as no will was able before it had rectitude to seize it if God did not give it, so also by forsaking what it received, one is not able to regain it unless God restores it" (DLA 10; S I, 222:10-14).[4]

Luther clearly agreed with these thoughts, although he does not spend much effort discussing sin in the abstract. One generally finds his substantial agreement with Anselm on the culpability of sin before God more in the clear assumptions he makes than in extended explanations, with the most notable exception being his catechisms. Yet even there, it is his primary concern not generally to assert that all are sinners, but rather to bring readers to recognize their own sin.

Perhaps the easiest reference from which to ascertain Luther's view is the catechism. With regard to the Ten Commandments, Luther affirms that no one

---

[3]"Virgo tamen ipsa unde assumptus est, in iniquitatibus concepta est, et in peccatis concepit eam mater eius, et cum originali peccato nata est, quoniam et ipsa in ADAM peccavit, in quo omnes peccaverunt—Nevertheless the Virgin from whom he was assumed, was conceived in iniquities, and in sin did her mother conceive her, and with original sin she was born, because she sinned in Adam, in whom all have sinned."

According to Anselm, the purity of the mother of Christ is not the means by which he himself is pure (CDH II:16; S II, 119:34-35), but rather she is purified by his future death (CDH II:16; S II, 120:4). She was cleansed by faith (*per fidem*) before his conception (DCV 18, S II, 159:23-24). In spite of this denial of the immaculate conception, Anselm gives clear dedication to the most honorable estate of Mary, and even invokes her (there are three extant *Orationes ad sanctam Mariam*, S III, 18-25). His Marian devotion springs out of a deeply incarnational theology.

[4]"Quippe sicut nulla voluntas, antequam haberet rectitudinem, potuit eam deo non dante capere: ita cum deserit acceptam, non potest eam nisi deo reddente recipere."

can keep any one of them, (LC Concl.; Trigl., 670)[5] since the Ten Commandments are "so high that no one can reach them by human strength" (LC Concl.; Trigl., 672).[6] In explaining the abundant provision of God under the Creed, Luther declares that "we sin daily with eyes, ears, hands, body and soul, money and goods and with everything we have" (LC Creed, Art. I; Trigl., 682).[7] Indeed, even one who has "begun to believe" cannot keep the Ten Commandments perfectly (LC Lord's Prayer; Trigl., 696).[8] Our flesh is "foul and inclined to evil, even if we have accepted God's Word and believe" (LC Lord's Prayer, Third Petition; Trigl., 714).[9] The petition of the Lord's Prayer on forgiveness is necessary to Luther because "if [God] does not forgive without letting up, we are lost" (LC Lord's Prayer, Fifth Petition; Trigl., 722).[10] This is why without Baptism "we cannot be saved" (LC Baptism; Trigl., 732).[11] Further, to any who experience no hunger for the Sacrament of the Altar, Luther's well-known advice is that they "reach into their bosom, to see whether they yet also have flesh and blood" (LC Sacrament of the Altar; Trigl., 770),[12]

---

[5]"Kein Mensch es so weit bringen kann, dass er eins von den zehn Geboten halte, wie es zu halten ist, sondern noch beide der Glaube und das Vaterunser zu Hilfe kommen muss—No one can get so far that he keeps one of the Ten Commandments as it is to be kept, but both the Creed and the Our Father must come to help."

[6]"so hoch sind, dass sie niemand durch Menschenkraft erlangen kann."

[7]"Wir sündigen täglich mit Augen, Ohren, Händen, Leib und Seele, Geld und Gut und mit allem, das wir haben."

[8]"Kein Mensch die zehn Gebote vollkommen halten kann, ob er gleich angefangen hat zu glauben."

[9]"Unser Fleisch ist an ihm selbst faul und zum Bösen geneigt, ob wir gleich Gottes Wort angenommen haben und glauben."

[10]"Summa, wo er nicht ohne Unterlass vergibt, so sind wir verloren."

[11]"Wir uns müssen taufen lassen, oder sollen nicht selig werden."

[12]"in ihren Busen greifen, ob sie auch Fleisch und Blut haben."

and thence to heed St. Paul's description of the flesh in Galatians 5. For Luther, we are "unworthy," and "have deserved wrath and condemnation, and hell also" (AE 31, 298; StL 10, 1265).[13]

Moreover, Luther likewise upheld the Augustinian *non posse non peccare*, as is evident especially from *De Servo Arbitrio* (1525), where Luther refers with approval to Augustine's teaching "that free choice by its own power alone can do nothing but fall and is capable only of sinning" (AE 33, 108; WA 18, 665).[14] Luther admits that Augustine uses the term *liberum arbitrium* in *De spiritu et litera* while he himself does not, but notes that Augustine's use of that term is in reference only to the freedom to sin, and that Augustine's position is essentially the same as his own. Thereupon Luther contends, more in criticism of Erasmus than of Augustine,

> For when it has been conceded and agreed that free choice, having lost its liberty, is perforce in bondage to sin and cannot will anything good, I can make no other sense of these words than that free choice is an empty phrase, of which the reality has been lost (AE 33, 116; WA 18, 670:33-38).[15]

Thus Luther and Anselm are agreed on the extent and sway of sin, that it covers the entire human race, on the culpability of sin before God, that it needs to be

---

[13]Sermon on "Two Kinds of Righteousness" (1518): "Darum ist alles das unser, das der Herr Christus hat, das uns Unwürdigen und Unverdienten alles aus lauter Barmherzigkeit gnädiglich und umsonst geschenkt ist, weil wir doch nicht mehr denn Zorn, Verdammniss und Hölle verdient hätten." This reference, found within a context describing the unmerited mercy of God, provides an example to demonstrate my contention that Luther's discussions of sin are generally set within the context of salvation, rather than as detached or abstract discourses.

[14]Cf. Augustine, *De spiritu et litera*, III, 5: "For Free choice is not capable of anything but sinning if the way of truth is not known." Migne 44, 203 (St. Augustine, vol. 10). Cited in AE 33, 108n.

[15]"Postquam enim concessum ac ratum est, liberum arbitrium amissa libertate cogi in servitute peccati nec posse quicquam velle boni, ego ex his verbis nihil aliud possum concipere, quam liberum arbitrium esse inanem voculam, cuius res amissa sit."

atoned, and that it cannot be overcome by human ability. Luther's disagreement is on the essence of sin, which must be dealt with below.

(~ 2) God's Justice

It is on the matter of God's justice that Anselm has received the greatest criticism. He maintains that God must be just, and that this justice can in no wise be set aside, as it would be unfitting for God to do so. The concept of fittingness is critical to Anselm, whose cognizance of it is precisely what provides the order and structure so characteristic of his works. God must be just because it is fitting for God to be just and Anselm cannot conceive of God otherwise than in connection with what is fitting. "Even the smallest unfittingness in God is impossible" (DIV 10; S II, 26:4).[16]   Forde, (1984) while maintaining that Anselm employed ideas from the realm of law and justice, (22) admits that Anselm's understanding of justice is "the more aesthetically tinged Augustinian concept of *order* rather than strict justice and law" (42). But here Forde is guilty of understatement, for the notion of aestetics is germane to Anselm's approach, inasmuch as beauty is fitting and the lack of it is unfitting. When in the *Cur Deus Homo* Anselm considers the idea of whether God could forgive sin out of pure mercy, without satisfaction, he calls at once upon the notion of what is fitting. "it is certainly not fitting (*non decet*) for God to forgive something inordinate in his kingdom. . . . Nor, therefore, is it fitting for him to forgive sin which is unpunished" (CDH I:12, S II, 69:15-17).[17] Anselm goes on to say, *sola ratione*, i.e., by rational argument unaided by appeals to authoritative

---

[16]"Quamlibet parvum inconveniens in deo est impossibile."

[17]"Deum vero non decet aliquid inordinatum in suo regno dimittere. . . . Non ergo decet deum peccatum sic impunitum dimittere."

statements, that as human justice is subject to law, so if injustice is overlooked, i.e., not subject to law, then it is freer than justice—which is unfitting and therefore cannot be (69:21-30). He concludes his rejection of the idea that God might forgive without satisfaction by standing squarely on the ground of its unfittingness.

> Therefore if it is not fitting for God to do something unjustly or inordinately, so it does not pertain to his liberty or kindness or will to forgive, unpunished, one who does not pay God what he has stolen (70:27-30).[18]

Here Forde (1984) charges that this takes from God even the opportunity to be merciful, for once he receives satisfaction, he is "satisfied" that the demands of his justice have been met, and there is no longer any need for mercy (23).[19] But Forde's charge would only be admissible were Anselm to deny the deity of Christ, since affirming this means considering God to be not only the one who receives satisfaction, but who makes satisfaction, wherein his mercy is clearly demonstrated. Still, although Forde is wrong here, we can at least say that his argument understands Anselm's point about justice. In that sense of mercy which entails leniency of justice, indeed it makes God quite unmerciful. But the mercy of which Anselm speaks is defined otherwise. For Anselm, mercy cannot mean dispensing with justice any more than fittingness or propriety can allow it. It is precisely this point on which Anselm's argument about the necessity for Christ hinges, and without which it collapses. But Anselm is most clear on this issue.

> Therefore, know most certainly that without satisfaction, that is without voluntary payment of the debt, God is neither able to dismiss the sin unpunished, nor can the sinner arrive at happiness, or happiness such as

---

[18]"Quapropter si non decet deum aliquid iniuste aut inordinate facere, non pertinet ad eius libertatem aut benignitatem aut voluntatem, peccantem qui non solvit deo quod abstulit impunitum dimittere."

[19]This is actually a repetition of the charge made first by Ritschl (1966, 262f).

he had before he sinned. For man could not in this way be restored, or become such as he was before he sinned (CHD I:19; S II, 85:28-32).[20]

So there are for Anselm some things not even God can do, not because he lacks ability or strength, but because they are inconceivable for God. He cannot do what is not fitting, not because he is impotent in this regard, but because there is no way he would be found doing what is unfitting. It is in this sense that Anselm contends that God cannot do without atonement if he desires to save his people. There are for Anselm only two options open to God. Either his honor must be repaid or he must punish. Any other option is inadmissible, for the reason that neither of the inescapable conclusions that would result would be tenable: either it would mean that God is not just to himself, or that he is powerless. Both of these conclusions are *nefas vel cogitare*—monstrous even to think of (CDH I:13; S II, 71:24-26),[21] making the atonement the only fitting alternative available. Anselm thus turns on its head the suggestion that he is limiting God. No, he responds, the alternatives are what limit God.

In order rightly to consider whether Luther agrees with Anselm's concept of God's justice, we must acknowledge from the outset that Luther's very definition differs, lest an illegitimate comparison result. Luther insists that when the term "God's justice" is used in Scripture, it is not to be taken to refer to God's self-existing, immanent justice, though he admits that this is the position of many of the fathers; rather, it is that justice, or righteousness, which God

---

[20]"Tene igitur certissime quia sine satisfactione, id est sine debiti solutione spontanea, nec deus potest peccatum impunitum dimittere, nec peccator ad beatitudinem, vel talem qualem habebat, antequam peccaret, pervenire. Non enim hoc modo repararetur homo, vel talis qualis fuerat ante peccatum."

[21]"Necesse est ergo, ut aut ablatus honor solvatur aut poena sequatur. Alioquin aut sibi deus ipsi iustus non erit aut ad utrumque impotens erit; quod nefas est vel cogitare—It is therefore necessary that either the honor taken away be repaid, or that punishment follow; otherwise, either God will not be just to himself, or he will be impotent to do either, which it is monstrous even to think."

gives freely to sinners in the Gospel (StL 11, 16; AP 1, 33).[22] Thus wherever Luther refers to the justice or righteousness of God, his definition is likely to differ from that of Anselm. In order therefore to determine any correspondence of Luther to Anselm's understanding of God's necessary justice, the precise definition must be compared rather than simply the term or like terms. For Anselm, God's justice is that particular attribute of God which prevents him from overlooking sin, as we have seen. This justice is strictly forensic, understood as deriving from the conviction that God is the perfect Judge. It is of penultimate significance to Anselm's conception of the necessity for Christ's vicarious satisfaction. This stage of my analysis therefore requires that this definition of justice be compared with Luther's view, to see if notwithstanding his difference in usage of the term, he would agree with Anselm that God cannot dispense with his rules of forensic justice in dealing with sinners. Are Aulén and Forde correct in saying that Luther's line of thought contradicts the forensic emphasis of Anselm leading to the necessity for the vicarious satisfaction?

Luther's position can be derived from a number of corollary assertions he makes relative to Christ and the removal of sins through him. To be sure, Luther's expression of a position similar to Anselm's is made from an entirely different perspective. He was not given to any form of abstract considerations of necessity, nor to the kind of *sola ratione* reasoning seen in Anselm. Unlike Anselm, Luther tended to look at the revelation itself for verification of the revelation, and evidently felt no need to verify it from the use of Anselm's intentionally blinded (*sola ratione*) kind of reasoned considerations. But if these differences are ignored, for the time being, Luther's essential correspondence in principle with Anselm's understanding of divine justice may be made by reference to a number of related ideas in Luther.

---

[22]Sermon for the First Sunday in Advent.

It is to be remembered that the roots of Luther's theology are often found in what he assumes. Luther admits this on occasion. In *De Servo Arbitrio*, for example, he passes over without elaboration additional arguments which could be made to drive home his point against free choice, arguments which he nonetheless calls "*fortissima*—very strong" (WA 18, 772:36; AE 33, 272). So much of Luther's position can be derived not only from what he directly states, but from what he clearly assumes the reader should already know.

Luther's adamant and repetitive rejection of merits before God indicates his general agreement with Anselm's conception of divine justice. Merits are rejected not because Luther rejects the concept of merit, but because the merits of sinners are unacceptable to God. "We poor sinners obtain the heavenly kingdom through Christ's keys, by the forgiveness of sins, given to us through Christ's death, and not through the merit of our own works" (AE 40, 330; WA 30/II, 470:1-3).[23] Far from being meritorious, every deed of the law, in spite of its outward appearance, is inwardly sin (WA 1, 227:35-36; AE 31, 14).[24] In a sermon on the two greatest commandments (Mt 22:34-46, the Gospel for the first Sunday in Advent), Luther takes pains to point out that attainment of the knowledge of this truth is the very purpose for which the law of God was given. From the law of God we learn that we are unable to fulfill it (StL 11, 1695; AP 5, 178), for God's aim through the law is to force us to see that "no matter how well we try we are unable to fulfill a letter of the law" (StL 11, 1696; AP 5, 180).[25] Therefore one cannot merit the Holy Spirit, "but Christ has earned

---

[23]"The Keys" (1530): "[Das eine himelreich ist das ewige leben,] dazu uns armen sünder die schlüssel Christi helffen durch vergebung der sünden, so uns Christus durch seinen tod und nicht durch unser werck erworben hat."

[24]"Disputation against Scholastic Theology" (1517), Thesis 76.

[25]"Wir auch, so viel an uns ist, nicht einen Buchstaben am Gesetz erfüllen mögen."

and acquired it" (StL 11, 1698; AP 5, 182).[26] Luther's rejection of works,
merits, and the idea of righteousness arising from obedience to the law is due to
his conviction that only Christ's works, merits and righteousness avail before
God.

> What a fine, constructive, and inoffensive doctrine that would be, if
> people were taught that they could be saved by works, as well as faith!
> That would be as much as to say that it is not Christ's death alone that
> takes away our sins, but that our works too have something to do with it
> (AE 35, 197; WA 30/II, 642:30-34).[27]

This conviction leads Luther in his 1535 Galatians commentary to say, "Our sins
are not removed by any other means than by the Son of God given into death,"
and this is because of the very fact that "He *was* given for them" (emphasis
Luther's). On the basis of this revealed truth Luther can say that "we cannot
remove [our sins] by works of our own."   Following this assertion comes
another, sounding very much like Anselm's *nondum considerasti, quanti ponderis
sit peccatum*:

> From this it follows that our sins are so great, so infinite and invincible,
> that the whole world could not make satisfaction for even one of them.
> Certainly the greatness of the ransom—namely, the blood of the Son of
> God—makes it sufficiently clear that we can neither make satisfaction for
> our own sin nor prevail over it (AE 26:32f: WA 40, 83).

Luther's references to the gross insufficiency of our merits, together with his
stress upon the greatness of Christ's merit and ransom, which for him is a clear
demonstration of our inability to make our own satisfaction, certainly find him

---

[26]"Den Geist kannst du dir selbst nicht verdienen, sondern Christus hat ihn dir verdient und
erworben."

[27]"On translating: An open letter" (1530): "O wie solt es so gar ein feine, besserliche,
unergerliche lere sein, wenn die leute lernten, das sie neben dem glauben, auch durch werck frum
möchten werden, Das wer so vil gesagt, das nicht allein Christus tod unser sunde weg neme,
sondern unsere werck thetten auch etwas da zu."

speaking in terms agreeable to Anselm's insistence that the requirements of divine justice must be met.

Luther also bases certainty of salvation upon the recognition that Christ's work is of infinite value, which implies beneath such certainty a realization that this work is necessary under the justice of God. "If I could obtain one, single work, just one-millionth part of the smallest work of Christ, I would be sure of eternal salvation" (AE 31, 221; WA 1, 610:35-37).[28] This conviction of infinite value attached to Christ's work leads Luther to say that it "gives life to the whole world by the destruction of sin" (AE 31, 243; WA 1, 623:38).[29]

In his "Disputation against Scholastic Theology" (1518), Luther contends against the view of William of Ockham who held that God could accept the sinner without justifying grace (WA 1, 227: 4-5; AE 31, 13).[30] Luther's position amounts to a rejection of Ockham's adaptation of Duns Scotus' distinction between *potentia absoluta* and *potentia ordinata*, which is also found in Gabriel Biel. Luther's contention here makes it clear that he, like Anselm, recognizes that there are certain things which not even God can do if he is to be true to himself. But Luther is not hereby saying that God is limited in his potency, any more than such was the case for Anselm. For Luther God could do without his appointed means of doing things, in terms of his ability, but it would be contrary to his will. Luther makes this clear in *De Servo Arbitrio*, where he declares that

---

[28]"Explanations of the Ninety-Five Theses" (1518), Thesis 58: "Ego enim si unicum opus, immo milies milesimam partem unius minimi operis Christi possem obtinere, securus sum et de redemptione aeterna."

[29]"Explanations," Thesis 79: "Christi crux vivificat totum mundum occiso peccato."

[30]"Explanations," Thesis 56: "Non potest deus acceptare hominem sine gratia dei iustificante. Contra Occam."

God could for example impart his Spirit without the Word, but he does not will to work this way (AE 33, 155; WA 18, 695:28-34).[31]

By considering therefore both Luther's recognition of the infinite value of Christ's work and his insistence that no consideration of the *potentia absoluta Dei* is allowable, a view emerges in Luther which begins to look very Anselmian in these respects. Luther bears an implicit agreement with Anselm's insistence that atonement be sufficient according to justice, as is perhaps best seen in his frequent references to the righteousness of faith. By this he means the righteousness which Christ has earned. Faith *per se* is not really sufficient alone; its sufficiency is derived entirely from the sufficiency of Christ in whom it trusts (so Althaus 1966, 232, Siggins 1970, 149, Schlink 1961, 99, Pesch 1972, 25, von Loewenich 1976, 103-6). In his 1518 sermon on "Two Kinds of Righteousness," Luther declares that the "alien righteousness" of Christ is bestowed upon the sinner "from without," and this is "the righteousness of Christ by which he justifies through faith." It is not the believing which in itself constitutes righteousness before God, but rather the Christ in whom one believes, for faith is nothing other than receiving and trusting him.

> Through faith in Christ, therefore, Christ's righteousness becomes our righteousness and all that he has becomes ours; rather, he himself becomes ours. . . . This is an infinite righteousness, and one that

---

[31]"Sic placitum est Deo, ut non sine verbo, sed per verbum tribuat spiritum . . . quae tamen absque verbo facere posset, sed non vult. Iam qui sumus nos, ut voluntatis divinae caussam quaeramus? Satis est nosse, quod Deus ita velit, et hanc voluntatem revereri, diligere et adorare decet, coercita rationis temeritate—It has thus pleased God to impart the Spirit, not without the Word, but through the Word . . . thus doing things that he could of course do without the Word, though he does not will so to do. And who are we that we should inquire into the cause of the divine will? It is enough to know that God so wills, and it is becoming for us to reverence, love, and adore his will, putting a restraint on the rashness of Reason."

swallows up all sins in a moment [*Augenblick*], for it is impossible that sin should exist in Christ (AE 31, 298; StL 10, 1265f).[32]

Luther's placement of so much stress on the fact that this righteousness of Christ is that by which sin is cancelled points to a tacit agreement in principle with Anselm's refusal to skirt the justice of God. To say that Christ's righteousness swallows up sin, and that this righteousness becomes ours through faith is to imply that sin cannot be dealt with except by means of this righteousness. The Anselmian corollary would be to say that God's justice is only satisfied because of Christ's work. Althaus (1966) agrees: "God cannot simply forget about his wrath and show his mercy to sinners if his righteousness is not satisfied. Luther, like Anselm, views Christ's work in terms of satisfaction" (202).[33]

---

[32]"Derhalben wird durch den Glauben an Christum die Gerechtigkeit Christi unsere Gerechtigkeit, und alles, das sein ist; ja, er wird selbst der unsere. . . .

"Dieses ist die unendliche Gerechtigkeit, die alle Sünden im Augenblick verzehrt; denn es ist unmöglich, dass eine Sünde in oder an Christo hafte und hange."

This, says Luther at the outset of this treatise, is the first of the two kinds of righteousness: "The first is alien righteousness, that is the righteousness of another, instilled from without. This is the righteousness of Christ by which he justifies through faith—Die erste Gerechtigkeit ist eine fremde und von auswendig eingegossen, das ist die, durch welche der Herr Christus gerecht ist und durch den Glauben rechtfertigt" (AE 31, 297f; StL 10, 1264).

[33]Anselm here translates, from Luther's 1522 Christmas sermon on Titus 3.4-7: "All this does not take place for nothing or without the satisfaction of God's righteousness; for mercy and grace cannot be thought of as being effective over us and in us or helping us to eternal blessings and salvation unless God's righteousness has previously been completely satisfied . . . for no one can come to God's rich grace unless he has absolutely and completely satisfied God's commandments." This is from WA 10/I/1, 121:16-122:9: "Solchs allis nit umbsonst odder on gnugthun seiner gerechtickeit geschehe; denn der barmherzickeit und gnade ist kein rawm ubir unss und inn unss zu wircken, odder unss zu helffen inn ewigen guttern und selickeit; der gerechtickeit muss zuvor gnug geschehen sein, auffs aller volkomlichst . . . darumb mag niemant zu der reichen gnade gottis kummen, er habe denn gottis gepotten auffs aller eussirst gnugethan."

A second reference Althaus translates as follows: "Now although God purely out of grace does not impute our sins to us, still he did not want to do this unless his law and his righteousness had received a more than adequate satisfaction. This gracious imputation must first be purchased and won from his righteousness for us." This is from WA 10/I/1, 470:18-22: "Ob nu wol uns wirt lautter auss gnaden unser sund nit zugerechnet von got, so hat er das dennoch nit wollen thun, seinem gesez und seiner gerechtickeit geschehe denn zuvor aller ding und ubirflussig gnug. Es must seiner gerechtickeit solchs gnedigs zurechnen zuvor abkaufft und erlanget werden fur uns."

Righteousness is required, which is exactly why the righteousness of Christ is for Luther so central. The reason faith justifies is precisely because it embraces Christ. Thus can Luther say that faith "will fill believers with so great a righteousness that they will need nothing more to become righteous" (AE 31, 347f; WA 7, 52:17-19).[34] When Luther declares that God requires only faith (e.g., WA 2, 718:35-37; AE 35: 16),[35] or says that everything depends upon faith (WA 2, 733:37-39; AE 35:38),[36] it must be remembered that he is here pitting faith against works, and not basing forgiveness or divine mercy on the mere act of believing, over against the work of Christ. That is, Luther does not advocate a kind of faith which would require only Forde's brand of mercy. Even the Word which faith trusts is not itself a means of redemption but a means of grace (WA 26, 40, 9; so Siggins 1970, 74; contra Forde 1984, 68). Faith reconciles "because it lays hold on the reconciliation which Christ has performed for us" (AE 36, 177; WA 8, 519:19-20).[37] Faith justifies not on account of itself, nor on account of the Word, but on account of him whom the Word proclaims, namely Christ. Luther's concept of mercy is simply not what Forde claims it is, a mere divine decision to forget what is owed. Faith for Luther

---

For an abundance of supporting references and favorable comparison to Anselm on this point see also Althaus 1966, 202-4.

[34]"The Freedom of a Christian" (1520): "Fides, quae est brevis et consummata plenitudo legis, tanta iustitia credentes replebit, ut nulla alia re ad iustitiam opus habeant."

[35]"Sacrament of Penance" (1519): "Szo wir doch ym gantzenn Evangelio nit eynen lessen, von dem er ettwas anders hett gefodert, dan den glauben."

[36]"Holy Sacrament of Baptism" (1519): "Aber allein durch den unglauben yrs wercks wirt sie [die tauff] zu nichte, und der glaub bringt erwidder die selben hinderniss yres wercks, alsso gar ligt es alles am glauben."

[37]"The Misuse of the Mass" (1521): "[Nicht das der glawb an yhm selbst versünet, ssondern] er ergreyfft und erlanget die versünung, wilche Christus fur uns gethan hatt."

trusts the merit and sacrifice of Christ as the basis and enabler of mercy, and not in any kind of mercy which would be devoid of such basis.

For a definitive statement from Luther regarding his implication that justification by faith means justification by Christ and his atonement, we may consider a sermon entitled, "The Sacrament of the Body and Blood of Christ— Against the Fanatics" (1526), which contains Luther's defense of the real presence of the flesh and blood of Christ in the Sacrament against the fanatics' contention that it is unnecessary. He declares, in a sarcastic tone so characteristic of his polemics, "You might as well tell me also that because faith alone justifies, Christ is not necessary," which is to say, the notion is absurd. The sarcastic diatribe thus continues,

> So let us say to God: You had sin, death, devil, and everything in your power; what need was there to send down your Son, and permit him to be treated so cruelly and to die? You could indeed have allowed him to remain on high; it would have cost you only a word, and sin and death would have been destroyed, along with the devil. For you are certainly almighty. Again, let us conclude that Christ was not born of the Virgin, and say: Of what use was it? Could not God have caused him to be born of a man just as well, and still be fashioned so that he would have been conceived without sin and have remained innocent? Indeed, let us even go further and say that it is not necessary that Christ be God. For through God's power he could just as well have risen from the dead and saved us, even if he had been purely human. Thus the devil blinds people, and the result is, first, that they are incapable of seeing any work of God in the right light, and second, that they also fail to regard the Word, and accordingly want to find out everything with their own minds. If you were to search out everything about a kernel of wheat in the field, you would be so amazed that you would die. God's works are not like our works (AE 36, 344; WA 19, 495:15-496:12).[38]

---

[38]"So sage mir auch, weil der glawbe alleine rechtfertigt, das Christus nicht not sey, So wollen wir zu Got sagen: Du hattest sund, tod, teuffel und alles yn deiner gewalt; was war es nutz odder not, das du dein son herab sendest, liessest yhn so greulich handlen und sterben? hettestu doch yhn wol kunden lassen droben bleiben; hette dich nicht mehr denn ein wort gekostet, so were sund und tod vertilget mit dem teuffel. Denn du bist yhe almechtig. Item, also wollen wir schliessen, das Christus nicht geboren sey von der Junckfrawen, und sagen: Was war es von noten? kund yhn nicht Gott eben so wol von einem man lassen geboren werden? und gleich wol

Here we see clearly Luther's fundamental agreement with Anselm's insistence on the necessity for Christ, as Luther's essential concurrence with Anselm's insistence on the necessity for the atonement is made clear. First he mocks and rejects the idea that God in view of his omnipotence could perform salvation without Christ. Next he rejects by mockery the question whether God could have been born of a man, and finally, again by ridicule, spurns the notion that Christ is not necessarily God. Rather than provide reasoned arguments why these ideas are untenable, which would certainly have been Anselm's course, Luther simply rejects them as coming from the devil, who blinds people so that they have no regard for the Word.

In his (1535) commentary on Galatians 2:20 ("For me"), he speaks in more personal terms than Anselm, but aside from this he comes across sounding very much like him.

> If I, an accursed and damned sinner, could be redeemed by some other price, what need was there that the Son of God should be given for me? But because there was no price in heaven or on earth except Christ, the Son of God, therefore it was extremely necessary that He be given for me (AE 26:177; WA 40/I, 296:34-297:13).[39]

Luther stresses the necessity for the atonement forcefully here because he is speaking as one personally in desperate need of it, something Anselm was not wont to do; yet one can see just as clearly here as in Anselm a distaste for

---

so schaffen, das er on sund entpfangen und unschuldig bliben were? Ja, weiter wollen wir sagen, es sey nicht not, das Christus Gott sey. Denn er hette eben so wol durch Gottes krafft kunden vom tod widder aufferstehen und uns erlosen, wenn er ein lauter mensch were gewesen. Also verblendet der Teuffel die leute, das sie kein Gottes werck recht ansehen kunden; Zum andern, das sie auch das wort nicht ansehen, wollen darnach mit yhrem kopff alles erforschen. Soltistu ein körnlin auff dem feld ausforschen, du soltist dich verwundern, das du sturbest. Gottes werck sind nicht unsern wercken gleich."

[39]"Si ego perditus et damnatus peccator potuissem alio quodam pretio redimi, quid opus fuisset pro me tradi filium Dei? Sed quia nullum erat in coelis nec terris praeter Christum filium Dei, ideo summa fuit necessitas eum pro me tradi."

speculative and impious notions about other avenues of redemption God might have had available to him.

From these references it is clear that the necessity for atonement by a divine Christ is just as clear in the mind of Luther as it is in that of Anselm, though his mode of expression is generally in different terms.

(~3) The Vicarious Satisfaction

For Anselm, in order for salvation to be accomplished, remission of sin is necessary (CDH I:10; S II, 67:18-19).[40] Further, "the world could not be saved" except by Christ's atonement (CDH I:10; S II, 66:2-3).[41] And what is also true, to provide the final link in Anselm's chain of argument for the necessity for the vicarious satisfaction, is that God cannot allow the world to go unsaved. God must "complete what he began" with human nature (CDH II:4; S II, 99:2).[42] So as not to have created in vain, "it is therefore necessary that God complete what he began with human nature" (99:9).[43] If God does not accomplish this, his creation is foiled rather than vindicated, and such an outcome is inadmissible, being unfitting. He must save the world, "so that he might not appear contrary to what is proper (*deceat*) by failing in what he began" (99:12-13).[44] Therefore the vicarious satisfaction of God's justice is required, inasmuch as the satisfaction cannot be made by those who owe it.

---

[40]"Necessaria est igitur homini peccatorum remissio, ut ad beatitudinem perveniat—Therefore remission of sins is necessary for man, in order for him to attain happiness."

[41]"Mundum erat aliter impossibile salvari."

[42]"de humana natura perficiet deus quod incepit."

[43]"Necesse est ergo, ut de humana natura quod incepit perficiat."

[44]"ne aliter quam deceat videatur a suo incepto deficere."

Moreover it is required that man make this satisfaction, since it was man who sinned. By sinning, man stole God's honor away; this must be repaid by the one who stole it (CDH I:11; S II, 68:29-69:2).[45] Anselm has only two options available to him: either the honor must be repaid or punishment must result (CDH I: 13; S II, 71:24-25).[46] It is unjust (*iniustus*) for a man not to pay what he owes someone else, and more so for him not to pay God what he owes (CDH I:24; S II, 92:6-7).[47] Therefore only man can make satisfaction for sins: *nec facere illam debet nisi homo* (CDH II:6; S II, 101:14).

For this reason, Hopkins' (1976) justification for translating *cur deus homo* with the indefinite article—"Why God became *a* man," rather than "Why God became man"—cannot be allowed to stand unchallenged. His argument rejects the latter translation by reason of its implication that Jesus assumed unindividuated, universal human nature, in order as *man* to pay *man's* debt. This is wrong, he declares; for "Anselm's view is that *a* man paid this debt—doing so on behalf of all other men" (6). Hopkins enlists *De Incarnatione Verbi* 11 to prove this. There Anselm is pre-empting any absurd charge that his position makes Jesus no more the Word than anyone else:

> *Quapropter non dicimus verbum et simpliciter hominem eandem esse personam, ne non magis dicamus illum hominem eandem esse personam cum verbo quam quemlibet hominem, sed verbum et illum assumptum hominem, id est IESUM*—On this account we do not say that the Word and man, simply, are the same person, lest we should say that that man

---

[45]"Sic ergo debet omnis qui peccat, honorem deo quem rapuit solvere; et haec est satisfactio, quam omnis peccator deo debet facere—So therefore everyone who sins must repay the honor of God which he stole, and this [repayment of honor] is the satisfaction, which every sinner must make to God."

[46]"Necesse est ergo, ut aut ablatus honor solvatur aut poena sequatur—Therefore it is necessary either that the stolen honor be repaid or that punishment follow."

[47]"Si homo dicitur iniustus, qui homini non reddit quod debet: multo magis iniustus est, qui deo quod debet non reddit—If a man who does not pay [another] man what he owes is called unjust, how must more unjust it is if a man does not pay God what he owes."

is no more the same person than any other man; rather, we say that the Word is the same person as that assumed man, namely Jesus (S II, 29:26-29).

Anselm must make himself clear here so as not to allow the likes of a Roscelin to ridicule his position. The *De Incarnatione Verbi* is itself a polemic against Roscelin, and it must therefore be remembered that the arguments found therein are not of the same nature as the discussions of the *Cur Deus Homo*. In the former work, Anselm must guard his expressions against open ridicule he can expect from a cynical enemy who might well charge Anselm with saying the person of the Word has assumed a personal unity with the human race. Thus he must make his position clear. He would undoubtedly not feel obliged to make the same assertion in the *Cur Deus Homo*, whose tone is more reflective.[48] The assertion he makes here in the *De Incarnatione Verbi* is really nothing more than stating what would otherwise be assumed as obvious: Christ is incarnate as an individual man, namely Jesus, and the incarnation of the Word is nothing apart from that. But now what Hopkins has done is to have Anselm say that the humanity which Christ assumed has no existential unity with the human race, thus confusing the personal union with an ontological unity in kind between Christ and the human race. He has forgotten that Anselm was a realist, not a nominalist. For Anselm the miracle of the incarnation is that in it there is indeed a constituent unity brought about between God and humanity, understood in a manner a nominalist would have difficulty accepting. *Homo* is not for Anselm merely a *flatus vocus*—a vocal sound. It is a *res* in itself; not merely the sum total of all *homines*. The realist mindset conceives the meaning of *cur deus homo* in an altogether different manner than the nominalist mindset. Where Anselm makes his realist perspective clear, and with it his understanding of *homo* in *Cur Deus Homo*, Hopkins mistranslates, in order to force Anselm into the nominalist

---

[48]Admittedly, an argument *e silentio*.

mindset. In II:8 (S II, 102:23-104:28), Anselm declares in no uncertain terms that Adam's race must rise and be lifted up *per se*—by itself (103:9).[49] But Hopkins cannot allow this, if he is to maintain his position. So he translates *per se* as "by its own efforts," thus skirting his embarrassment at Anselm's realism. But if the human race must be raised up *per se*, then a necessity obtains of God's assumption of human nature, i.e., the very same nature as Adam. Hopkins will not have this, so he translates *assumere hominem* (102:25) in the chapter title as "to assume a human nature," destroying Anselm's realism both by using the indefinite article and by refusing to employ a more natural translation of *homo*. This chapter, as its title indicates, is demonstrating precisely what Hopkins does not want it to demonstrate, namely the necessity that God assume human-ness, the same humanness, ontologically, as Adam's, in order to become existentially united with the human race. The vicarious substitution of Christ is for Anselm not "x for y," but "x for x." In Christ, man makes satisfaction for himself, which was what was required. With Hopkins' rearrangement, not only is this point missed, but the beauty of Anselm's argument is lost and it becomes a legalism, much closer to what Aulén, Moltmann, and Forde see in Anselm. The necessity that the vicarious satisfaction be made by man is a necessity whose key ingredient is the fittingness of it. In fittingness is beauty, which is of central importance to Anselm. Thus in Anselm's view of satisfaction we must qualify our use of the term *vicarious*, which we customarily employ for the labelling of his view. The satisfaction is vicarious in the sense that Christ is the substitute for the human race in atoning; it is not vicarious in a sense which would allow God to renege on his original charge: sinners must themselves pay what they owe.

---

[49]S II, 103:7-9: "Amplius. Sicut ADAM et totum genus eius per se stetisset sine sustentatione alterius creaturae, si non peccasset: ita oportet ut, si idem genus resurgit post casum, per se resurgat et relevetur—Furthermore, as Adam and the entire race would have stood by itself without assistance from another creature, had they not sinned, so it is fitting that, if the same race rises after the fall, it is raised and lifted up by itself."

Christ pays therefore not as another, but as the sinner, in a way which fulfills the original requirement. This is the implication of Anselm's requirement that the satisfaction be made by man.

But what of the necessity that this vicarious satisfaction be made by God? Has Anselm yet answered the question *cur deus homo*? Aulén (1969) contends that for Anselm, the work of Christ is not God's from start to finish. Rather, Aulén insists, because Anselm places so much emphasis on the necessity that the satisfaction be made by man, there is no real need in his thought for the incarnation at all, but only that God provide that Man who would be able to make sufficient satisfaction (86f). If this contention is allowed to stand, then Forde's charge that Anselm prohibits God from having true mercy gains merit, since God in essence merely becomes the recipient of satisfaction before dispensing with punishment. Thus Aulén's charge is serious.

But Aulén is wrong; he has misread Anselm, for reasons which, I believe, become clearer when Anselm's method and purpose are weighed in the balance. It is clear, if one can read Anselm on his own terms and without any preconceived bias concerning what Anselm is supposed to have held, that for him the mercy of God stems precisely from the fact that it is God himself who pays the debt. One wonders whether Forde bought Aulén's claim without investigating it for himself.

What Aulén is trying to show is that Anselm is guilty of failing to answer his own question. The satisfaction must be made by man, says Anselm, because it is man who has sinned; but there is really no corollary requirement here, in terms of the claims of justice, that the satisfaction be made by God; at least that is what Aulén's contention assumes. Therefore, he concludes, the necessity for the atonement is in effect removed. God must provide the sacrifice, but not necessarily *be* the sacrificial victim—so Aulén charges that Anselm has not proven the necessity for the incarnation.

But Aulén misses some keys to Anselm's thought. First there is Anselm's pervading and more or less tacit conviction of the necessity that there be beauty and symmetry in all things pertaining to God. For Anselm fittingness, which turns out always to be requisite in conceiving of God, has to do with symmetry and order. As the human race is God's most precious work (*pretiosum opus*, CDH I:4; S II, 52:8), for which on this account his plan could not be allowed to fail, therefore it is also fitting that God be the one performing its redemption. "[God's] proposition could not be brought into effect, unless the human race was liberated by its Creator himself" (CDH I:4; S II, 52:10-11).[50] The need for God himself to make the atonement is strictly in keeping with what is fitting. Fittingness must always obtain for the work of God, in Anselm's thought, which means that there *is* as much requirement for the *deus* in the *deus-homo* as there is for the *homo*, even if the requirement is not exactly correlative with the requirement for the *homo*. That is, it is not for a correspondingly *similar* reason that the satisfaction be made by God as that it be made by man, but there is nonetheless a reason every bit as acceptable.

Secondly, working from logic, Anselm reasons that there is no one other than God available to make satisfaction anyway, because the work of salvation can only be accomplished by something greater than every thing that is not God (CDH II:6; S II, 101:7-8).[51] This is because it is God's honor which must be maintained: *quia hoc facit necessitate servandae honestatis* (CDH II:5; S II, 100:23-24). Therefore as it is true that nothing except God surpasses everything

---

[50]"[Nonne satis necessaria ratio videtur, cur deus ea, quae dicimus, facere debuerit: quia genus humanum, tam scilicet pretiosum opus eius, omnino perierat, nec decebat, ut, quod deus de homine proposuerat, penitus annihilaretur,] nec idem eius propositum ad effectum duci poterat, nisi genus hominum ab ipso creatore suo liberaretur?"

[51]"Maiorem esse necesse est quam omne quod non est deus—It is necessary that it be greater than everything which is not God."

that is not God (101:10),[52] the necessity for the atonement is shown: *"Non ergo potest hanc satisfactionem facere nisi deus*—Therefore only God can make this satisfaction" (101:12). Whether the argument is accepted or not, Anselm is here making what his interlocutor Boso quickly recognizes as *magnum quiddam*— a major point (101:20), and Aulén's contention fizzles.

Indeed for Anselm the satisfaction must be made by man, as Aulén stresses. But it is quite irresponsible for Aulén to jump from this to a consequent rejection of the possibility of God's performing of the satisfaction. Aulén denies a priori the possibility of the very point Anselm is trying to prove.[53] It is man who must perform the satisfaction—therefore it cannot be God? The deftness of this *non-sequitur* has evidently convinced Forde. Aulén's argument, moreover, that the "classic" view provides a greater organic necessity (Aulén 1969, 87) for the incarnation is equally unacceptable, using his own reasoning. If Anselm's reason for maintaining the necessity that God himself be the vicariously satisfying victim is unacceptable to him, why should Aulén's own reason for maintaining the necessity that God be the Victor over his enemies be any less unacceptable? One can argue just as well (or poorly, actually) that God could send an agent to conquer satan. In fact it might even be argued that an angel would be *more* appropriate, since satan is an angel. By Anselm's reasoning the necessity for the deity of Christ is greater when considered in connection with the vicarious satisfaction than when considered in connection with the "classic" view. Would it not be fitting for an angel to defeat an angel, in keeping with symmetry? Of

---

[52]"Nihil autem est supra omne quod deus non est, nisi deus—Nothing, however, is greater than everything which is not God exept God."

[53]This, like the position of Forde, follows Ritschl's (1969, 262f) nineteenth-century lead. Ritschl made a similar charge, saying that Anselm's juridical conception of divine justice precludes the possibility of reconciliation.

course, this is not Anselm's position,[54] but Aulén surely ought not to have charged him with making the atonement less than God's work from start to finish. This is no less a charge against his own position, by Anselm's reckoning.

The whole point of the vicarious satisfaction rests for Anselm with the necessity for the *deus-homo*. One cannot reject Anselm's argument with an either-or proposition having no basis. In fact, if we accept Aulén's line of reasoning that Anselm's great emphasis on Christ's humanity disqualifies anything he says about Christ's divinity, then we must leave Aulén with a Christ who is as little human as he allows Anselm's Christ to be divine. Although Anselm's stress on the incarnation of God is made from an entirely different perspective than Luther's, the incarnation itself must nonetheless be recognized as an integral element in the thought of the former.

Forde's (1984) attack on Anselm's conception of mercy (23) rests squarely on Aulén's charge that Anselm's Christ is not fully God.[55] Forde's charge that the tradition of Anselm places roses on the cross (11), not allowing for any real mercy, stems likewise from a refusal to accept what Anselm affirms about the incarnation. The fact that the vicarious victim is God is precisely what makes the sacrifice an act of God's mercy. It is only without the *deus* in the *deus-homo* that Forde's criticism of Anselm obtains; and in fact Anselm's affirmation of the incarnation makes his claim of mercy more appropriate, not less so. Forde's kind

---

[54]Anselm is also able to speak in terms of Aulén's "classic" view, a point which Aulén will not allow. Anselm speaks in terms not unlike those of Irenaeus, of God's restoration of life to the world, in CDH I:1; S II, 48:2-5, and also on Christ's conquering of the devil through his suffering, in CDH I:3; S II, 51:9-12; CDH I:22; S II, 90:9-25; and CDH I:23; S II, 91:9-14.

[55]It is tempting to suppose that Forde let Aulén do his homework for him here, for it appears also to be the case with regard to Anselm's relation to Abelard (1079-1142). Forde claims Abelard "gained the historical reputation of being Anselm's great antagonist" (23), probably thinking of Aulén's (1969) contention that historical studies of dogma have commonly emphasized a rivalry between the two (95). Abelard certainly attacked Anselm's view—see Peter Abailard: "Exposition of the Epistle to the Romans: An Excerpt from the Second Book," II (Fairweather 1956, 280-283)—but personal antagonism was found rather between him and some of his closer contemporaries, especially Anselm of Laon and Bernard of Clairvaux.

of sheer mercy, by which God is supposed to forgive without exacting prior satisfaction (1984, 23), may have more claim to be called mercy than the kind of mercy he attributes, erroneously, to Anselm—a mercy which is in fact no mercy at all. But the mercy of which Anselm actually speaks is far more appropriately called mercy than Forde's brand, for it involves sacrifice on the part of the benefactor himself, whereas Forde's conception of mercy does not.

Turning now to Luther, we note first that the debate over the question whether Luther accepted the idea of the vicarious satisfaction is not new. We recall the nineteenth century battle between Hofmann and Theodosius Harnack, the latter arguing for Luther's acceptance of the vicarious satisfaction and the former arguing against it. Since then Aulén has argued against it, as has Moltmann, and recently Forde. As the debate has already been hashed out for over a hundred years, it will not be treated in great detail here, yet something needs to be said in favor of Luther's basic acceptance of the Anselmic vicarious satisfaction. Yet again we have arrived at an area on which comparison is somewhat elusive, due to the fact that Luther's method and purpose are quite plainly at variance with Anselm's. Indeed this is probably the very reason Luther has been so frequently misrepresented on this point. So once again we must attempt to filter out the elements of purpose and method which enter Luther's expression, to enable as it were a comparison of purely smelted substances. Style, purpose, and method will be taken up in earnest below. We can find basic agreement between Luther and Anselm on the vicarious satisfaction if we strain out for now his clearly different approach. To be sure, Luther says much that Anselm does not, providing an additional reason his agreement is difficult to recognize; but the agreement can nonetheless be found woven into the fabric of his primary foci of discussion.

For Luther, justification by faith is the *Hauptartikel* of the Christian faith (WA 40/I, 441; AE 26, 282), and can be expressed in an abundance of images, all of which are generally quite compatible with Anselm's thought. Luther's discourse on justification most frequently speaks in terms of an exchange—the celebrated *fröhliche Wechsel*—between Christ and the sinner. In "The Freedom of a Christian," we find a text which provides a good example of this. Luther uses the metaphor of Christ as the bridegroom and the soul as the bride. The bride/bridegroom metaphor was a favorite image of Luther's,[56] being for him a most fitting vehicle for his explanation of the *fröhliche Wechsel* between Christ and the Christian. As bride and bridegroom share all things in common, so also do the church and her Christ.[57] By faith "we are in Him, and He is in us. This Bridegroom, Christ, must be alone with His bride in His private chamber" (WA 40/I, 241:13-14; AE 26, 137).[58] The church as a bride is *lilium inter spinas*—a lily among thorns (WA 2, 604:36; AE 27, 391).[59] The exchange which occurs is of course a severely unbalanced one: we receive all good, and he receives all evil; we receive from Christ grace, life, and salvation; that is, all that which Christ has earned by his atonement; as Christ receives in exchange our sin, death, and damnation in his passion.

---

[56]Other references, in addition to the quotation below, for Luther's use of this metaphor can be found in WA 22, 339:9-20; WA 22, 337:29-34; WA 57/III, 224:13-15 (AE 29, 226); WA 7, 597:13ff (AE 21, 351).

[57]Luther can be found occasionally and rather consistently rendering "spiritual" or allegorical interpretations of sermon texts in which the woman in the text is to be understood as referring to the church. For instance, the mother of Jesus is allegorized in this way (StL 11, 474; AP 2, 66), and even the woman in Mt 13:33 who hid leaven in meal is interpreted not as Christ, but as the Church (WA 2, 569f; AE 27, 340).

[58]Galatians commentary (1535): "In illo sumus per fidem et ipse in nobis, Ioan. 6. Oportet hunc sponsum Christum esse solum cum sponsa in sua quiete."

[59]Galatians commentary (1519).

The believing soul can boast of and glory in whatever Christ has
as though it were its own, and whatever the soul has Christ claims
as his own. Let us compare these and we shall see inestimable
benefits. Christ is full of grace, life, and salvation. The soul is
full of sins, death, and damnation. Now let faith come between
them and sins, death, and damnation will be Christ's, while grace,
life, and salvation will be the soul's; for if Christ is a bridegroom,
he must take upon himself the things which are his bride's and
bestow upon her the things that are his (WA 7, 54:36-55:4; AE
31, 351).[60]

The *fröhliche Wechsel* has been occasionally misunderstood and criticized

as immature Luther, based on the mistaken premise that it occurs through the

mystical presence of Christ, i.e., *propter Christum in nobis*, which would create

a tension with forensic justification (so Forde 1984, 53; Hoffman 1976, 171;

Green 1980, 204). That is, if the exchange is mystical, then it becomes in effect

akin to the scholastic *gratia infusa*, according to which the righteousness by

which the Christian stands before God is inherent in the Christian's nature. To

be sure, it comes from Christ, but it is infused into the believer so that it now

becomes an intrinsic attribute; the exchange is one which gives to the Christian

an inherently pure heart from which the righteousness *coram Deo* flows. But

Luther's preference for the *fröhliche Wechsel* cannot be called supportive of this

position; rather, for him the exchange is actually quite forensic. Christ need be

no more mystically present with the soul for the exchange of righteousness to

occur than the soul need be mystically present with the crucified Christ for the

exchange of sin to occur. If the exchange happens both ways, then it cannot be

called an infused exchange of sin for righteousness, for the notion that sin is

---

[60]"Quaecunque Christus habet, de iis tanquam suis praesumere et gloriari possit fidelis anima,
Et quaecunque animae sunt, ea sibi arroget Christus tanquam sua. Conferamus ista, et videbimus
inaestimabilia. Christus plenus est gratia, vita et salute, Anima plena est peccatis, morte et
damnatione. Intercedat iam fides, et fiet, ut Christi sint peccata, mors et infernus, Animae vero
gratia, vita et salus: oportet enim eum, si sponsus est, ea simul quae sponsa habet acceptare et ea
quae sua sunt sponsae impartire."

infused mystically into Christ is clearly absurd. Rather, it is imputed forensically to him; and thus the reverse exchange must also be seen as one of imputation. For Luther, then, the *fröhliche Wechsel* occurs only by imputation; it may in fact be termed Luther's version of the vicarious satisfaction.

Indications of this can be found in great abundance throughout Luther. His 1535 Galatians commentary is rife with such references. There he declares that sin is not imputed to the Christian, because "His righteousness is yours; your sin is His" (AE 26, 233; WA 40/I, 369:25).[61] Christ is wrapped up in our sins (WA 40/I, 434:26-28; AE 26, 278),[62] sin was imposed upon him (WA 40/I, 569:15-16; AE 26, 279),[63] indeed he clothed himself in our person—*induere personam nostram*—and laid our sin upon his shoulders—*imponere in humeros suos peccata*—and said, I have committed the sins which all men have committed—*et dicere: Ego commisi peccata quae omnes homines commiserunt* (WA 40/I, 442:31-443:14; AE 26, 283f). Thus Christ became guilty of all laws, curses, sins, etc., because he "stepped in between—*venit medius*" (AE 26, 290; WA 40/I, 452:14). This makes him a Mediator who "sets himself against the wrath of the Law and abolishes it" (AE 26, 325; WA 40/I, 503:20-21).[64] Therefore he "interposed himself as Mediator between two most different parties" (WA 40/I, 504:15-16; AE 26, 325).[65] He performed and bore the Law, thus conquering it (AE 26, 373; WA 40/I, 436:18).[66] Thus all doubts

---

[61]"Cuius iustitia est tua, peccatum tuum est suum."

[62]"Nos vero debemus involvere Christum et involutum cognoscere ut carne et sanguine, ita peccatis, maledictione, morte et omnibus malis nostris."

[63]"Peccato ei imposito."

[64]"Sed opponit se irae legis et tollit eam et satisfacit legi in suo corpore per Semetipsum."

[65]"Ibi ergo interposuit Christus sese Mediatorem inter duos diversissimos."

[66]"Hoc ipso, quod fecit et sustinuit legem, vicit eam in Semetipso."

may be laid to rest in the knowledge that "if I am a sinner and err, He is righteous and cannot err" (WA 40/I, 578:30-31; AE 26, 379).[67] Christ earned expiation, remission of sins, righteousness, freedom, and life for us by His death and resurrection (WA 40/II, 22:23-25; AE 27:19).[68]

Luther's sermons are also full of this exchange. The conscience may rejoice "if you . . . recognize the Lamb of God carrying your sin" (AP 1, 133; StL 11, 117);[69] Christ's satisfaction has "through his blood and death paid for our sins and reconciled God" (StL 11, 707; AP 2, 332);[70] thus we are encouraged to believe "that Christ made satisfaction for our sins and that his satisfaction is ours" (AP 3, 131; StL 11, 884f).[71] Christ is the Savior come

---

[67]"Si ego peccator sum et erro, Ipse iustus est, errare non potest."

[68]"[Qui excidit a gratia, amittit simpliciter] expiationem, remissionem peccatorum, iusticiam, libertatem, vitam, etc., quam Christus sua morte et resurrectione nobis emeruit."

[69]"Kannst du nun [glauben, dass solche Stimme Johannis wahr sei, und seinem Finger nachsehen, und] das Lamm Gottes erkennen, dass es deine Sünde auf sich trage: [so hast du gewonnen, so bist du ein Christ, ein Herr über Sünde, Tod, Hölle und alle Dinge; da muss dein Gewissen froh werden, und dem zarten Lamm Gottes aus Herzen hold werden.]"

[70]"[Und zwar das Wort, *satisfactio*, Genugthuung, haben wir ihnen zu Willen lassen hingehen, der Hoffnung, ob wir sie könnten mit Glimpf zu der rechten Lehre bringen . . . doch es heisse, nicht unsere Genugthuung, wie wir denn in der Wahrheit keine haben, sondern Christi, damit er] für unsere Sünde durch sein Blut und Sterben bezahlt und Gott versöhnt hat."
This reference is of interest because it appears to allow the term *satisfactio* more as a concession than as a chosen label, demonstrating my contention that although Luther's position can be shown in essence to agree with that of Anselm, his perspective differs in other significant respects. Luther continues, in this reference, to complain about the great abuse of the term under the papal church, and concludes by going so far as to announce that the term ought not henceforward be used at all!: "Darum soll auch dies Wort 'Genugthuung' in unsern Kirchen und Theologie fürder nichts und todt sein, und dem Richteramt und Juristenschulen, dahin es gehört und daher es auch die Papisten genommen, befohlen sein." It appears, however, that Luther did not follow his own counsel, for this Easter Tuesday declaration is succeeded by an indication of his continued use of the term as soon as the Fourth Sunday after Easter, as can be seen in the following reference in my text. It is admittedly possible, though not likely, that he wrote the second of the two sermons first.

[71]"[So wir glauben,] dass Christus für unsere Sünde hat genug gethan und dass sein Genugthun unser sei."

from heaven, who has "taken upon himself our sins and made himself a sacrifice
to the everlasting wrath of God which we had merited by our sins" (AP 3, 448;
StL 11, 1188).[72] The abundance of references in Luther to the concepts of
sacrifice and exchange exchange lead one to wonder how Hofmann, Aulén, Forde
and company could have convinced so many that their position is even worthy of
consideration. Althaus (1966) rightly contends that for Luther justification itself
is seen as a transfer of Christ's righteousness to the sinner (266); the notion that
this is incompatible with Anselm's vicarious satisfaction is nothing short of absurd
(so Althaus 1966, 202).[73] What has evidently fooled some into believing the
absurdity are the glaring differences in method, purpose, and intention between
Anselm the early medieval archbishop and monk of Canterbury and Luther the
sixteenth-century preacher and reformer from Wittenberg. Once these have been
examined, a comparision concerning the greater questions of doctrinal substance
becomes clearer, and we will come away from our comparative study with far
different results, having made our approach in this way, than those who have not
considered them as seriously.

Correspondence, Looking from Luther to Anselm

Three areas of correspondence emerge when comparing Anselm and
Luther, looking from the latter to the former, which are 1) the doctrine of Christ,
2) the love of God, and 3) faith. Each of these will now be examined in turn.

---

[72]"[Das Heisst aber eigentlich dies Herniederfahren des Sohnes Gottes, dass er sich herunter
geworfen hat in unser Elend und Noth, das ist,] Gottes ewigen Zorn, mit unsern Sünden verdient,
auf sich genommen und ein Opfer dafür worden."

[73]See also WA 39/I, 219, 250, 366, 375, 380, 435f, 478f.

(~1) Christ

For Luther, Jesus Christ is God, emphatically. He is the full incarnation and revelation of God, and since he is the full incarnation of God, God can be found nowhere else, and there is "no other God than this Man Jesus Christ" (AE 26, 29; WA 40, 78).[74] So consistently does Luther aver this that we may call it the shibboleth of Luther (so Siggins 1970, 79).[75] Luther's Christology is of the highest kind, and his stress on the full divinity and honor of the man Jesus is consistent throughout his life, and unexcelled. One finds much less reference to the true humanity of Christ in Luther, simply because it is less scandalous to reason (so Siggins 1970, 199, but see Harnack 1969:II, 139-146). Not only does Luther follow the Chalcedonian tradition of calling Mary *mater Dei* (e.g., StL 11, 436; AP 2, 25); he unpacks this: God is laid in a manger, Mary makes broth for God, God suffers, and God dies. Luther follows completely Augustine's declaration that "the Father, in sending the Son, sent his other self."[76] Siggins (1970) sees the strongest stress in Luther's doctrine of Christ to be the unity of Christ's person (227,232). He quotes Luther's assertion that Christ's being in the Father is "the chiefest article and cardinal point" of Christian faith, to support this contention (85; WA 45, 589:25). Further, Siggins declares, "Luther insists that Christ's history is His own and no one else's" (81). As the knowledge of God is in Christ, Christ is the pledge, token, and testimony of God's grace (79-107). Althaus (1966, 19) agrees with Siggins' contention, noting Luther's assertion that through Christ "we learn to look straight into the face of

---

[74]See also WA 20, 727:6; 30/III, 132:23; 35, 456:14; 31/I, 63; 40/II, 256:20; 45, 550:13; 45, 589:1; 46, 763:2; et al.

[75]I have found no better treatment of Luther's Christology than that of Siggins.

[76]Augustine, *Tract. in ev. Ioh.*, XIV, 11; quoted in Siggins 1970, 81.

God" (WA 46, 669, 672; AE 22, 153, 157). The revelation of God is in Christ only (WA 45, 520:37-521:2; DBD, 89).[77]

Yet there are more Luther scholars who contend that justification ought to be called for Luther the heart of all theology, referring in their contentions to Luther's own admission that it is "the article on which the Church stands or falls."[78] I too have declared, above, that justification is for Luther the *Hauptartikel* of the Christian faith (p. 44). Moreover, Luther contends that justification itself includes all the other doctrines of the faith, "and if it is sound, all the others are sound as well" (AE 26, 283; WA 40/I, 441:30-31).[79] But inasmuch as justification is for Luther a transfer of the righteousness of Christ,[80] the difference in contentions ought not to be pushed too far. There were for Luther many ways of expressing the major or central point of the Christian faith. Since Luther tended to do his theology "from below," it meant far more to him to say that Christ is in the Father than it would have meant for the masters of the medieval schools, whose theology was routinely done "from above."[81] The same may be said for Luther in relation to Anselm, whose

---

[77]"Denn ynn dieser person (spricht S. Paulus) wonet warhafftig die gantze Gottheit und ist ausser im kein Gott, also das ich yn treffen möge oder zu im kome (wie wol er sonst allent halben ist)."

[78]WA 40 III, 352:1-3 (1540); cf. WA 40/III, 335:5-10. See also WA 50, 199.

[79]Galatians commentary (1535): "Eoque salvo salvi sunt et reliqui."

[80]WA 39/I, 219, 250, 366, 375, 380, 435f., 478f. See Althaus 1966, 266.

[81]Peter Lombard's *Sentences* provides an epitomal example of the medieval tendency to discuss the second person of the Trinity from above. I say epitomal because the legitimacy of the *Sentences* derives primarily from its general faithfulness in carrying on earlier catholic traditions. In Fairweather's (1956) words, "as for the doctrine of the atonement, while Anselm's assumptions reappear in Hugh of St. Victor, Peter Lombard does little more than reproduce the pre-Anselmian symbols" (230f). By "from above," I mean a Christology which takes God rather than man as its point of departure. The Lombard deals at great length with the traditional and catholic explanations of the doctrine of the Trinity. Unlike Luther, who is brought continually back to the incarnation and work of Christ, the Lombard can go on for thirty-three chapters (distinctions) discussing the Trinity in the abstract, and devote only twenty-three to the incarnate Christ, giving

thought likewise tended to approach Christology from above. For Luther to say that Christ is in the Father is for him to imply that our justification has been accomplished by God (so Harnack 1969:II, 245), whereas Anselm's discourse on the relation of Christ to the Father cannot be said to have included the same notion, inasmuch as Anselm deals with the *opera ad intra*[82] more abstractly. Since Luther was not given to dealing in abstract thought, more can be said about his expressions which place Christ on an equal plane with the Father. Luther tends to do his theology looking from earth's vantage point; Anselm, from heaven's.

This contrast is a point of great significance which needs mention here, lest the points of Christological agreement between Luther and Anselm be overdone. Although there is in Luther abundant reference to the work of Christ, what causes Luther to stand out in bold relief against the scholastic approach is Luther's constant accent on Christ himself who does the work. It is for Luther not enough to say that the work was done, or to analyze the work done, as Thomas Aquinas had done so meticulously.[83] One gains from Luther a sense

---

evidence of his greater affinity for such speculative thought in comparison to Luther. He was quite evidently comfortable with abstract discussions, and it must be admitted at the very least that an abundance of this, whether on the Holy Trinity or on any other topic, lends itself well to the speculative mindset common in the scholastic period.

There is of course a certain sense in which any discussion of the Trinity could be called abstract, as in the Trinitarian controversies of an earlier age, or as in the Athanasian Creed. Whenever the divine *opera ad intra* (see n. 82, below, on this term) are confessed, some abstract discussion is unavoidable, inasmuch as these are not empirically discerned. Discussions of the *opera ad intra* are by their nature bound to be more abstract than a theology from below which begins with the history of the person of Jesus.

[82]This term is arguably is somewhat inappropriate here, since *opera* in itself implies expressions of God in the world. I have notwithstanding this employed it, only because it has been customarily in use among Lutheran dogmaticians to refer to the inner-Trinitarian relationships.

[83]Luther's emphasis on Christ's person is actually a point of contrast with the emphasis which Thomas had placed on the work of Christ (so Ebeling 1970, 156f). Where Thomas took to unpacking every detail of Jesus' passion and resurrection, Luther makes no systematic attempt to deal with such speculative questions pertaining to Holy Week as are found in the *Summa*

that the facts of the atonement are not as necessary to stress as that which makes the it it the wonderful work it is, namely, the truth that God himself is the one who does this work. It is in this truth that the significance of the atonement lies for Luther, who prefers continually to emphasize the incarnation when dealing with soteriology. His points of stress are always those generally considered more germane to Christology proper than to the redemptive work of Christ. The impression derived from this is that Luther cannot bring himself to do analysis on the work in abstract because he is too impressed with the reality of the incarnation in it. What makes the work of Christ truly wondrous is the fact that this Man Christ is fully and bodily God, making the work that of God himself and no one less. In calling Christ Victor over sin, death, and damnation, Luther means to say concurrently that this Christ is God by nature (WA 40/I, 441:31-33; AE 26, 283).[84] Discussions of the source and cause of our salvation tend to end with Christ himself, rather than with the Father: "Christ Himself is our Reconciliation, Righteousness, Peace, Life, and Salvation" (AE 26, 151; WA 40/I, 261:26-27).[85] For Luther, Christ is the "quintessence" of God's relation to man (WA 46, 637:31; AE 22:117, cf. n90; WA 33, 19:27; AE 23:16).[86] Luther is so consistent in his expressions of the divinity of Christ as to lead his readers to the understanding that even when he does not say so explicitly, he wants it understood.

Theologiae.

[84]"Quare cum docemus homines per Christum iustificari, Christum esse victorem peccati, mortis et aeternae maledictionis, testificamur simul eum esse natura Deum—When we teach that men are justified through Christ, Christ being the Victor over sin, death, and the eternal curse, we are testifying at the same time that he is by nature God."

[85]"Ipse Christus enim est reconciliatio, iustitia, pax, vita, salus."

[86]Siggins (1970, 85) contends that quintessence a better translation of *ausbund*, a rare term, than "exemplar" as rendered by AE 22, 117, cf. n90, and AE 23, 16.

The Christological agreement between Anselm and Luther is to be expected in view of the appreciation both had for their Western tradition, and particularly for Augustine. That Anselm's Christology was as Chalcedonian as Luther's is beyond legitimate dispute. The difference of approach between them, though significant, ought not to obscure their general Christological agreements. Aulén's suggestion that for Anselm the work of Christ is not God's work from start to finish can claim only the support of Aulén's own mistaken inferences. The primary difference is simply that Anselm prefers to speak "from above."

Anselm declares, "the Lord Jesus Christ, we say, is true God and true man, one person in two natures, and two natures in one person" (CDH I:8; S II, 59:20-22).[87] In Anselm's explanations and defense of the Trinity, it is easy to see his affirmation of full divinity of the Second Person. In the *Monologion*, the full divinity of the Son is emphasized repeatedly. The Son is the essence of the Father, the strength of the Father, the wisdom of the Father (M 45; S I, 61:26-7), the understanding, wisdom, knowledge, and cognition of the Father (M 46; S I, 62:20-1,23). Indeed, "the Father and the Son and their Spirit exist equally in one another" (M 59; S I, 70:2),[88] and therefore "the Son considered by himself . . . is the Supreme Being" (M 77; S I, 84:7-8).[89]   The *De Incarnatione Verbi* is Anselm's most polemical work, having been written to defend the doctrine of the Trinity against Roscelin, and in it Anselm is just as clear, in just the same sort of terms: the Son, he says repeatedly, is God, and this same Son, "through unity of person, is man" (DIV 10; S II, 26:14).[90]   The

---

[87]"Sed dominum Christum IESUM dicimus verum deum et verum hominem, unam personam in duabus naturis et duas naturas in una persona."

[88]"Quod pater et filius et eorum spiritus pariter sint in se invicem."

[89]"Et singulus pater et singulus filius et singulus eorum spiritus est summa essentia."

[90]"Homo per unitatem personae filius est dei."

Son is Jesus; that is, "both God and man, Son of God and Son of the Virgin" (DIV 11; S II, 29:10).[91] Anselm nowhere denies this; as we have seen, Aulén bases his claims exclusively on Anselm's stress on the humanity of the Christ, but nowhere does Anselm indicate that he means thereby to deny Christ's divinity. Anselm is as little vulnerable to a charge of Arianism as Aulén would be to a charge of docetism, and perhaps the latter charge is more appropriate than the former. To repeat an earlier point, any charge that stressing the humanity of Christ in itself amounts to a denial of his divinity is tantamount to a denial of the possibility of the incarnation altogether.

(~2) The Love of God

According to Luther, the love of God is the reason for the accomplishment of the atonement, but the scope of matters which are attributed to the love of God is wider than that. The love of God for his people is behind everything he does. Every good we receive from him, as well as every escape from trouble is evidence of God's "fatherly heart and abundant love toward us" (LC Creed: I, Trigl., 682).[92] Yet the pinnacle of evidence for the love of God is seen in Christ. "There was no counsel, help, nor comfort, until this only and eternal Son of God out of boundless goodness had pity on our misery and utter poverty and came from heaven to help us" (LC Creed: II, Trigl., 684).[93] This boundless goodness (*grundlose Güte*) is manifested in that over and above all our temporal goods, God has in his incarnation and work of redemption "completely

---

[91]"deus et homo, filius dei et filius virginis est."

[92]"Was uns vor Augen kommt und Gutes widerfährt, und wo wir aus Nöten oder Fährlichkeit kommen, wie uns Gott solches alles gibt und tut, dass wir daran spüren und sehen sein väterlich Herz und überschwengliche Liebe gegen uns."

[93]"Da war kein Rat, Hilfe noch Trost, bis dass sich dieser einige und ewige Gottessohn unsers Jammers und Elends aus grundloser Güte erbarmte und vom Himmel kam, uns zu helfen."

poured himself forth and held nothing back that he has not given to us''
(Ibid.).[94] Christ, says Luther, was given for me *summa charitate*—by the
greatest love (AE 26, 177; WA 40/I, 297:13-14). The love and faithfulness of
God, which the Holy Spirit teaches by bringing us to the conviction that Christ
has accomplished everything, removing sin and overcoming every enemy, is so
great that "I cannot fully fathom [it]'' (AP 3, 279; StL 11, 1024).[95] Not only
God himself, but his angels have great love for us (StL 11, 142; AP 1, 158).

Like Luther, Anselm attributes the work of Christ to the love of God,
although he is more inclined to attribute it ultimately to fittingness. Beauty and
order lie behind both divine love and the atonement, and here is a point of
emphasis not seen in Luther. Because of Anselm's heavy stress upon fittingness
as requisite in all things pertaining to the divinity, Anselm can be found
emphasizing divine justice over divine love.

In a chapter of the *Cur Deus Homo* dealing with the willingness of Christ
to die, Anselm manifests a separation in his thinking between the requirements
of obedience which Christ met and his willingness to die. Anselm is here
refuting the notion that Christ was compelled to die more because of the
constraints of obedience than freely (CDH I:9; see I:8; S II, 61: 1-2). The first
step of his refutation is to make a distinction between what might be called active
and passive obedience.[96] He enjoins Boso to distinguish ''between that which

---

[94]"Er sich ganz und gar ausgeschüttet hat und nichts behalten, das er nicht uns gegeben
habe."

[95]"Lieber Vater, ist das dein Wille, dass du mir so grosse Liebe und Treue erzeigest, die
nicht genug zu ermessen ist."

[96]Lutheran dogmaticians have with regularity made this distinction in their discussions of the
obedience of Christ, but without making the differentiation as sharp. Francis Pieper was even
careful, in his early 20th century dogmatics (Pieper 1951, 373), to dissociate himself from Anselm
on the issue, charging that the latter did not include the active obedience of Christ in the
satisfaction Christ rendered. He further cited with approval early Lutheran dogmaticians Gerhard

he did out of the requirement of obedience and that which, happening to him
because he remained obedient, he endured without the requirement of obedience"
(CDH I:9; S II, 61: 8-10).[97]   Anselm explains that God would not have
required death of man had he not sinned (61:32-62:2), and upon this basis
contends,

> Therefore God did not coerce Christ, in whom there was no sin, to die;
> but Christ willingly endured death, not by an obedience [requiring] the
> forsaking of his life, but on account of the obedience of keeping
> righteousness, in which he persevered so steadfastly that he incurred death
> from it (62: 5-8).[98]

In the distinction Anselm is making it is evident that he sees a difference between
Christ's obedience and his willing sacrifice, although he sees the latter as the
unavoidable outgrowth of the former. What this means is that Anselm does not
view obedience as having fundamentally to do with love, for if he did, he would
have seen the willingness of Christ's sacrifice as the ultimate expression of
precisely that love for all humanity which the law requires. But Anselm declares
only that God did not compel Christ to die, evidently not considering that God did
not compel Christ to be obedient at all. He distinguishes the active obedience of
Christ from his willingness to suffer. If the nature of Christ's active obedience
is seen as a fulfillment of that command to love as God loves, then one can see
no more active expression of it than in the ultimate sacrifice. Luther does not
make the distinction between active and passive obedience in Christ which

---

and Quenstedt against the charge that they had overlooked the "intimate connection between the
obedientia activa and the *obedientia passiva*" (378).

[97]"[Ut mihi videtur, non bene discernis] inter hoc quod fecit exigente oboedientia, et quod
sibi factum, quia servavit oboedientiam, sustinuit non exigente oboedientia."

[98]"Non ergo coegit deus Christum mori, in quo nullum fuit peccatum; sed ipse sponte
sustinuit mortem, non per oboedientiam deserendi vitam, sed propter oboedientiam servandi
iustitiam, in qua tam fortiter perseveravit, ut inde mortem incurreret."

Anselm has made here, and here is a somewhat subtle nuance of difference between them.

Nonetheless Anselm does speak in no uncertain terms about the love of God as the cause of the work of redemption, and in this he exhibits fundamental agreement with Luther. Anselm declares, through Boso his interlocutor, that Christ "redeemed us from sins and from his wrath and from hell and from the power of the devil, whom, because we were not able, he vanquished, and returned to us the kingdom of heaven" (CDH I:6; S II, 53: 8-11),[99] sounding at this point remarkably similar to Luther's familiar *Small Catechism* explanation of the Creed.[100] He goes on to maintain that this exhibits the love of God: *"et quia haec omnia hoc modo fecit, ostendit quantum nos diligeret*—and because he has done all these things in this way he demonstrates how much he loves us" (53:11-54:1).

Anselm must deal with the objections to his insistence that payment obtain before God can be merciful, objections in the very vein in which we have seen the objections of Forde, which contend that the necessity of payment obviates the possibility of mercy. Against these Anselm contends that "it is a mockery to

---

[99]"Redemit nos a peccatis et ab ira sua et de inferno et de potestate diaboli, quem, quia nos non poteramus, ipse pro nobis venit expugnare, et redemit nobis regnum caelorum." This refutes Forde's (1984, 22) contention that Anselm never speaks of the wrath of God.

[100]Luther: Christ "has redeemed me, a lost and condemned creature, purchased and won me from all sins, from death, and from the power of the devil, not with gold or silver, but with his holy precious blood, and with his innocent suffering and death, that I may be his own, and live under him in his kingdom—[Christus] mich verlornen und verdammten Menschen erlöst hat, erworben und gewonnen von allen Sünden, vom Tod und von der Gewalt des Teufels, nicht mit Gold oder Silber, sondern mit seinem heiligen, teuren Blut und mit seinem unschuldigen Leiden und Sterben, auf dass ich sein eigen sei und in seinem Reich unter ihm lebe." *Small Catechism* II:4; Trigl., 544f.

Note the striking similarities: Both speak of redemption; Luther calls himself "condemned" (*verdammten*) and Anselm speaks of God's wrath; Luther says "purchased" (*erworben*), Anselm says "bought"; Luther's redemption is from sins, death, and the power of the devil, while Anselm's is from sins, wrath, hell, and the power of the devil; Luther refers to Christ's kingdom, and Anselm refers to the "kingdom of heaven."

attribute such a mercy to God" (CDH I:24; S II, 93:20),[101] and that it is
"impossible for him to be merciful in that manner" (93: [26,] 27-28).[102]
Still Boso objects that "if the righteousness of God is reasonable, there is no way
by which [this] miserable little man can escape, and the mercy of God seems to
be lost" (94:8-9),[103] to which Anselm replies,

> You have requested a reason; [now] hear a reason. I do not deny the
> mercy of God, for he saves men and beasts, as he has multiplied his
> mercy. But we are speaking about that ultimate mercy, by which he
> makes a man happy after this life (94:10-13).[104]

In this reference to Psalm 35 (36),[105] Anselm implies that the kind of divine
mercy to which he refers is greater than that against which he argues. Thus his
response to a claim that he lessens or denies the love of God with his insistence
on the justice of God—the claim, indeed, of Forde—would be that his version of
divine love is in fact the greater.

A further instance of Anselm's assumption that divine love is behind the
atonement can be seen following another occasion of Anselm's insistence on the
necessity for payment of debt to God, when Boso the interlocutor asks,

> Then how will man be saved, if he does not pay what he owes, if [it be
> that] he cannot be saved without paying what he owes? Or how can we

---

[101]"Sed derisio est, ut talis misericordia deo attribuatur."

[102]"[Quapropter quemadmodum deum sibi esse contrarium, ita] hoc modo illum esse
misericordem impossibile est."

[103]"Si rationem sequitur deus iustitiae, non est qua evadat miser homuncio, et misericordia
dei perire videtur."

[104]"Rationem postulasti, rationem accipe. Misericordem deum esse non nego, qui homines
et iumenta salvat, quemadmodum multiplicavit misericordiam suam. Nos autem loquimur de illa
ultima misericordia, qua post hanc vitam beatum facit hominem."

[105]Psalm 35 (36):7-8: "Homines et iumenta salvabis, Domine, Quaemadmodum multiplicasti
misericordiam tuam, Deus." This is a good example of Anselm's style of weaving the text of
scripture into his speech, with which my next chapter deals.

brazenly claim that God is rich in mercy beyond human understanding, if he is unable to perform this mercy? (CDH I:25; S II, 94:26-28)[106]

Now that Boso has raised the idea of the richness of God's mercy—mercy implicitly agreed by both to be beyond human understanding—Anselm directs him, or those he is here representing, to Christ. "Let them (the scoffers in whose place Boso is speaking) believe with us in Christ, that they might be saved" (95: [1-5,] 6).[107]

(~3) Faith

Luther's emphasis on the love of God is bound together with his emphasis on faith, because he is most concerned to express the love or goodness of God where sight is denied, as a component of his theology of the cross. Luther is concerned to honor God as good and gracious, "even if he acts and speaks otherwise, and all our understanding and feeling be otherwise" (AP 2, 63; StL 11, 471).[108] Indeed sometimes God acts in a way which appears contrary to love and kindness, yet then faith must rise and still say, "He acts sour, but he is

---

[106]"Quomodo ergo salvus erit homo, si ipse nec solvit quod debet, nec salvari, si non solvit, debet? Aut qua fronte asseremus deum in misericordia divitem supra intellectum humanum, hanc misericordiam facere non posse?"

[107]"[Hoc debes ab illis nunc exigere, qui Christum non esse credunt necessarium ad illam salutem hominis, quorum vice loqueris, ut dicant qualiter homo salvari possit sine Christo. Quod si non possunt ullo modo, desinant nos irridere, et accedant et iungant se nobis, qui non dubitamus hominem per Christum posse salvari, aut desperent hoc ullo modo fieri posse. Quod si horrent,] credent nobiscum in Christum, ut possint salvari—[This you ought now to ask those who believe that Christ is not necessary for human salvation, those in whose stead you speak, to say how man can be saved without Christ. If they cannot at all do this, let them stop mocking us, and draw near {cf. Heb. 4.16}, and unite themselves with us, who do not doubt that human salvation is possible through Christ, or else let them despair of its being possible by any other means. If that is abhorrent to them,] . . ."

[108]"Darum ist dies Stück des Evangeliums das höchste und wohl zu merken, dass wir müssen Gott die Ehre geben, dass er gütig und gnädig sei, ob er gleich selbst sich anders stellt und sagt, und alle Sinne und alles Fühlen anders gedächten."

sweet I know" (StL 11, 471; AP 2, 64).[109] It is especially during times of temptation that faith becomes requisite, leading Luther to exhort that we "regard God in no other light than that of a merciful God" because "faith lays hold of things that are not seen and of things that are not matters of experience, Heb. 11,1" (AP 5, 144f; StL 11, 1662).[110]

Thus it is clear that for Luther, faith is essentially trust, *fiducia*, and is especially at its strongest when it must be exercised, as it were, in the darkness. It is the character of faith to believe where sight is denied, and in such darkness to manifest itself. In his sermon for the first Sunday in Advent (1540), Luther takes Jesus' humble entry on an ass into Jerusalem as an example of how everything that concerns faith is against reason and nature ("How does such an advent become a great king?"), declaring that "faith is of the nature that it does

---

[109]"Sauer stellt er sich, doch ist er süss, das weiss ich." This is what the mother of Jesus means to say at the wedding of Cana, in Luther's sermon on John 2.1-11, for the Second Sunday after Epiphany, 1540.

[110]"[Das ist uns alles zum Exempel vorgestellt, dass wir lernen fest bleiben im Glauben und] Gott nicht anders einbilden, denn einen barmherzigen Herrn, [der uns wohl lässt versuchen, und stellt sich, als zürne er mit uns und lache mit der Welt; aber man hüte sich nur vor demselben Lachen und erschrecke nicht vor dem Zorn, damit er die Seinen ansicht. Es scheint wohl, als halte ers zuweilen mit den Bösen und verfolge die Frommen ohne alle Gnade; aber es schadet nicht und ist nur um einen Blick zu thun. Das ist aber ein blinder und geistlicher Blick, den man muss sehen mit blinden Augen, das ist, mit dem Glauben, der nichts sieht: *Fides enim est invisibilium*,] der Glaube redet von den Sachen, die man nicht sieht, und von unerfahrnen Dingen, Hebr. 11,1—[All this is presented to us as an example, that we may learn to remain steadfast in faith and regard God in no other light than that of a merciful God who, indeed, may permit us to be tempted, as if he were angry with us and were laughing at us with the world; but let us guard ourselves against such laughter and not become terrified at the anger, with which he attacks his people. It may appear as if at times he were on the side of the wicked and persecuted the godly without mercy; yet it does no harm and it depends only upon a glance. But it is a blind and spiritual glance, which we must give with blind eyes, that is, with the eyes of faith, which sees nothing; For faith is invisible.] Faith lays hold . . ."

not judge nor reason by what it sees or feels but by what it hears. It depends upon the Word alone and not on vision or sight" (AP 1, 22f; StL 11, 5).[111]

So also in a sermon for the Sunday after Christmas (1540), on the presentation of Christ, Luther takes the example of Joseph and Mary, who, if they had judged according to outward appearances,

> would have considered Christ no more than a poor child. But they disregard the outward appearance and cling to the words of Simeon with a firm faith, therefore they marvel at his speech. Thus we must also disregard all the senses when contemplating the works of God, and only cling to his words, so that our eyes and our senses may not offend us (AP 1, 259; StL 11, 236).[112]

In a sermon for Epiphany (1540), Luther similarly refers to the wise men as ones who would never have found the Christ Child had they followed the light of reason and nature, and who, upon finding and worshipping him, manifest great faith, since they thus treat the humble child as a king. "This was a strong faith indeed, for it casts aside many things which impress human nature. . . . This is the kernel of the Gospel, in which the nature and character of faith is explained

---

[111]"[Alles, was den Glauben betrifft, die Vernunft und Natur verachtet und ihr ganz uneben ist; als, dass dieser sollte sein der König von Jerusalem, der so arm und gering daherfährt, dass er nur auf einem fremden gedingten Esel reitet, wie möchte das Natur und Vernunft erkennen?] Wie reimt sich das Einreiten zu einem grossen Könige? Aber der Glaube ist der Art, dass er nicht richtet noch folgt, darnach er hört. Am Wort hanget er allein, und gar nichts am Gesicht oder Geberde—[Everything that concerns faith is against reason and nature; for example, how can nature and reason comprehend that such an one would be king of Jerusalem who enters in such poverty and humility as to ride upon a borrowed ass?] How does such an advent become a great king? But faith is of the nature . . ."

[112]"[Hätte Joseph und Maria sollen urtheilen nach dem Gesichte, so] hätten sie nicht mehr Christum geachtet denn ein armes Kindlein. Aber nun lassen sie das Gesicht fahren und hängen an den Worten Simeons mit einem festen Glauben; darum verwundern sie sich der Rede. Also müssen wir auch alle Sinne fahren lassen in Gottes Werken, und nur an seinen Worten hangen, auf dass unser Auge oder Sinne uns nicht ärgern."

as an assurance of things not seen" (AP 1, 363; StL 11, 336).[113] In these and countless other examples Luther returns repeatedly to his theme of faith's trusting where nature and experience cannot see. For Luther, then, faith is blind trust, not in the Kierkegaardian sense, but in the sense of trust where sight and experience are denied and only the promise remains.

The faith of which Luther generally prefers to speak would be classified as *fides qua creditur*, the faith by which the Gospel is believed. He speaks with contempt about mere *fides historica*, saying that "it is of no value only to believe that this history is true as it is written; for all sinners, even those condemned believe that" (AP 1, 143; StL 11, 126).[114] He then continues, manifesting his well-known stress on the *pro nobis* of the Gospel,[115] to contend that

> the right and gracious faith which God demands is, that you firmly believe that Christ is born for you, and that this birth took place for your welfare. The Gospel teaches that Christ was born, and that he did and suffered everything in your behalf (Ibid.).[116]

Thus Luther's version of faith as *fiducia* might be summed up in two ideas, a blind trust in the Gospel and, correlatively, a confidence that the Gospel is *pro nobis*.

---

[113]"O wie ein mächtiger Glaube ist das gewesen, wie viel Dinges hat er verachtet, das die Natur bewegt hätte.

. . . Hier liegt nun der Kern des Evangelii, darin es uns lehret die Art und Eigenschaft des Glaubens, dass er sei *argumentum non apparentium* (eine gewisse Zuversicht dess, das man nicht siehet)."

[114]Sermon on the Gospel for Christmas Day (1540): "Derselbige Glaube ist nicht allein, dass du glaubest, diese Historie sei wahr, wie sie lautet; denn das hilft nichts, weil alle Sünder, auch die Verdammten solches glauben."

[115]See Siggins 1970, 269; Green 1980, 139. But Bertram's (1989, 182f) statement that "faith is equivalent to truth for Luther" goes too far.

[116]"Sondern das ist der rechte gnadenreiche Glaube, den Gottes Wort und Werk fordert: dass du festiglich glaubest, Christus sei dir geboren, und dass seine Geburt dein sei, dir zu gut geschehen. Denn das Evangelium lehrt, dass Christus sei um unsertwillen geboren, und alle Dinge um unfertwillen gethan und erlitten."

Anselm's references to faith, on the other hand, are generally not as complex as Luther's, being more apt to be made in reference to what is believed, i.e., *fides quae creditur*. Faith seeking understanding—*fides quaerens intellectum* —is a premium example of Anselm's regular use of the term. The debate among Anselm scholars over the relationship of faith to reason would be much easier to follow, I believe, if precisely what is meant by faith were made clear. When Barth (1960, 18) asserts that for Anselm faith is "utterly and completely independent of the validity of . . . human propositions"—propositions which are the product of faith's seeking—he is evidently referring to *fides qua creditur*, the faith by which one believes;[117] yet when McIntyre (1954, 33) counters, against Barth, that the *probare* of faith determines the form of its *intelligere*, i.e., that the rational proving of Christian truth is what makes up the contours of its understanding, he is evidently referring to *fides quae creditur*, or the faith which is expressed in the creeds. Thus it appears to me that while McIntyre may have misunderstood Barth, he does not seem to have misread Anselm. Anselm's conception of *fides*, though broad enough to include both *fides qua* and *fides quae*, more regularly focuses on the latter.

In the *Cur Deus Homo*, for example, Boso redirects the focus of the exercise at a strategic point coming at the end of his first entire section of the work, where he leads as well into his second entire section. Here he tells Anselm, "I did not come for you to remove from me doubts about my faith, but in order that you might show me the reasons for my certainty" (CDH I:25; S II, 96:6-7).[118] Boso is interested in the rationale of the faith which is believed; he is not concerned about the condition of his own faith. He requests further that

---

[117]Admittedly, Barth's own perspective is able to say that *fides quae creditur* is also independent of human propositions, since in his view the Word of God is itself independent of them. Thus Barth's position on Anselm is not expressed in terms which are altogether clear.

[118]"Non ad hoc veni ut auferas mihi fidei dubitationem, sed ut ostendas mihi certitudinis meae rationem."

Anselm help him to understand by rational necessity (*rationabili necessitate*) all those things "which the catholic faith commands us to believe about Christ" (96:9-10).[119] Anselm's *Cur Deus Homo* itself, then, is largely devoted to answering Boso's request. The terms in which Boso makes his request indicate that he is thinking of articles of faith, and not of the nature of faith as believing or trusting.

Yet Anselm is not at all fundamentally at odds with Luther's conception of faith as trust, either. Though he is certainly far less apt to focus thereon, a point which to be sure is not insignificant, he nonetheless is found referring to faith as trust, in essence *fides qua*. There is no evidence, however, of a notion in Anselm of faith as trusting *in darkness*, unlike Luther. While Luther relies on *faith* alone when sense experience is denied, Anselm is found to rely on *reason* alone when the faith, i.e., *fides quae*, is removed. Still, aside from this rather glaring omission when compared to Luther, Anselm does manifest basic agreement with the notion of faith, *fides qua*, as holding to Christ for salvation, or more precisely as holding Christ against the demands of God for salvation. This can be seen at the end of the *Cur Deus Homo*, where Anselm explains how great and just is the mercy of God. Though he does not employ the term *fides*, he surely has it in mind when he pictures the mercy of God.

> Certainly, what could be understood as more merciful than for God the Father to say to a sinner, condemned to eternal torments and having no way to redeem himself, "Receive my Only-begotten son and offer him in your stead," and for the Son himself to say, "Take me and redeem yourself" (CDH II:20; S II, 131:29-132:3)?[120]

---

[119] "Ita me volo perducas illuc, ut rationabili necessitate intelligam esse oportere omnia illa, quae nobis fides catholica de Christo credere praecipit—So I wish you to lead me through to the point where by rational necessity I ought to understand all those things which the catholic faith commands us to believe about Christ."

[120] "Nempe quid misericordius intelligi valet, quam cum peccatori tormentis aeternis damnato et unde se redimat non habenti deus pater dicit: accipe unigenitum meum et da pro te; et ipse filius: tolle me et redime te?"

This statement appears to reveal in Anselm a mindset conducive to the prevailing understanding of the sacrifice of the mass (so Forde 1984, 22), but Luther can actually be found to say something very similar, in a sermon on the Gospel for St. Stephen's Day.

> It is not sufficient for one who is to stand before the judgment of God, to say, I believe and have grace; for all that is within him is not able to protect him; but he proffers to this judgment Christ's own righteousness which he permits to plead for him at the judgment seat of God. . . . Under this righteousness he creeps, crouches, and stoops, he confides in Christ's righteousness and believes without the least doubt that it will sustain him (AP 1, 283; StL 11).[121]

In both of these references—both Anselm's and Luther's—the Christian offers Christ or the righteousness of Christ to God, and while Luther's reference is more clearly to faith, it would be stretching matters to hold that Anselm's reference is to the mass and not to faith; thus I conclude he is referring to faith, to *fides qua*, and in a manner not unknown to Luther, notwithstanding the latter's aversion to the sacrifice of the mass.

Anselm's prayers manifest a similar emphasis on faith as holding to Christ; his *Prayer to Christ*, being largely a string of connected quotations from the Psalms and elsewhere, speaks with great eloquence (the eloquence of Scripture itself, being largely taken directly therefrom) of the desire of faith for Christ. Christ is the "hope of my heart, strength of my soul, help of my weakness" (Ward 1973, 93:12-13; S III, 6:10),[122] while Anselm pines away concerning his own weakness and "lukewarmness" (*teporem*, S III, 7:21), finally pleading with Christ after the fashion of the bride in Solomon's song:

---

[121]"Denn wer vor Gottes Gericht bestehen soll, ist nicht genug, dass er sage, ich glaube und habe Gnade; denn alles, was in ihm ist, mag ihn nicht genugsam schützen: sondern er bietet demselbigen Gerichte entgegen Christi eigene Gerechtigkeit, die lässt er mit Gottes Gerichte handeln . . . Unter dieselbe kreucht, schmuckt (schmiegt) und duckt er sich, traut und glaubt ohne allen Zweifel, sie werde ihn erhalten."

[122]"Spes cordis mei, virtus animae meae, auxilium infirmitatis meae."

What shall I say? What shall I do? Whither shall I go?
Where shall I seek him? Where and when shall I find him?
Whom shall I ask? Who will tell me of my beloved?
      for I am sick with love.
The joy of my heart fails me;
      my laughter is turned into mourning;
My heart and my flesh fail me;
      but God is the strength of my heart, my portion for ever.
My soul refuses comfort, unless from you, my dear.
Whom have I in heaven but you,
      and what do I desire upon earth beside you? (Prayer 2; Ward 1973,
97:143-153; S III, 9:72-79)[123]

This manner of speech is quite common in Anselm's prayers, where the most

abundant indications are found of the yearnings of faith. Still, although these are

instances of an emphasis in Anselm on *fides qua*, it is admittedly rather difficult

to find much on this in his main treatises. So again, though we can claim some

fundamental agreement here between them, yet there is something to be said for

Luther's far greater theological stress on the point.

---

[123]This prayer weaves the words of several portions of Scripture into its text, as was
Anselm's custom in his earlier years. My next chapter deals with this style in detail, and this
prayer will be taken up again there; for Latin original see below, p. 76.

Chapter III

Points of Some Similarity:

on Style of Expression

Anselm's Use of Scripture, to Achieve Pulchritude

Gillian Evans, I believe, has done more to make possible a fair reading of Anselm than anyone including Sir Richard Southern, to whom she dedicated her *Anselm and Talking about God* (1978).[1] This work is particularly helpful because Evans uncovers in it something critical to a correct reading of Anselm, namely his attention to beauty, *pulchritudo*. Karl Barth (1960) had considered the simplicity of his rational method of proving theological truths to be the key to Anselm. "Anselm's theology," he declared frankly, "is simple. That of the plain secret of his 'proving'" (68). But Evans points out that there is more to it than this. Anselm, she says, "displays a simplicity of conception and exposition hard won through many years of discussion and private thought, which had been systematically directed towards making things plain" (1978, 139).

---

[1] I am indebted to Dr. Wanda Cizewski of Marquette University for recommending that I give careful attention to Evans' work in my research.

Barth was attracted to the simplicity of Anselm's theology, but evidently failed
to understand that the simplicity in itself is one of the most compelling traits of
Anselm, something intentional on Anselm's part. In giving due attention to
method of expression, Anselm becomes a craftsman of words, with the expressed
intention of compelling the reader, in part by virtue of the pleasure gained from
appreciating simple beauty in speech. Evans points to his interplay of sounds and
cadences, by which he tries to "woo his readers into enjoyment not only by
virtue of the pleasure gained from appreciating simple beauty in speech." Evans
points to his interplay of sounds and cadences, by which he tries to "woo his
readers into enjoyment not only by presenting them with satisfying arguments, but
also by pleasing them with elegant writing" (144f).[2]

When this is considered alongside his attention to fittingness, we begin to
see a pattern. Anselm's first concern, it appears, is for fittingness in all things:
in God, in created order, and even in the use of language. Since beauty is fitting,
Anselm is being internally consistent to devote such effort to propriety in
expression and choice of words.   The chain-of-arguments reasoning so
characteristic of his method contributes to this propriety of expression. Coupled
with Anselm's choice of words, it brings forth a manner of speaking unparalleled
in appearance of fittingness and beauty. Attention to means of expression when
talking about God was evidently a serious matter to Anselm, as this was for him
the most important purpose of language. Evans points out that for Anselm, in the
tradition of Augustine (cf. *De Doctrina Christiana*, Book IV), it is only proper
that such a beautiful subject matter should be reproduced in appropriate style
(Evans 1978, 145).

As we have seen, Luther was aware of Anselm's heavy stress upon beauty
and propriety, and even cites him with approval in a 1518 sermon on penitence

---

[2]Brian Stock (1983, 333) notes that Anselm is "one of the first authors to conceive of a
reading public in the modern sense."

(WA 1, 319-324), where Luther speaks of a *speciossima iusticia*, a most beautiful propriety, which arises out of intuition and contemplation, and becomes the love of wisdom, whose beauty (*pulchritudo*) is apparent. This makes for true penance, because to love propriety is to do that penance, and those who do love propriety are therefore considered worthy of absolution.[3] Yet Luther goes on to distinguish abstract intuitive virtue from concrete intuitive virtue, saying of the former that as virtue for its own sake it appeals to carnal men, and calling the latter the truly holy kind, seen in Christ.[4] Luther then contends that it is this latter kind to which Anselm refers in his teaching that one ascends to the love of God from the love of good men.[5] Thus Luther was, at least as late as 1518, not openly opposed to Anselm's reasoned contemplation of the beautiful, although it certainly is not a frequent topic of Luther's discourse.

Anselm's singular devotion to the framing of his thoughts in appropriate words can be seen more clearly in his earlier works, when he was less bothered by the need to defend Christian truth against its enemies. Thus we see it more clearly in the *Monologion* and the *Proslogion*, both written between 1076 and 1078, while he was still Prior of Bec. Both of these works speak the language of devotion, and are marked by Anselm's careful efforts at expressing himself as beautifully as he was able. Thus when he sent the *Monologion* to his old master

---

[3]"Secundo paratur per intuitum et contemplationem speciosissimae iusticiae, qua quis in pulchritudine et specie iusticiae meditatus in eam ardescit et rapitur, incipitque cum Salomone [Wisdom of Solomon 7.29] fieri amator sapientiae, cuius pulchritudinem viderat. Haec facit vere poenitentem, quia amore iusticiae id facit, et hii sunt digni absolutione" (WA 1, 319:27-31).

[4]"Sed hic regula talis notanda est, quod intuitus virtutum fit dupliciter. Abstractive seu per se, et sic carnalem hominem parum movent: quo modo traditur per verbum praedicationis. Sic enim non nisi speculative videtur. Concretive sive per aliud: hoc est (exempli gratia) ut intuearis homines, qui tali virtute lucent, quorum omnium speculum primum est Christus, deinde sancti in caelo. Verum rudem et incipientem maxime movent exempla praesentia et sui saeculi" (WA 1, 319:36-320:4).

[5]"Sic enim B. Anshelmus docet ascendere ad amorem dei ex amore hominis boni" (WA 1, 320:6-7).

and predecessor in the archbishopric of Canterbury, and received at length an unexpected criticism and suggestion for changing it, Anselm was faced with a difficult choice. Lanfranc felt that not enough attention was given to the authority of Scripture or the Fathers (Evans 1978, 16; Southern 1983, 19; see Letter 77; S III, 199-200), which indicates a failure either to grasp or to accept Anselm's chosen method. For Anselm the decision to omit authorities was undoubtedly taken because his method was generally to make his case *sola ratione*. This, it seems, was due to his conviction that balanced chain-of-arguments reasoning was more instrumental in the pursuit of faith's understanding, since this style of expression more appropriately highlighted the pulchritude of the faith (cf. Evans 1989, 38). So Anselm, while admitting to Lanfranc that he could have expressed himself better, chose nonetheless not to spoil the beauty of the whole by inserting authorities where his method called for resisting appeals to authority and his style called for concise and simple words. Thus he chose to leave the work as it was, though not without some apparent distress on having thus to dispense with the advice of his mentor. His inner turmoil over whether to reject Lanfranc's counsel or to add unwanted leavening to his method he resolved by opting for the former; which tells us that even Lanfranc meant less to him than his chosen method of aiming at a beauty of expression appropriate to talking about God.

Attention to beauty may be called an integral component in the mind of Anselm. It provides reasons both for his *sola ratione* method and for his abundant use of Biblical phrases and grammar. It also explains why he was so averse to controversy. Harmony and consistency were always important to him (so Evans 1978, 96), so he took no pleasure in controversy (98). This is, of course, a point of great contrast with Luther.

For Anselm, unlike Luther, the faith was not so much a matter which because of its substance would require defending; rather, what required either expression or defense was its pulchritude. Beauty of language was requisite because of the beauty of the faith, and the beauty of the faith is the ultimate basis of Anselm's *sola ratione* method.

In spite of this, there is a certain similarity of style between Luther and Anselm, resulting in each from separate convictions. Luther's vocabulary, like Anselm's, was frequently that of Scripture, and for him this was due to his convictions about the power of the Scriptures as the Word of God. But although Anselm's vocabulary is similar, there is a different reason. The method of Anselm involves a strict adherence to the Sacred Scriptures, both in terms of the boundaries they provide for the *sola ratione* method, and in terms of the language Anselm prefers to use. The reason for this preference appears to be Anselm's reasoned awareness of the beauty of the Biblical language and grammar. Anselm was interested in beauty, and hence he could find no better resource for adding beauty to his own words than Scripture itself.

It was, to be sure, a rather stock custom by Anselm's time to extract portions of psalms for use in the Hours of prayer, and in this respect Anselm's contributions are really nothing new. For example, in one eleventh-century book of prayers are found prayers which each follow a psalm and employ its words. Thus Psalm 23, "The Lord is my Shepherd," is followed by the words "Lord, be our shepherd, and we shall lack nothing. We desire no other leader than you, no pasture other than your glory. Lead us in the paths of righteousness, and we shall not go astray. In the valley of the shadow may we not be overcome" (Ward 1973, 37). Ward points out that it was customary even since the fifth century to give Old Testament words a New Testament meaning in similar fashion (36). What appears novel in Anselm is the attention he pays specifically to beauty, providing a rationale both for his *sola ratione* method and for his Biblical style.

In the use of the Biblical vocabulary Luther and Anselm appear very much alike, following the patristic tradition of Augustine. When one is so familiar with

the Scriptures, and so conscious of their sacred status as these men were, the
manner in which the Scriptures are so cherished is seen by the frequent use of
their expressions in one's own work. Anselm's method led him to attempt to
reconstruct the Biblical truths without the Bible, but his style of expression, which
betrays his great love for the sacred page, is not entirely true to his method. As
was not uncommon in his day, Anselm weaves implicit reference to Scripture
throughout his language, not so much as though he were given to providing the
authoritative word on the subject, but rather because this was the beautiful
language Anselm knew so well and therefore could not have avoided, even when
his expressed intentions were to argue *remoto Christo*, as if nothing at all were
known about Christ. Yet his devotion to beauty explains this tension in Anselm's
method, for it is this devotion which leads him both to construct *sola ratione*
chains of argument (which he considers most appealing to reason), and to employ
the vocabulary and phrases of Scripture in his speech.

This is not generally true of his philosophical works, however, which is
perhaps an indication of how Anselm understood philosophy to be the *ancilla
theologiae*, the handmaid of theology. References to Scripture in the *De
Grammatico*, the *De Veritate*, the *De Libertate Arbitrii*, and the *De Casu Diaboli*
are scant. In producing philosophical works which did not deal directly with
theological, i.e., Biblical matters, Anselm was not inclined to employ the
language of Scripture; the subject matter did not warrant the use of such
language, and perhaps therefore a lower quality of speech was deemed acceptable
in dealing with philosophical matters, in spite of their clear relation and aid to
theology.   Anselm's lack of Biblical language in his philosophical works
should not mislead his readers into thinking they were intended as ends in
themselves. That they were indeed *ancillae theologiae* can be seen in brief
references from each. The *De Grammatico* was evidently written to aid in
arguing against the dialecticians of the day, who are mentioned in its closing

words (DG 21; S I, 168:8-12). But the dialecticians' attack was to Anselm primarily one with theological consequences, as is seen especially in his defense of the Trinity against Roscelin in the *De Incarnatione Verbi*.[6] The *De Veritate* is clearly meant as an philosophical excursus arising out of theological matters, as is clear from the opening words of chapter one: "*Quoniam deum veritatem esse credimus*—inasmuch as we believe that God is truth" (S I, 176:4).[7] The *De Libertate Arbitrii* phrases the student's desire for further explanation in the familiar terms *Credo, sed intelligere desidero* (DLA 3; S I, 211:1) so reminiscent of the *Proslogion*'s famous *credo ut intelligam*. Further, the subject matter of the *De Libertate Arbitrii* in itself provides an example of Anselm's philosophical works as excurses intended to benefit theological thought: the freedom of the will. Such is also the case with the *De Casu Diaboli* and the *De Concordia Praescientia et Praedestinationis et Gratiae Dei cum Libero Arbitrio*;[8] these are

---

[6]Eugene Fairweather (1956) notes that Anselm's approach was a middle course between the radical dialecticians and the Gregorian reformers of his day. On the side of the extreme dialecticians were Berengar of Tours and Roscelin of Compiègne, and on the side of the reformers were Peter Damian, Bruno of Segni, and Manegold of Lautenbach, for whom dialectic was the *ancilla theologiae* in the most radically subordinate sense, as they tended to repudiate everything which lay beyond the simplest rational explanations. Anselm's response, says Fairweather, was more judicious. Following Lanfranc through the Berengarian controversy, he chose to answer the misuse of dialectic by "exemplifying, even more wholeheartedly than Lanfranc, its proper Christian use, which he took so seriously as to consider it part of the responsibility of the mature believer" (48).

[7]Here is an interesting instance of an employment of Biblical grammar. The manner of speaking employed in calling God truth is identical to that found in I John 4:8, which declares that God is love. Neither expression intends an ontological equation of God with the qualities of truth or love, but rather to state in a grammatically vivid way the necessity of connecting ultimate truth or love with God. Nowhere else in this treatise is such use of the Biblical grammar seen in the same way; there are references to Scripture, to be sure, but no evidence of the use of Biblical grammar in the framing of Anselm's own thoughts. This, I surmise, is due to the fact that it is a philosophical, not theological, work.

[8]I also admit that the *De Concordia* in particular could be considered a theological, and not a philosophical work, inasmuch as it deals with the very question with which Luther deals in his *De Servo Arbitrio*. However, the approach of Anselm in the *De Concordia* bears similarity in style to his other philosophical works, being rather unlike that of Luther in *De Servo Arbitrio*; hence I have chosen to classify it with Anselm's philosophical works and not to deal with it,

philosophical questions arising from the attention given Biblical matters. So it is
clear that Anselm's philosophizing was intended as an aid to his theology; the
lack of Biblical vocabulary is due both to the non-devotional nature of
philosophical works and to Anselm's seeing no necessity to garnish his
philosophical language with the *pulchritudo* generally reserved for his theological
works.[9]

Turning to the latter, I shall examine them briefly in chronological order,
for it will be easier thus to note that the Biblical grammar is most especially seen
in the earlier works.

The Prayers of 1070 and 1072

Among the earliest extant writings of Anselm is the 1070 collection of
seven prayers he sent to one Princess Adelaide, to accompany the "Flowers of
the Psalms" she requested of him (Letter 10; S III, 113-4; Ward 1973, 172f).
The language of Scripture is profuse therein, as is the case in all of his prayers
generally. Anselm pays more attention to the pulchritude of Biblical speech in
the prayers composed while at Bec than he will at any point later in his career.
Perhaps it is for this reason that his "prayers and meditations . . . were more
popular during the Middle Ages than anything else he wrote" (Evans 1989, 27).

---

though my choice is somewhat debatable, even to me. A comparison of Luther and Anselm on
the question of free will would have to be somewhat extensive, in order to do the matter justice,
and while well worth the undertaking, would seriously challenge the limits of my scope of
comparison here. Briefly (and inadequately), Luther's conception of the bondage of the will
derives from his reading of Scripture with a unified conception of grace (*gratia sola*) and the
Gospel foremost in mind, while Anselm's approach is to make an effort to reconcile, *sola ratione*,
seemingly opposed statements of Scripture on grace and free will.

[9]I admit that this was quite probably a less-than-fully conscious choice of language on Anselm's part.

His employment of Scripture appears in general to follow one of two patterns. Either he will employ at will disjunct Biblical phrases, as from the psalter—this will most clearly be seen, for example, in the *Proslogion*, or he will mold the prayer around some Biblical references, as in these prayers to Biblical saints considered in connection with events of their lives in particular. The use of the Bible is in the latter case somewhat more straightforward, but still not straightforward enough to find Anselm giving exact location. In this way Anselm refers in his prayer to St. Stephen to the martyrdom of Stephen and expands upon it in meditation:

> Your venerable face shone with the nobility of an angel, for purity made your heart so clear that your blessed eyes saw God in his glory; and you were on fire with so much love that in your goodness you prayed for the evil men that surrounded you. It was so, good Stephen, it was indeed so, and I rejoice, praise, and exult that I know this of you (Prayer 13, Ward 1973, 174; S III, 50:6-11).[10]

Thus also his *Prayer to St. John the Baptist* refers to him simply as "praised by an archangel before you were begotten by your father" (Ward 1973, 127; S III, 26:4),[11] and refers to his leaping in the womb as showing his mother the mother bearing God—*tu monstrans matri gravidam matrem dei* (Ibid.). So also his *Prayer to St. John the Evangelist* refers to him as "best beloved—*dilectissime*"—and as the one who "reclined familiarly on the glorious breast of the Most High—*cui familiare fuit recumbere supra illud gloriosum pectus altissimi*" (Prayer 11, Ward 1973, 157; S III, 42:5-8), combining the reference to John 13.23 (*Erat ergo recumbens unus ex discipulis eius in sinu Iesu, quem diligebat Iesus*) with the popularly familiar *Qui habitat*, Psalm 91 (90): *Qui*

---

[10]"Venerabilis vultus tuus angelica dignitate fulgeret; quod tanta cordis munditia nituisti, ut beati oculi tui deum in gloria sua viderent; quod tanta caritatis pietate arsisti, ut pium os tuum pie pro impiis te perimentibus oraret. Sic fuit, bone STEPHANE, sic fuit, sic gaudeo fuisse; et sic gaudeo, laetor, exulto te cognovisse."

[11]"prius ab archangelo laudatus quam genitus a patre."

habitat in adiutorio Altissimi. Next he makes reference to John 19.26, Jesus'
giving of his mother to John, following with some emphatic self-deprecation. In
his straits *(angustiis)* he calls to John, "although I am so tepid, yet with all the
affection of my mind—*quamvis tepido, toto tamen affectu mentis meae*" (S III,
42:15-16), combining a reference to the lukewarm church of Apocalypse 3.16
with Jesus' command to love God with all the mind (Matthew 22.37).

So continues this style through all the prayers sent to Adelaide, as well as
those sent to Gundolf in 1072, prayers to St. Mary. Not only is an abundance
of such language easily seen; the lilt of a careful use of cadence and meter is
evident throughout. Anselm's attention to beauty blends his Biblical vocabulary
with his own creative writing. His Prayer to God, for example, employs the
sounds of the words and the number of their syllables in a careful poetic style of
repetitive rhyme:

> Omnipotens deus et misericors pater et bone domine, miserere mihi
> peccatori.
> Da mihi veniam peccatorum meorum.
> Cavere, vincere omnes insidias et tentationes et dilectationes noxias;
> Perfecte mente et actu vitare quae prohibes,
>   facere et servare quae iubes.
> Credere, sperare, amare, vivere quod et quantum et ut scis et vis (Prayer
> 1; S III, 5:3-7; Ward 1973, 91:1-10).[12]

This style is also seen in Anselm's Prayer to Christ, a block from which, having
been cited above, is given here again with indication of its various sources. Here
the poetry of Scripture becomes the poetry of Anselm.

> Quid dicam? Quid faciam? Quo vadam?
> Ubi eum quaeram? Ubi vel quando inveniam?

---

[12]"Almighty God, merciful Father, and my good Lord, have mercy on me, a sinner.
Grant me forgiveness of my sins.
Make me guard against and overcome all snares, temptations, and harmful pleasures.
May I shun utterly in word and in deed, whatever you forbid,
And do and keep whatever you command.
Let me believe and hope, love and live, according to your purpose and your will."

Quem rogabo? Quis nuntiabit dilecto quia amore langueo?
Defecit gaudiam cordis mei,
  versus est in luctum risus meus.
Defecit caro mea et cor meum,
  deus cordis mei et pars mea deus in aeternum.
Renuit consolari anima mea nisi de te, dulcedo mea.
Quid enim mihi est in caelo,
  et a te quid volui super terram?
Te volo, te spero, te quaero.
Tibi dixit cor meum:
  quaesivi vultum tuum, vultum tuum, domine, requiram;
  ne avertas faciem tuam a me (S III, 9:72-79; Ward 1973,
97:143-153).[13]

Anselm's deft literary skill is here at its best (so Evans 1989, 27).

The *Monologion* (1076)

The *Monologion*'s statement of method is most clear on the intention to
exclude Scripture from the argument, and so Anselm is not seen to employ the
terms or phrases of Scripture until he is well into his treatise. Not until chapter

---

[13]"What shall I say? What shall I do? Whither shall I go?
 Where shall I seek him? Where and when shall I find him?
 Whom shall I ask? Who will tell me of my beloved?
  for I am sick with love.
 The joy of my heart fails me;
  my laughter is turned into mourning;
 My heart and my flesh fail me;
  but God is the strength of my heart, my portion for ever.
 My soul refuses comfort, unless from you, my dear.
 Whom have I in heaven but you,
  and what do I desire upon earth beside you?
 You do I want, you do I hope for, you do I seek.
 My heart said to you: I will seek you face, your face, Lord, will I seek; hide not your
  face from me."
In this prayer, again, Scripture is woven in throughout. "Quia amore langueo" is from Cant.
2.5; "Deficit gaudiam cordis mei, versus est in luctum" is from Lam. 5.15; "Defecit caro mea
. . . deus in aeternum" is from Ps. 73 (72).25; "Renuit consolari anima mea" is from Ps. 77.2
(76.3); and "Tibi dixit cor meum . . . ne avertas faciem tuam a me" is from Ps. 27 (26).8 in the
Roman Psalter. The Vulgate of Ps. 26.8 reads: "exquisivit te facies mea . . .''

29 (of 80), is Anselm seen to employ here and there the language of Scripture in
his own speech. Up until this point, the discussion has waxed philosophical, and
hence the Biblical vocabulary is not seen. But when a considerable number of
points have been established *sola ratione*, Anselm feels free to refer to them by
means of Biblical vocabulary. Though his method in the later chapters remains
consistently the *sola ratione* method, he now feels at greater liberty to employ the
Biblical language, once the points emphasized by it have been established *sola
ratione*. But rather than referring directly to a text, Anselm will simply insert
brief phrases from the Bible at will into his own composition, which is indicative
of his thorough familiarity with and love of Sacred Scripture. It may be that
Anselm's characteristic lack of references is at least partly due to a deep influence
of the vocabulary of Scripture on his own thought-patterns, causing him to refer
to various texts and phrases without full awareness that he was doing so. The
patristic mindset, still very much alive in Anselm's day, and certainly in Anselm
himself, was so conditioned by deep immersion into and meditation upon the
Bible as to frame the very patterns of devotional thought and prayer.

So it is that the later chapters of the *Monologion* begin to see a bit of a
stylistic breakdown, as it were, from his original intent to argue *remoto Christo*.
Now, for example, the expression of the Supreme Spirit (i.e., the Word), is
called that through which all things were made—*per quam omnia facta sunt* (M
29; S I, 47:6), taken from John 1.3.[14] So also does Anselm declare that the
Word is with God—*apud ipsum* (M 32; S I, 51:17), a clear reference to John 1.1:
apud Deum. Next, he calls the Word God's image—*imago* (M 33; S I, 53:4), a
reference to Colossians 1.15. So also does he label the Word God's figure—
figura (ibid.), from Hebrews 1.3. Likewise he calls the Word life and truth—*vita
et veritas* (M 35; S I, 54:9-10), found in John 1.3-4. Further, whatever the

---

[14]See also 30; S I, 48:12 and 31; 50:18.

Highest Spirit creates, the Word likewise creates—*Quare quaecumque summus spiritus facit, eadem et verbum eius facit et similiter* (M 37; S I, 55:19-20), a reference to John 5.19: *Quaecumque enim ille fecerit, haec et Filius similiter facit.* Or again, as the Father has life in himself, so has he granted the Son to have life in himself—*Sicut enim pater habet . . . vitam in semetipso, . . . ita . . . dat filio habere . . . vitam in semetipso* (M 44; S I, 61:1-5), from John 5.26. The mind is referred to as its own mirror—*speculum*—for contemplation of what it cannot see face to face—*facie ad faciem*, from 1 Corinthians 13.12 (M 67; S I, 77:27-28),[15] and everyone should strive toward God by loving the good with all the heart, soul, and mind—*toto corde, tota anima, tota mente amando*, from Matthew 22.37 (M 74; S I, 83:7-8). Or again, faith without love is dead—*fides sine dilectione mortua*, compare James 2.20: *fides sine operibus mortua* (M 78; S I, 85:3-4), and faith works by love—*fides quae per dilectionem operatur* (M 78; S I, 85:6), a line taken from Galatians 5.6: *fides quae per charitatem operatur.* And again, God alone is he from whom and through whom and in whom are all things—*ex quo et per quem et in quo sunt omnia* (M 80; S I, 87:6-7), a reference to 1 Corinthians 8.6: *quoniam ex ipso, et per ipsum, et in ipso sunt omnia.*

From these examples it is clear that in the later chapters of the *Monologion*, in which Anselm's expressed method is to set Scripture aside, Anselm has not escaped the terms of Scripture, in keeping with his desire for beauty of expression. In his method itself he appears consistent with his expressed statement on his method; but in his style, in the later chapters, the vocabulary and phrases of Scripture are seen in abundance. But both his method and his style, while seemingly inconsistent with each other, are consistent with his aim to achieve beauty and fittingness in language. Moreover, in view of the lack of any of this Biblical vocabulary until nearly halfway through the treatise, it is likely

---

[15]See also M 70; S I, 81:1.

that Anselm considered that when his chain-of-arguments has blossomed to the point where it stood alongside the Biblical record, he felt compelled to express himself in the best terms available, namely those of Scripture itself.

The *Proslogion* (1077-8)

The kind of implicit scriptural references seen as an element of style in the *Monologion* are far more abundant in the *Proslogion*, which perhaps is due to the even more highly devotional character of the latter. The *Proslogion* is itself a prayer, a word with God, i.e., a λόγιον πρὸς τὸν θεόν—the title may have been intended as a play on the words of John 1.1, though Anselm's knowledge of Greek was limited at best. Therefore an even greater abundance of stylistic artistry is to be expected, and the words of Scripture, being words of the *Word*, would be the best words from which to choose. In the *Proslogion*, the pages are literally filled with the vocabulary and phrases of Scripture, even more so than in the later chapters of the *Monologion*. Here Anselm's love of the sacred page is most clearly demonstrated, and it is helpful to remember that his established method of setting the authority of Scripture to the side in attempt to reason its truths separately from it, was in no way intended to cast any aspersion on Scripture, nor to suggest that it was less than most sacred. Though we may wish to call the method of Anselm characteristic of scholastic thought in general, we must see his language as rightly earning for him the appellation, "last of the fathers." At the risk of over-generalization, one might even suggest that this is the very point at which Anselm can himself be seen as a bridge between the patristic and scholastic era.

A brief look at the Biblical language of Anselm in the *Proslogion* will demonstrate something in his method which ought not be overlooked, namely that his use of reason, though freed from the need to appeal to authority in spite of

Lanfranc's criticism, was nonetheless closely bound to what the authority of Scripture had first revealed. Anselm's method was not given to allowing a mischievous free-play to reason; rather, reason must be disciplined to follow the exact steps of Scripture, yet without appealing to Scripture's authority. These exact steps were taken not only in what Anselm expressed, but also in how he expressed it, in his use of the Biblical vocabulary. If this was evident in the case of the *Monologion*, it is much more so in the *Proslogion*, where Anselm strings together an abundance of Biblical phrases.

Taking by way of example the *Proslogion*'s opening reference to Matthew 6.6 (*intra in cubiculum . . . clauso ostio*), we see this style employed from the outset. The reference is followed immediately by an implicit reference to Psalm 27 (26). Anselm says, "Speak now, my whole heart . . ."—*totum cor meum*, a reference to *cor meum* in the verse 8 of the psalm—". . . speak now to God: I seek your countenance; your countenance, Lord, I seek"—*Quaero vultum tuum; vultum tuum, domine, requiro* (M 1; S I, 97:9-10), a further reference to the same verse: *te quaerit facies mea; Faciam tuam, Domine, quaero*. The very next thought contains a reference to God's dwelling in unapproachable light—*lucem inaccessibilem* (98:4), from I Tim. 6.16, leading Anselm to ask what shall be done to seek his face, employing the terms of Psalm 84 (83): "Your servant . . . longs to come to you—*accedere ad te desiderat*," but "your dwelling place—*habitatio tua*—is inaccessible" (98:10-11), a reference to Psalm 84 (83).1-2: *Quam dilecta habitatio tua, Domine exercituum! Desiderat, languens concupiscit anima mea atria Domini.*

This line of speech continues here and there throughout the book; the words and language of one Biblical text are woven into Anselm's manuscript, followed immediately with the words of another. Space does not permit an expanded exposition of all the texts Anselm has woven into his work. Even Francis Schmitt, in providing the apparatus of the critical Latin edition, could not keep up with all the texts to which Anselm refers. Anselm's style here is not exactly one which quotes Scripture, but rather which is so at home with the text of Scripture that its vocabulary and terms are blended at will into the text of the treatise. Clearly, Anselm would not have been free to write in this manner without a thorough familiarity with the Sacred Scriptures. Anselm was not inclined so much to *quoting* Scripture as rather to *employing* Scripture and its words, in his own syntax and vocabulary.

The *De Incarnatione Verbi* (1092-4)

The *De Incarnatione Verbi* is for a theological treatise rather short on references to Scripture, due undoubtedly to the fact that it is a polemic against Roscelin. A man of peace, Anselm did not like polemics and avoided argumentation whenever he could; he always preferred the meditative repose of a monk. The work was written during the period when Anselm was forced against his will to become archbishop of Canterbury, a period of some considerable personal turmoil. Lanfranc had recently died, and Anselm found himself taking up the mantle of his mentor. So the *De Incarnatione Verbi* is by the nature of the work unable to be as devotional as Anselm preferred his works to be, and hence instances of the use of Biblical style are few.

The exception to this is the opening chapter, where Anselm provides a flourish of his former devotional style before launching into his attack on Roscelin. Anselm declares there that his adversary should not be accused "if he was once darkness, but now is light in the Lord—*aliquando tenebrae, nunc autem lux in domino*" (DIV 1; S II, 5:24-5), a reference to Ephesians 5.8. Next, after a paragraph on his intended purpose, Anselm provides another string of Biblical phrases so common in the *Proslogion*: before examining, *sola ratione*, the deep matters of faith, the heart must be cleansed by faith, for God says, "cleansing their hearts by faith—*fide mundans corda eorum*'' (8:7-8), a reference to Acts 15.9: *fide purificans corda eorum*; and the eyes must be enlightened through keeping the precepts of the Lord, because the precept of the Lord is light, enlightening the eyes—*praeceptum domini lucidum, illuminans oculos* (8:9), from Psalm 19.8 (18.9); through humble obedience we ought to become as little children—*debemus fieri parvuli* (8:10), a reference to Matthew 18.3: *efficiamini sicut parvuli*—that we may learn the faithful testimony of the Lord, giving wisdom to the little ones—*testimonium domini fidele, sapientiam praestans parvulis*, from Psalm 18.8 (8:11-12). The string of Biblical language continues thus for a couple of paragraphs, followed by a reference to the dialecticians whom Anselm means to refute, rounding out the chapter.

The remainder of the treatise is then devoted to the defense and hence does not contain strings of Biblical phrases. Thus as soon as Anselm turns directly to the task of polemics before him, he drops the language of Scripture. One must wonder why. Perhaps his distaste for polemical argumentation, as necessary as he thought it was, led him somewhat unconsciously to drop the language of Scripture, as if to suggest that the *pulchritudo* of divine truth must be reserved only for those who would appreciate it. This, as we shall see, is one of the distinguishing points of great difference between Anselm and Luther. While Anselm's polemics provide the least evidence of the Biblical vocabulary, Luther's by contrast provide a great deal of evidence of a likeness to the approach of Scripture. Luther was at home with polemics, and his choice of Biblical vocabulary was very much a part of his polemical style; Anselm was not given to polemical speech, and only employed it when the beauty of reason was less likely to convince. So his Biblical vocabulary is reserved for his more meditative works.

The *Cur Deus Homo* (1094-8)

In the *Cur Deus Homo*, Anselm's manner of employing the Biblical vocabulary and phrases is much like that seen in the later chapters of the *Monologion*, in the opening chapter of the *De Incarnatione Verbi*, and more profusely throughout the *Proslogion*. Because the *Cur Deus Homo* is not presented in the form of a prayer, its use of the Biblical language is, as in the later chapters of the *Monologion*, more restrained than what is seen in the *Proslogion*; yet because it is not polemical, the Biblical language finds greater use than in the *De Incarnatione Verbi*. Further, like the *De Incarnatione Verbi*, it was written in a later period, from Canterbury, where Anselm no longer enjoyed the luxury of Bec's placid retreat. Nonetheless, examples of Biblical language and its corresponding pulchritude still abound. In the opening chapter, Anselm explains that the purpose of gaining understanding is that those who do "may always be ready to give a defense to everyone who asks you a reason for the hope that is in us—*parati semper ad satisfactionem omni poscenti se rationem de ea quae in nobis est spe*" (CDH I.1; S II, 47:10-11), a reference to 1 Peter 3.15, which has the plural *vos* for *se* and *vobis* for *nobis*. On Christian simplicity, he says that many believers "ponder it in their hearts—*in corde versare*" (48:25), a reference to Luke 2.19: "*Maria autem conservabat omnia verba haec, conferens in corde suo*," and Luke 2.51: "*Et mater eius conservabat omnia verba haec in corde suo.*" Anselm then complains that Boso has asked something which is above him, *a me supra me est*—taken from Psalm 139 (138).6: *Nimis mirabilis est mihi scientia haec*—and too lofty for him, *altiora me* (48:25), from Ecclesiasticus 3.22: *Altiora te ne quaesieris*. It is likewise something which his intellect is unable to grasp—*quam intellectum meum ad eam capiendam non sufficere* (49.1-2), another reference to Psalm 139 (138).6: *Sublimis: non capio eam*. Boso's words (let us assume the vocabulary of Boso in the manuscript is essentially that of Anselm, inasmuch as Anselm is its composer) refer to giving freely what has been freely received—*ea quae gratis accepisti libenter impertiris* (49:5-6), coming from Matthew 10.8: *Gratis accepistis, gratis date*. Anselm then refers to the subject at hand as being of a form fairer than the sons of man—*est de specioso forma prae filiis hominum* (49:18), from Psalm 45.2 (44.3): *Speciosus es forma prae filiis hominum*. Anselm's characteristic use of Biblical phrases and grammar continues thus throughout the *Cur Deus Homo*, yet to a somewhat lesser extent than in the *Monologion* and *Proslogion*.

The *De Conceptu Virginali* (1099-1100)

Evans (1978) contends that when Anselm wrote the *De Conceptu Virginali* as a sequel to the *Cur Deus Homo*, it did not bear as close an attachment to it as the *Proslogion* did to the *Monologion*. The *Proslogion* was meant to complete something Anselm felt he had left unfinished in the *Monologion*, but the necessity for the *De Conceptu Virginali* was not as urgent following the *Cur Deus Homo* (172).

Thus the character of the *De Conceptu Virginali* is much less comparable to that of the *Cur Deus Homo* than is that of the *Proslogion* to the *Monologion*. In the *De Conceptu Virginali*, Anselm refers frequently to Scripture and comments on it. He does not appear to be so given to employing the *remoto Christo* methodology of the *Cur Deus Homo*. On the other hand, he is far less inclined to use the phraseology of Scripture in the weave of his own speech. This treatise appears to be one simply designed to tie up some loose ends (so Evans ibid.). Now in the later years of his career, Anselm is producing less devotional material, and he appears less intent on paying attention to beauty in speech; again, this is probably due to the influence of change and upset since the quietude of Bec. We see from this perspective a clear reason why Anselm was so averse to taking the position at Canterbury: perhaps he knew this would happen to his

writing, or, put another way, perhaps his stylistic modifications are indicative of
the restlessness he knew he would feel once removed from his earlier peaceful
existence.

The *De Processione Spiritus Sancti* (1102)

This document was written to defend the *filioque* against the Greeks. Only
fifty years earlier was the Great Schism between East and West, whose major
point of contention this was. Once again Anselm has been called upon to perform
a task he considers somewhat odious, namely enter into debate in efforts to
convince opponents. "There are many who are more capable than I of
accomplishing this," he objects, adding that the task was imposed upon him by
many whose request "I dare not resist" (DPSS 1; S II, 177:10-13).[16] Here
we find a return to the *sola ratione* methodology of earlier works, in contrast to
the *De Conceptu Virginali*, where it is virtually absent. But similarly to the *De
Conceptu Virginali*, there is a conspicuous absence of the pulchritude and
vocabulary of Scripture found in the earlier works, with the exception, of course,
of the trinitarian names and terms of inner-trinitarian relationship. This work is,
like the *De Incarnatione Verbi*, necessarily given to polemics, though the tone
herein is considerably more conciliatory and respectful toward the Greeks than
the *De Incarnatione Verbi* is toward Roscelin. Yet in spite of the complete lack
of animosity expressed, the *De Processione Spiritus Sancti* still finds no room for
the threads of Biblical language so artistically woven into his earlier treatises.
Perhaps it was too far removed from Anselm's present world and therefore lost.

---

[16]"Quamvis igitur multi sint qui hoc melius me possint efficere, tamen quoniam mihi a
pluribus iniungitur, quorum petitioni cum pro debito veritatis amore tum pro eorum caritate et
religiosa voluntate non audeo resistere, invoco eundem spiritum sanctum, ut ad hoc me dignetur
dirigere."

Another striking case is Anselm's reply to a letter of a Bishop Walram to him (S II, 233-238), written between 1106-1107. Walram's letter abounds with the language of Scripture woven at will into the text, exactly as seen in the *Proslogion*, and throughout the letter. The style is precisely that of an earlier Anselm, and therefore might be expected to produce a reply in kind from the latter. But Anselm's reply to Walram (239-242) does not follow stylistic suit, suggesting that he was no longer given to his earlier style.

Luther's Use of Scripture, for Proclamation

The 'Unreasonable' Approach of Luther

Luther's thought is less reasonably structured than Anselm's. I am not entirely content to call his approach unreasonable, since that adjective is generally used derogatorily, and it is certainly contrary to my intent to appear critical of Luther's approach; I call his approach unreasonable simply for lack of a better term; I mean to say that Luther shows no evidence of following the Anselmian/scholastic pattern of arguments meant to appeal especially to reason.

Luther's difference of approach is most especially seen in the fact that he does not employ the Anselmian chain-of-arguments approach. For Anselm, the chain-of-arguments was employed as a means of appealing to reason through the fittingness and propriety of careful logic. This was for him a chief way of appealing to beauty. There is a somewhat inconsistent appearance to Anselm's thought here, since he also prefers to find beauty in the language and phrases of Scripture. We might wonder, that is, why he did not prefer as well the order of Scripture to that of reason. But Anselm considered reason—sanctified reason, to be sure—the organ which recognized *pulchritudo*, and thus the use of well-

reasoned and systematic arguments ought certainly be seen as appropriate means
of attracting reason. Anselm was interested in gaining adherents to the faith by
appealing to their reason. But Luther's agenda was different. He preferred not
to order his thought according to a pattern constructed by reason, but according
to Scripture. Though Anselm was also clearly wont to express himself in Biblical
terms and phrases, Luther took the use of Scripture a step further. Not only was
Luther conversant in the terms and phrases of Scripture; he was especially
concerned to present the message of Scripture with the agenda of Scripture.
Where Anselm's agenda was generally provided by sanctified reason, Luther
preferred to follow the agenda provided by the Word of God. His task was,
simply, *enarratio*:[17] exposition of the Word, under that Word's own
guidance.[18]

For Luther as a preacher, it was not so much of importance that the words
and message be beautiful, as clear.

> We need good, learned, spiritual, faithful preachers in every locality who
> without books can draw forth the living Word from the old Scriptures and
> make it plain and simple to the people, just as the apostles did (AP 1,
> 372; StL 11, 345).[19]

----

[17]I wish to acknowledge that the use of the term *enarratio* to sum up Luther's conception of
his task was suggested to me by Dr. Kenneth Hagen, whose manuscript (1989) on Luther's
Galatians commentary is still in preparation.

[18]It is well worth pointing out that Luther's use of the term "Word of God" differs markedly
from Anselm's use. For Anselm and generally for the Fathers before him, "the Word" was the
regular term for the Second Person of the Trinity, whereas Luther preferred to employ "Word
of God" to refer to the contents of the Sacred Scriptures. The Bible is for Luther the Word of
God, especially the Bible as it is orally proclaimed; for Anselm the Word is more commonly the
Son of God, i.e, God the Son. In this difference in usage, we find Luther employing the term
after the fashion of Luke-Acts, whereas Anselm's usage corresponds to the common occurrence
in John, as in "the Word was God" (John 1.1). This difference is discussed in chapter five.

[19]"[Darum ists gar nicht neutestamentisch Bücher schreiben von christlicher Lehre; sondern]
es sollten ohne Bücher an allen Oertern sein gute, gelehrte, geistliche, fleissige Prediger, die das
lebendige Wort aus der alten Schrift zögen und ohn Unterlass dem Volke vorbläueten, wie die
Apostel gethan haben."

The Gospel must be set forth publicly, in clear terms. The need for this public proclamation of it was what led Luther to translate the Scriptures into the vernacular, as well as to write his catechism in the simplest terms he knew. This is not to say that he wished to re-phrase the Gospel in his own terms, but the very opposite. His convictions about the power inherent in the words of the Gospel itself led him to the task of setting those words forth plainly, with the conviction that the words, once communicated, will themselves be at work in the formation of Christian faith. So Luther was intent on following as closely as he was able the agenda of Sacred Scripture. Consequently there is none of the meticulous outline division or point-by-point analysis, of the type seen abundantly in the scholastic era, the type budding in the chain-of-arguments approach of Anselm.

This is not to say that Luther had no use for categorical division. There is evidence in places of careful numbering of points, the Ninety-Five Theses being the most celebrated example. The Disputation Against Scholastic Theology (1517) and the Heidelberg Disputation (1518) likewise contain 97 and 40 numbered theses respectively. Yet even here, the numbering is not anything like the chain-of-arguments approach Anselm had taken. Furthermore, these early works do appear to be the only ones which evince a numerical division of sentences or short theses.[20] Luther's numbering of theses does not divide them according to an outline, but rather seems to be a simple listing of points of contention. It is reasonable to suppose, although admittedly it cannot be proven, that Luther's manner of numbering his points arises out of his familiarity with scholastic form, which may have naturally suggested his use of numerical point division. Given this supposition, one can nonetheless derive no sense of deliberate, reasoned ordering in Luther's method of numeration, and this sets it

---

[20]See my excursus on the "early" and "late" Luther, at the end of this chapter.

apart from the method of Anselm. In the three works listed above, he presents
his theses in a way in which he appears almost to have put them on the page in
the order in which they came into his mind, entirely unlike the chain-of-
arguments method of Anselm. For Luther, putting thoughts on the page appears
to have arisen out of a different necessity. Where Anselm prepared fruits of
contemplative effort, Luther was too busy with the task of *enarratio*, of bringing
the Word out into the public, for such serenity. He perceived his task as one
behind which the force of conviction always lay. For him the ordering of
thoughts was not as important as the expression of them, when these were
perceived to be the thoughts of a faith which must be defended. This
'unreasonable' approach is itself more like that of Scripture, where the ordering
of points is likewise not generally seen to be in chain-of-arguments fashion.[21]
Luther's convictions about the power of the Word of God are seen to have led
him to spend less time finding the right outline or form for it than simply
proclaiming it. Luther did not long for the kind of serenity the Wartburg offered
him, but soon found himself too driven by the necessity to preach to stay there.
His willingness to risk coming out in public to preach in his "Junker Jörg"
disguise, while yet an outlaw, is ample testimony to his desire for a return to the
fray. In this respect we see how very unlike Anselm Luther was: where the
former craved the life of a monk, the latter was ever eager to carry on the battles
of the Church Militant. As a result, with regard to the formal ordering of
arguments, Luther was rather unreasonable. But this is in keeping with his
understanding of the power and force of the Word. That is, a systematic
approach need not be superimposed on it, for the simple reason that the Word

---

[21]I admit that chain-of-arguments reasoning can be found in the Scriptures on occasion,
especially in the Pauline epistles, as, for example, in Romans 10.14-15: How then shall they call
on him in whom they have not believed? And how shall they believe in him of whom they have
not heard?, etc.

itself is purely given. Thus Siggins (1970) maintains, "Luther's choice of an unsystematic approach is part of his conception of the theological task" (267).

Luther's Use of Catechetical Division and Order

To say that Luther's approach was unreasonable is not to say that he had no use for division or ordering of thought. To the contrary, he is seen to have great concern about proper division of the Word, in a doctrinal sense. Luther is emphatic about the right division of law and gospel, and contends that great pains must be taken lest this be confused. For Luther the distinction between law and gospel is the greatest skill in Christendom (WA 25: 5f, 22).[22] The law delivers one to God's wrath and punishment (WA 19, 210:7; 226:12); the gospel forgives through the name of Christ. In this way law and gospel are seen as God's two testaments (WA 8, 103:35-37; AE 32, 223).[23] Siggins (1970, 65) points out that Luther's heavy stress on this point even appears to set him at odds with Augustine. But law and gospel are not equals, as Holl (1977, 54) has noted. The preaching of the law is for Luther "alien," and the wrath and love in God are not on the same level. Love is God's "proper" work, while wrath is not.

Luther was also careful and deliberate in his structuring of his catechism. When dealing with instruction for the young or uninformed, Luther becomes very orderly and concise. In the catechism he retained the traditional parts of Decalog, Creed, and Our Father, with the conviction that there is "no simpler nor better arrangement of this instruction of doctrine than the arrangement which has existed

---

[22]In a 1532 sermon on Galatians 3.

[23]"Against Latomus" (1521): "Scriptura divina peccatum nostrum tractat duobus modis, uno per legem dei, altero per Euangelium dei. Haec sunt duo testamenta dei ordinata ad salutem nostram, ut a peccato liberemur—Divine Scripture treats our sin in two ways, one by the law of God, the other by the Gospel of God. These are the two testaments of God ordained for our salvation, that we may be freed from sin." Althaus (1966, 260) discusses this.

since the beginning of Christendom, viz., the three parts, Ten Commandments, Creed, and the Lord's Prayer'' (WA 19, 76:7-10).[24] But Luther was probably aware that the Ten Commandments had only been included since the thirteenth century, and that they generally followed, rather than preceded, the Creed. Moreover, in the Creed Luther took pains to make divisions according to a threefold structure corresponding to the three Persons of the Trinity. This represents a rather new approach, as previous catechetical uses of the creed had divided it otherwise (see WA 30/I, 434).[25] Luther might well be seen to have taken deliberate steps to substitute his own order (see Bente 1921, 64), since he was convinced that the law should precede the gospel. In this altering of the structure one can see some similarity to Anselm's reasoned approach. Anselm's stated intentions behind carefully structured reasoning and order, seen in the *Monologion*, were to provide the ignorant with a persuasion from reason alone (M 1; S I, 13:5-11). Thus it becomes clear that Luther, while in one respect very unlike Anselm who was ever searching for the most appropriate and beautiful way of expression, was on the other hand similar to him in his concern for simplicity of order in connection with catechetical instruction. This order Luther derives from the subject of Scripture. It is Scripture which for Luther demands such division according to law and gospel, and according to the works of the triune God. Here he is seen to be subservient to the order he perceives in Scripture, and more so than Anselm had been. Similarly, Luther derives from Scripture's account God as Father, Son, and Holy Ghost his division of creed and catechism. A tremendous difference is seen between Luther's trinitarian emphasis in division of the creed and the trinitarian emphasis we saw in Anselm. For Anselm,

---

[24]"Dise unterricht odder unterweysunge weys ich nicht schlechter noch besser zu stellen, denn sie bereyt ist gestellet von anfang der Christenheyt und bis her blieben, nemlich die drey stuck, die zehen gebot, der glaube und das vater unser.'' See also WA 30/I, 434, 457; WA 7, 204:5-17.

[25]The ordering of the Latin Church Fathers was Creed, Our Father, and Double Command of Love (*Doppelgebot der Liebe*, the original alternate form of the decalog).

discussions of the Trinity centered on the *opera ad intra*[26] and hence were more abstract, providing fertile ground for speculative thought; in Luther, the *opera ad extra* are consistantly put forward, and especially the work of Christ. Luther does not care about God in the abstract, the *deus absconditus*. Rather, "God must . . . be left to himself in his own majesty, for in this regard we have nothing to do with him, nor has he willed that we should have anything to do with him" (AE 33, 139; WA 18, 685:14-15).[27]   For Luther God is known only as he reveals himself, and in dealing with his self-revelation, one must of necessity deal first with the external works of God.[28]   These cannot be discussed apart from the Word of God, however, and on this point Luther is emphatic. In keeping with his insistence that grace alone is at work in the work of salvation from beginning to end, Luther will not allow for discussions of God apart from what God has revealed about himself, nor even for treatments of theology whose focal point differs from that of Scripture, God's own treatment of himself. Scripture sets in order for Luther not only the doctrinal content of theology, but also its manner of presentation. But this means that theology must be entirely Christocentric, since Scripture itself is seen thus by Luther.

> Every prophecy and every prophet must be understood as referring to Christ the Lord, except where it is clear from plain words that someone else is spoken of. For thus He Himself says: "Search the Scriptures, . . . and it is they that bear witness to Me" (John 5:39). Otherwise it is most certain that the searchers will not find what they are searching for

---

[26]See p. 51, n. 82 on my use of this term.

[27]*De Servo Arbitrio* (1525): "Relinquendus est igitur Deus in maiestate et natura sua, sic enim nihil nos cum illo habemus agere, nec sic voluit a nobis agi cum eo."

[28]Althaus' (1966) compendium of Luther's thought follows Luther's lead, devoting only two pages to "the Trinity" (199f).

(Luther, "First Lectures on the Psalms" (c1513) AE 10, 7; WA 3, 13:6-9).[29]

Luther has been criticized on this score for proposing a canon within a canon, by those who fail to understand what is meant by a Christological hermeneutic.[30] Luther does not thereby mean to impose from the outside, as it were, a Christological structure on the content of Scripture, but the very opposite. He in fact warns against "making your own ideas into articles of faith" (WA 7, 455; AE 32, 98).[31] It is his conviction that Scripture itself has this Christological structure and purpose, and that it is meant to be interpreted, according to its own testimony, in this way. For Luther, Scripture is no textbook or catena of theological truth, but rather a unified whole. One cannot know what Scripture is saying until one knows what Scripture is talking about, namely Christ. If, as Von Loewenich puts it, "A re-evaluation of all values results from the cross"(von Loewenich 1976, 12), then the value of Scripture itself, which proclaims the cross, must likewise be re-evaluated. It must now be understood as the true manger which holds Christ (StL 11, 135; AP 1, 152).[32]

---

[29]"Omnis prophetia et omnis propheta de Christo domino debet intelligi, nisi ubi manifestis verbis appareat de alio loqui. Sic enim ipse dicit: Scrutamini scripturas: ille enim sunt, quae testimonium perhibent de me, alioqui certissimum erit, scrutantes deficere scrutinio."

[30]George Tavard (1959, 86-89), for example, charges that Luther is inconsistent when he charges that other teachers wish to have their own doctrines established by Scripture, claiming that Christians are to Luther only those who agree with "his version" of Christianity. Siggins' (1970, 18f) defense of Luther's Christological hermeneutic is worthy of mention.

[31]"Mach nit Artickell des glawbensz ausz deynen gedanckenn, wye der grewel zu Rom thut, das nit villeicht ausz deynem glawben eyn trawm werde." For more on this, see Althaus 1966, 4n.

[32]Strictly speaking, it is for Luther the Old Testament which is the manger holding Christ: "Christus in dem Tüchlein bezeichnet den Glauben im Alten Testament . . . Siehst du hier, wie fein Christus und der Glaube in der schlechten Schrift und Figur gewickelt ist?—Christ in swaddling clothes represents the faith in the Old Testament . . . Do you here see how, figuratively speaking, Christ and the faith are wrapped up in the plain Scriptures?"

The Structure and Thrust of Luther's Speech

Luther's use of language must be taken into account in order to gain an accurate reading of Luther. His cognizance of the Biblical content and subject matter was his guiding force in his own choice of vocabulary and manner of expression. Where Anselm followed especially the Biblical pulchritude, Luther followed especially the Biblical subject matter. Doing this led him occasionally to employ Biblical terms and phrases within the fabric of his own vocabulary, as was the case with Anselm, deriving mostly from his familiarity with and love for the Scriptures, and hence there is some similarity of Luther's vocabulary to that of Anselm. But Luther differs in that he employs also the very thrust or "punch" of Scripture in his own words. As Jesus' words in the Gospels deliver personal challenge to the hearers, so do Luther's. Siggins (1970) agrees: Luther's unfettered style, he contends, is due to the fact that the voice of the Gospel relies upon its graphic and dramatic power of portrayal. The *pro nobis* of the history of Christ must always be heard (268f).

For instance, the Baptist's and Jesus' calls for repentance seem to have had a profound effect upon Luther, as is most evident from the fact that he includes it in the first of his Ninety-Five Theses. This call for repentance means a complete change of heart: "Our Lord and Master Jesus Christ, saying, Repent, etc., willed the entire life of the faithful to be one of repentance" (WA 1, 530:16-17; AE 31, 83).[33] The term μετανοεῖτε is not only in the imperative mode, but encompasses the entire life of the hearer. This gives Luther license to be as forceful in his own preaching and writing. As the Scriptures proclaim, so will Luther feel compelled to proclaim, and in the same manner of speaking.

---

[33]"Dominus et magister noster Ihesus Christus dicendo 'poenitenciam agite &c.' omnem vitam fidelium poenitentiam esse voluit."

Some debate has been seen over whether or not Luther meant to understand the heart of the Reformation to be the question "how do I find a gracious God?" The question itself actually surfaces rather late, in a sermon on baptism preached in Wittenberg on Feb 1, 1534 (WA 37, 661:23-24; see Pesch, 15n).[34] The debate hinges on whether the question sounds too Pelagian to be the lynchpin of the Reformation. We will do well, however, to realize that Luther's use of rhetoric must necessarily sound quite Pelagian at times, inasmuch as the intention of such rhetoric is to move the hearers to response.

Luther scholars have likewise disagreed on what Luther considers justification to be. He calls it the *articulus stantis et cadentis ecclesiae* (WA 50,199), but has been shown to have used it in two different ways, referring either to imputation or to actually becoming righteous. This two-fold use of the word cannot be correlated, as some have attempted, with Luther's early and later theology; he uses "justification" in both senses at the same time, sometimes even shortly after each other in the same text (see Althaus 1966, 224-228). Luther's organic linkage here of the articles of faith has puzzled scholars who have failed to take his use of language into account. One must derive his meaning from his subject-matter taken as a whole, and cannot expect a fair reading of him to be gained from hearing only a short quotation here and there. Siggins' (1970) explanation is apropos:

> In the nominalist logic, which he espoused, whereas concepts are univocal, terms that stand for concepts in language vary flexibly with the nature of the discourse. As a result, the correct hermeneutical order, he insists, is from the subject matter to the grammar, and not vice versa (2; see WA 45, 548,10).

One must know therefore what Luther is talking about before one knows what he is saying. This is most especially true with theology as Luther understood it. In

---

[34]Luther asked himself after fifteen years as a friar, "O wenn wiltu ein mal from werden und gnug thun, das du einen gnedigen Gott kriegest?"

Ebeling's (1970) words, theology is responsible for its own language (91; see Althaus 1966, 8n).

Some scholars have attempted to drive a wedge between Luther's doctrine of Christ and his doctrine of justification; not, that is, to suggest a contradiction here in Luther, but rather to suppose that his thought can be neatly divided here. This is not possible, however. Luther's central assertion that Christ is in the Father should not be understood as an abstract contention, but rather, always as being *pro nobis*. As noted above, Luther tended to prefer doing theology "from below," as opposed to Anselm whose theology was typically done "from above." Scholars therefore who would pit Luther's admission that justification is the *articulus stantis et cadentis ecclesiae* against Siggins' contention that for Luther the person of Christ is central fail to see that for Luther Christology cannot be discussed statically. Siggins (1970) wonders whether Luther can even be said to have a Christology at all (268f). The One who is in the Father is for Luther the One who suffers, and through whom justification is accomplished; and for Luther it is not possible to ponder these thoughts in isolation from each other.

Scholars who fail to see this will tend not only to assume a difference in stress between the person of Christ and the work of Christ, but furthermore to contend that there is a tension between Luther's celebrated *fröhlicher Wechsel* and forensic justification. There are those who claim that Luther's reference to this "happy exchange" of Christ's righteousness and the sinner's sin in justification makes the doctrine of justification less than exclusively forensic, rejecting it as "early" Luther (so Hoffman 1976, 171; Green 1980, 194; see above, p. 45). But to contend that the *fröhliche Wechsel* requires an infusion of righteousness is to misunderstand Luther's preference for this language. The mystical presence of Christ in the believer should not be seen as a premise of this exchange, as Hoffman would have us believe. On the contrary, for Luther the language of exchange was simply another way of expressing the same thought as expressed elsewhere by the forensic terminology. In a letter to Johann Brenz in May 1531, Luther explains the sense in which the imputed righteousness of Christ is itself the righteousness of Christ *in nobis*.

> I also am accustomed, my dear Brenz, in order better to understand this problem, to imagine there exists no quality in my heart which bears the name faith or charity. But in their place, I put Jesus Christ, and I say: This is my righteousness. It is he, himself, who is the quality and (as they say) my formal righteousness; so that, in this way, I shall free and rid myself of the law and works, and even of the contemplation of that objective Christ, who is perceived as a doctor or giver. But I want him, by himself, to be, for me, both the gift itself and the doctrine itself, so that I may possess all things in him. Thus he says, I am the way, the truth and the life; but he does not say, I give unto you the way, the truth, and the life, as if, standing outside of me he worked such things within me. It is within me that he should be, should remain, live and speak and not through or in me, etc., 2 Cor. 6, so that we should be God's righteousness in him, and not in love or subsequent gifts (WA, Br 6, 100:49-101:59, see McDonough 1963, 55).[35]

Thus Luther can by his own admission speak of the Christ *in nobis* and mean something entirely other than the mystical presence of Christ; the *Christus in nobis* is the *Christus pro nobis*, and is clearly not meant by Luther to be understood as an enabler of virtuous habits which justify. Luther can employ a variety of terms to express identical thoughts.

Luther's terms must always be understood contextually, and his mastery of language includes an versatility such as is common in Scripture itself. Therefore great care must be exercised when comparing and contrasting Luther to his scholastic forebears. To contend with Holl (1977, 76f) that Anselm opted

---

[35]"Et ego soleo, mi Brenti, ut hanc rem melius capiam, sic imaginari, quasi nulla sit in corde meo qualitas, quae fides vel charitas vocetur, sed in loco ipsorum pono Iesum Christum, et dico: Haec est iustitia mea, ipse est qualitas et formalis (ut vocant) iustitia mea, ut sic me liberem et expediam ab intuitu legis et operum, imo et ab intuitu obiectivi illius Christi, qui vel doctor vel donator intelligitur. Sed volo ipsum mihi esse donum vel doctrinam per se, ut omnia in ipso habeam. Sic dicit: 'Ego sum via, veritas et vita'; non dicit: ego do tibi viam, veritatem et vitam, quasi extra me positus operetur in me talia. In me debet esse, manere, vivere, loqui, non per me aut in me etc. 2. Cor. 6, ut essemus iustitia Dei in illo, non in dilectione aut donis sequentibus."

for the *satisfactio* element in Christ's work while Luther chose the *poena* element, and then to charge that these ideas are mutually exclusive is not only to misunderstand Anselm's *aut satisfactio aut poena*, but to forget Luther's adaptability in using forms of speech. For Luther, the true meaning of Christ's work can be found in *either* or *both* concepts.

Luther's Use of the Biblical Texts

In Luther's Explanations of the Ninety-Five Theses (1518), he opens by stringing several references to Scripture together in support of his position. Unlike Anselm, he employs the texts of Scripture here primarily to explain his position. Anselm's employment, we recall, was primarily to provide fitting vocabulary or *pulchritudo*. Both weave strings of Biblical texts into their own writing, but for Luther the intent is strictly *enarratio*; he wishes to set forth from the Scriptures the message of the Scriptures.

So in his explanation to the first of the Ninety-Five Theses, Luther states that he shall prove his meaning of Jesus' term "repent" (Matthew 4.17) "for the sake of those who are misinformed." Since he will argue in his second thesis against the contention that "repent" is a reference to the sacrament of penance, we know that he is deliberately attempting here to set forth his interpretation of *metanoiete* in opposition to the Vulgate's *poenitentiam agite*. Thus he begins by substituting his own translation of *metanoiete*, which is *transmentamini*. This leads him to Romans 12.2 which in the Vulgate has the similar *reformamini*: Be transformed by the renewal of your mind (*reformamini in novitate sensus vestri*). This text is now employed to demonstrate the meaning of repentance. Here Luther demonstrates that as it were his mental concordance deals not so much in exact words as in concepts. First he rejects the Vulgate's rendering, but then he proceeds to tie the meaning of the text to Romans 12.2 without finding correspondence either in the Latin or in the Greek terms. The Greek term in the Romans 12 text is μεταμορφοῦσθε, not μετανοεῖτε. Thus it is clear that Luther was not employing Romans 12.2 as a proof-text. Otherwise we might well wonder how Luther can adduce here the Romans 12 passage in support of his interpretation of the term, for we see that word used there is different. But Luther is thinking conceptually, and hence will not quibble over exact correspondence of individual terms; his definition of a term must be derived from the context in which the term appears.

There is a clear and certain likeness to Anselm in Luther's grammar. Neither of them used proof-texts, but both of them tied strings of texts together into their own discourse. Although Luther frequently gives the reference, at least generally, when he uses or refers to a Biblical text, the original manuscripts contain no quotation marks around the Biblical quotations, as Pelikan has also noted (Pfürtner 1964, 8). As Schmitt provided the quotation marks not originally supplied in Anselm, so did the Weimar editors provide for Luther. The American edition even makes bold to provide in brackets every reference it finds Luther making to Scripture; even when he provides book and chapter, the brackets are inserted in order that we may know the exact verse. But this is not to represent accurately the mind of Luther, who needed no concordance for his work. His fluent familiarity with all the parts of Scripture allowed him to import at will relevant texts.

So his explanation of the first of the Ninety-Five Theses continues:

It is evident, however, that this recovery or hatred of oneself should involve one's whole life, according to the passage, He who hates his soul in this life, preserves it for eternal life. And again, He who does not take his cross and follow me, is not worthy of me. And in the same chapter, I have not come to bring peace, but a sword. In Matthew 5, Blessed are those who mourn, for they shall be comforted. And Paul in Romans 6 and 8 and in many other places orders us to mortify the flesh and members of the body which are upon earth. In Galatians 5 he teaches us to crucify the flesh with its lustful desires. In II Corinthians 6 he says,

Let us show ourselves in much patience, in many fastings, etc. I produce these citations so extensively because I am dealing with those who are unacquainted with our teachings (AE 31, 84; WA 1, 530:25-531:3).[36]

Here we see both a similarity and a dissimilarity with Anselm. Luther is more apt to show at least roughly to what in Scripture he is referring; this is, as he says, to educate the uninformed. Luther is not driving at pulchritude, but at instruction. His purpose is to enarrate, to proclaim Christ.

In *De Servo Arbitrio (1525)*, Luther refers continually to Scripture in order to demonstrate the source of his teaching, and on occasion will employ Biblical phrases or terms without giving the reference, in a vein quite similar to Anselm's technique. For example, in a section on the hiddenness of the true church, Luther declares,

> For the Church is ruled by the Spirit of God and the saints are led by the Spirit of God (Rom. 8) [v.14: "For as many as are led by the Spirit of God, they are the sons of God."] And Christ remains with his Church even to the end of the world [cf. Matthew 28.20: "and lo, I am with you alway, even unto the end of the world."] and the Church of God is the pillar and ground of the truth [I Timothy 3.15: "the church of the living God, the pillar and ground of the truth."] These things, I say, we know, for the creed that we all hold affirms, I believe in the holy catholic church (AE 33, 85; WA 18, 649:30-650:3).[37]

---

[36]"Certum est autem, quod ista resipiscentia seu odium sui tota vita fieri debeat, iuxta illud: Qui odit animam suam in hoc mundo, in vitam aeternam custodit eam. Et iterum: Qui non accipit crucem suam et sequitur me, non est me dignus. Et ibidem: Non veni pacem mittere, sed gladium. Matt: v. Beati qui lugent, quoniam ipsi consolabuntur. Et Paulus Ro: vi. et viij. aliisque multis locis iubet mortificare carnem et membra, quae sunt super terram. Et Gal: v. docet carnem crucifigere cum concupiscentiis eius. Et ij. Corin: vi. dicit: Exhibeamus nosmetipsos in multa pacientia, in ieiuniis multis &c. Haec sic late profero, tanquam cum eis agam, qui nostra ignorant."

[37]"Ecclesia enim spiritu Dei regitur, Sancti aguntur spiritu Dei, Rom. 8. Et Christus cum Ecclesia sua manet usque ad consummationem mundi. Et Ecclesia Dei est firmamentum et columna veritatis. Haec, inquam, novimus. Nam sic habet et symbolum omnium nostrum: Credo Ecclesiam sanctam catholicam." Vulgate references are as follows: Romans 8.14: "Quicumque enim spiritu Dei aguntur, ii sunt filii Dei"; Matthew 28.20: "et ecce ego vobiscum cum omnibus diebus, usque ad consummationem saeculi"; I Timothy 3.15: "Ecclesia Dei vivi, columna et firmamentum veritatis."

Here it is also evident that Luther is not employing the language of Scripture for the reasons Anselm had done so; rather, his purpose is to teach, and where he is at liberty to assume that his audience has some awareness of the Scriptures, he does not feel the need to demonstrate the source of his assertions. Moreover, Scripture is not for Luther a proof-text book, but rather a Word which is meant for proclamation; therefore if he in his teaching is tending to the very task of proclaiming what Scripture says, his task may be considered accomplished even if he does not list the Scriptural reference; hence he evidently did not feel the need to be entirely meticulous about it. Thus when Luther's editors on occasion take it upon themselves to "correct" Luther where he is perceived to be in error, they are actually misrepresenting him somewhat (so Hagen 1989, 16f).

Luther's mental concordance is clearly in use in his sermons as well. No matter what text he is preaching, he will regularly employ abundant references from anywhere in the Scriptures, and usually only as if in passing, as if briefly to bolster the words of his interpretation. That is, his interpretation with great regularity employs words of Scripture found elsewhere. He, like Anselm, often prefers the very words of the Bible to his own words. Luther's sermons will normally have a dozen or more references to passages of Scripture other than the lesson on which he is preaching, in which he gives exact location (besides this, he occasionally provides references in which he will not bother to give the location of the verse he is quoting other than to provide its source, e.g., Jesus, or St. Paul).

For example, in his sermon on Matthew 21.1-9 (First Sunday in Advent), Luther will interpret the apostles' setting of Christ on their garments as teaching that they do not preach themselves but Christ; then, Luther's means of emphasizing this point is to refer to a string of texts from the epistles to demonstrate this truth: 2 Corinthians 1.24: "Not that we have lordship over your faith," 2 Corinthians 4.5: "We preach not ourselves, but Christ Jesus as Lord, and ourselves as your servants for Jesus' sake," and 1 Peter 5.3: "Neither as lording it over the charge allotted to you" (AP 1, 54; StL 11, 39f).

Or again, in a sermon on Matthew 20.1-16, the Gospel for Septuagesima Sunday, warning against pride, Luther refers to the fears of even the greatest saints, and how some of them fell. In this connection he cites David's complaints in Psalm 131.2: "Surely I have stilled and quieted my soul; like a weaned child with his mother," Psalm 36.11: "Let not the foot of pride come against me," and Psalm 119.21: "Thou hast rebuked the proud that are cursed." Next he mentions Paul in 2 Corinthians 12.7: "That I should not be exalted overmuch there was given to me a thorn in the flesh"; then he refers to "to-day's Epistle" in which "we have heard . . . what honorable men have fallen" (1 Cor. 9.24 - 10.5: ". . . with many of them God was not well pleased: for they were overthrown in the wilderness.") Finally he sums up with "Behold, how Saul fell! How God permitted David to fall! How Peter had to fall! How some disciples of Paul fell!" (AP 2, 110f; StL 11, 513)[38]

Examples of this nature are abundant throughout the sermons of Luther, and the few cited here should in no way be supposed to be the bulk of proof for my contentions of Luther's preference for employing strings of Scripture references in service of his instruction.

So Anselm and Luther were both able and inclined to employ Scriptural phrases and passages at will in their own composition; the difference is that Anselm's purpose in doing so was primarily to achieve pulchritude, and thus to appeal to reason, whereas Luther's purpose was to proclaim in the best way possible the message of Scripture. What better way than to recite and refer repeatedly to the words themselves?

---

[38]"Siehe, wie ist Saul gefallen! Wie liess er David fallen! Wie musste Petrus fallen! Wie fielen etliche Jünger Pauli!"

Excursus:

The "Early" and "Late" Luther

The question of Luther's development has entertained scholars for years, and has not been a primary focus of this investigation, but a certain aspect of the issue deserves mention here, inasmuch as it has bearing on this study.

Ian Siggins' (1970, 4f) assessment of the two primary schools of thought is apropos.

> Scholars on both sides continue to argue the importance of the continuities and discontinuities between the "young" and the "mature" Luther. . . .
>
> We may decide, with Professor Rupp, that "it is clear, in all essentials, his theology was in existence before the opening of the church struggle of 1517." [E. Gordon Rupp, *Luther's Progress to the Diet of Worms* (Greenwich, 1951), p. 39.] Or we may conclude, with Professor Cranz, that "the differences between the early and the mature works are so great that only confusion results from the assumption that we are dealing with a single, unified position." [F. Edward Cranz, *An Essay on the Development of Luther's Thought on Justice, Law, and Society*, Harvard Theological Studies, 19 (Cambridge, Mass., 1959), p. xiv.] In either case the answer makes an undeniable difference to the shape of Luther's doctrine.

Some scholars from among Rupp's side in the debate have noticed a shift in Luther, notwithstanding their conviction that Luther's theology remained intact from 1517 on. Siggins reminds us that proponents of the one school do not deny that Luther refined his thoughts (6). Of these scholars, some evaluate this shift in terms of development or maturation in Luther, while others refuse to make that judgment, maintaining instead that Luther's thought was fully developed in 1517. Among the first group is Paul Althaus, who refers to two "stages of development" in Luther pivoting on the year 1524 (Althaus 1966, 375). His use of the term 'development' is questionable, however, since he acknowledges that the occasion of the Anabaptists called Luther to a different front (350f), and notes Luther's own explanation of how he preached differently in the first period of the Reformation because of the prevailing theological climate (262n). Althaus is essentially agreed with Rupp. "The development of [Luther's] thought from his earlier to his later years is discussed only at some very important points. Apart from this, his theology is understood as unified and consistent at all important and decisive points throughout all stages of his development" (v-vi). Ernest Schwiebert (1950) refers similarly to a maturation in Luther, yet he takes it as a result, in part, of his struggle with the "Heavenly Prophets" in 1524. Schwiebert maintains that Luther was not fully mature until 1528 (282; 449). Werner Elert holds likewise that after 1523 Luther overcame many one-sided views as his theology progressed (see Schütte 1980, 54).

Scholars who have noticed the shift without evaluating it as evidence of development include Walther von Loewenich (1976), who refers to a "slight" shift in Luther, which von Loewenich terms a reshaping of the "back parts of God" on the basis of the theology of the cross (49). Siggins (1970) agrees that Luther shifted in his descriptions of the *theologia crucis* (80f). Both scholars see this as a shift away from a ready reference to a *deus absconditus*, a God who remains hidden in revelation, to the much stronger Christology of Luther's later years, during which he more readily portrays Christ as the full revelation of God. Holsten Fagerburg (1972, 178f) holds that Luther emphasized the promise in his earlier writings, but the elements of the sacraments later.

I agree that the Anabaptist controversy marks the period after which Luther seems to have shifted his focus, but there does not appear to be sufficient evidence to conclude that this points to development or maturation in the Reformer. Allegations of development made purely on the basis of revisions are unwarranted. It is safer to say that the overall character of Luther's thought appears to have been intact by 1517, despite the fact that the writings of his later years tend to manifest a greater stress upon the objective elements of the faith. Luther's focus of concentration appears to have shifted in at least some subtle but significant respects, which is to be expected in consideration of the fact that different parties opposed him from 1523 on.

In his years prior to 1523 his major adversary was Rome, and the first object of his attack was the indulgence traffic. This he began to criticize in sermons on October 31, 1516, and February 24, 1517. Soon afterward his attacks intensified, in the Ninety-Five Theses (1517) and the Leipzig Debate (1519). The indulgence issue was from the start foremost among the papal abuses against which Luther railed. Luther saw that where indulgences were sold, the Gospel was minimized. "For those indulgences are prompted so extensively and exclusively that the gospel is treated as an inferior thing and is hardly mentioned" (AE 31:176; WA 1, 585:20-21).[39] It seems that the main issue at stake here was the significance of faith, and its omission in the current teachings of the church. Since the nub of contention was the Roman circumvention of faith in their advocacy of the *ex opere operato* communication of sacramental grace, Luther's point of greatest emphasis was the importance of faith and, correlatively, of the Word of God as that which creates and maintains faith. The essence of the problem may be seen to have lain primarily in Rome's heavy stress upon the objective element of sacramental activity, viz., the sacramental offering of grace, to the extent that the subjective element, viz., the appropriation of grace by faith, was excluded.

In response to this, Luther gave highest emphasis to the subjective element, the reception of grace by faith. Thus, especially in his earlier years,

---

[39]"Explanations of the Ninety-Five Theses," Thesis 28.

Luther seldom spoke of the merit of Christ, the atonement, or the distribution of grace in the sacraments, without including the reception of grace by faith. For Luther, who understood his ordination vows to have laid upon him the requirement to be a defender of the faith on every front, it became for him critical to stress the absolute necessity of faith, in dealing with the issues at hand in this controversy. Luther's battle for faith necessitated his treatment of theology from the angle of its point of contact with its beneficiaries, since it was this point at which for Luther the Roman errors centered. Thus he commonly attributed to faith the highest supremacy. This stress and verbal emphasis upon faith itself (*fides qua creditur*) necessarily meant that the content of faith (*fides quae creditur*) should receive less attention. In this controversy by which his "early" years are marked, Luther spoke of theology from the subjective angle, viz., the appropriation of grace, and he steered notably clear of the objective angle, presumably both because the point of contention was not here, and because the problem, as Luther saw it, was precisely the exclusively objective (*ex opere operato sine bono motu utentis*) character of Roman theology. Luther's Sitz im Leben was the struggle for faith versus works, and for faith versus an understanding of the *ex opere operato* communication of grace which saw no necessity for faith.

The greatest difficulty with Luther's constant emphasis, in his earlier years, on the receiving end of justification (subjective justification) is that some of his statements appear to neglect the atonement and merit of Christ, especially where the Word of God, as the declaration of the justificatory verdict, is juxtaposed with faith as the acceptance of that verdict. Perhaps it was because errors concerning the objective value and necessity of the atonement were not directly affecting the laity that in spite of the questionable treatment of the necessity of the atonement by the late nominalists, Luther did not directly address these, in dealing with the issues at hand. Thus some statements of his in his earlier years appear to place faith and the Word in such a highlight as to give them a meritorious character which in later writings would tend to be attributed more exclusively to Christ alone. It is certainly not unreasonable to suppose that the Anabaptist controversy may have been a catalyst in what appears to have been a shift toward objectivity. Any perception that Luther in his earlier years failed to connect faith and its object may well be explained by considering the fact that he had so frequently to make faith's necessity his point of entry into debate. In his later years he found faith being confused with personal experience, and thus it is to be expected that a richer definition of it is found in his later thought, as he seeks to defend it from false ideas of what faith is.

Chapter IV
Points of Difference

On the Essence of Sin

Sin is for Anselm "nothing other than not to render to God what is due,"[1] generally labelled among scholars as a view seeing sin as privation, or absence of original righteousness. This tradition, which Scotus and Ockham would follow (see Froelich 1985, 146) was in opposition to the strict Augustinian idea of sin as concupiscence, a morbid quality of the soul (so Fairweather 1956, 58; Froelich 1985, 144-147). For Anselm, concupiscence is not sin. The sinful "appetites (*appetitus*)" are in themselves neither just nor unjust, and do not of themselves make one unjust; it is only if one consents to them by will (*voluntate*) that they render one *iniustum* (DCV 4; S II, 144:6-8). Anselm argues his case here, presumably because he knows of opposition to it, by maintaining on the basis of Romans 8.1 that there is no condemnation for Christians. If, he argues, the sinful appetites rendered one culpable in themselves, then damnation would

---

[1]"Non est itaque aliud peccare quam non reddere deo debitum." CDH I:12; S II, 68:10.

indeed result (144:10-11).[2] Since this is not the case, his conclusion is that
concupiscence is not sin. Therefore *"non eos sentire, sed eis consentire
peccatum est*—the sin is not to sense these, but to consent to them" (S II, 144:11-
12).

Tavard (1983, 32) contends that Anselm was handicapped by his
quantitative measurement of grace, and indeed Anselm declares that repayment
of what is owed to God must consist in more than what was stolen.[3] But where
Anselm's quantitive measurement appears even more readily is in his calculation
of sin. Anselm declares that satisfaction of punishment must follow upon every
sin: *"Necesse est ut omne peccatum satisfactio aut poena sequatur"* (CDH I,15;
S II, 74:1-2). Further, he has Boso ponder being caught in the necessity of
having to commit one sin or some greater one (*aut hoc aut maius facere
peccatum*, S II, 88:25). This atomizing of sin, quite indicative of quantitative
measurement, gives insight into Anselm's conception of sin. Sin for Anselm is
not in the affections, but in acts to which the affections lead, and it is for these
that debt to God is incurred (so Ritschl 1966, 340).

Luther voices agreement with the conception of sin as debt to God (contra
Aulén 1969, 116f; Forde 1984, 50) in as prominent a work as the Small
Catechism. Christ "suffered, died, and was buried, that he might make
satisfaction for me and pay what I owe, not with silver or gold, but with his own
precious blood" (LC, Article II; Trigl., 686).[4] To contend that in Luther's
view this satisfaction is made not to God but to the devil is not only to

---

[2]"Nam si sentientem sine consensu iniustum facerent, sequeretur damnatio—For if
experiencing them without consent made unjust, damnation would follow."

[3]"Nec sufficit solummodo reddere quod ablatum est, sed pro contumelia illata plus debet
reddere quam abstulit—Nor will it suffice merely to repay what was stolen, but because of the
wrong inflicted he ought to repay more than what he stole" (CDH I:11; S II, 68:22-23).

[4]"gelitten, gestorben und begraben, dass er für mich genugtäte und bezahlte, was ich
verschuldet habe, nicht mit Silber noch Gold, sondern mit seinem eigenen teuren Blut."

misunderstand Luther's use of the term "satisfaction" here, but to misrepresent his understanding of the atonement. In his postil for the epistle for the fifth Sunday in Lent, on Hebrews 9.11-15, Luther spells out clearly the recipient of Christ's offering, namely God. "Christ offered himself in the heart before God . . . He hung before the eyes of God, and is still there. The altar is also, spiritually, the cross" (StL 12, 462f; AP 7, 164).[5] In a sermon on Easter Sunday's epistle (1 Cor. 5.6-8), Luther in a passage remarkably indicative of some Anselmian logic, declares,

> The meaning of the phrase "sacrificed for us" . . . [includes the] necessity of considering the greatness and terror of the wrath of God against sin in that it could be appeased and a ransom effected in no other way than through the one sacrifice of the Son of God. Only his death and the shedding of his blood could make satisfaction. And we must consider also that we by our sinfulness had incurred that wrath of God and therefore were responsible for the offering of the Son of God upon the cross and the shedding of his blood.
>
> Well may we be terrified because of our sins, for God's wrath cannot be trivial when we are told no sacrifice save alone the Son of God can brave such wrath and avail for sin (AP 7, 190f; StL 12, 487).[6]

I am, quite frankly, rather amazed to find that some Luther scholars have been persuaded by the idea that Luther believed the offering of Christ's sacrifice was to the devil. Such scholarship is clearly irresponsible, for it is unquestionably

---

[5]"[Aber] Christus opferte sich selbst im Herzen vor Gott . . .
"Er am Kreuz [in keinem Tempel, sondern] vor Gottes Augen hing, und noch daselbst ist. Item, der Altar ist auch geistlich das Kreuz."

[6]"Was aber das heisse, dass er spricht: 'für uns geopfert', [haben wir in der Predigt vom Leiden Christi gehört, wie uns zwei Stücke darin vorgehalten werden sollen, Zum ersten,] dass wir bedenken den grossen, ernsten und erschrecklichen Zorn Gottes wider die Sünde, an dem, dass solcher Zorn durch keinen andern Weg hat mögen abgewendet werden und die Versöhnung durch keine Bezahlung hat mögen erworben werden, denn durch dies einige Opfer, das ist den Tod und Blut des Sohnes Gottes, und dass wir alle mit unsern Sünden solchen Zorn Gottes verwirkt, und Ursache gewesen sind, das Gottes Sohn hat müssen am Kreuz geopfert werden und sein Blut vergiessen. Solches soll in uns wirken, dass wir ernstlich erschrecken von unsrer Sünde wegen; denn es muss nicht ein geringer Zorn Gottes sein, weil du hörst, dass kein ander Opfer hat mögen gegen denselbigen stehen und für die Sünde Abtrag thun, denn der einige Sohn Gottes."

clear, if not from a general grasp of Luther's thought, at least from these references, that Luther believed Christ's offering to have been made to God the Father. Thus it should be just as clear that when Luther refers to sin as debt, or something owed, he means, as does Anselm, debt to God, and not to the devil.

But beyond this, Luther is quite clearly at odds with Anselm's conception of sin. His specific reference to and rejection of it is in the 1536 Disputation on justification. This document is framed after the pattern of the scholastics, with each *argumentum*, or point of contention, followed by Luther's rebuttal (*"Dilutio M. Lutheri"*). As in every case of such a scholastic pattern, the *argumentum* is given in the form of a statement expressed from the standpoint of error and perhaps a brief rationale providing some basis for the erroneous position, against which the response then argues. So here, there is an *argumentum* attempting to establish the scholastic definition of sin, followed by Luther's refutation, and here Anselm in particular is refuted. The *argumentum* attempts to establish the point that the scholastic definition of original sin is a good definition, and Luther rejects it out of hand, mentioning Anselm by name.

> When they [i.e., the scholastics[7]] say [original sin] is concupiscence, it is an insufficient definition. Anselm's definition is also too weak, when he says, it is the absence of original righteousness which ought to be present. It is indeed not so much the absence of righteousness as the inbred evil, making us fit for eternal death, even remaining after baptism, repulsive to the law of God and the Holy Ghost. The difference the papists do not understand, and therefore they do not define rightly. For whoever does not alter all these parts of original sin, does not understand sin. (WA 39/I, 116:17-117:7)[8]

---

[7]The reply translated here is of the Hamburg codex, which is the one variant of the eight codices of this treatise. The others specifically label the *scholastici* as the ones against which Luther is arguing.

[8]"Quando dicunt: est concupiscentia, est insufficiens definitio. Est et nimis tenuis Anshelmi definitio, quando dicit, esse carentiam iustitiae originalis, quae deberet inesse. Non enim est tantum carentia iustitiae, sed etiam ingenitum malum faciens nos reos aeternae mortis, manens etiam post baptismum, repugnans legi Dei et spiritui sancto. Has differentias papistae non intellexerunt, ideo non recte definierunt. Qui enim non novit omnes partes huius peccati

That Luther opposed Anselm's version of original sin is clear from this plain admission, which appears also to contain an implicit charge against Anselm of failure to understand sin. Here then is a twist of irony, as Anselm's famous rejoinder against the suggestion of redemption by fiat, "You have not yet considered how weighty a matter is sin" (CDH I,21; S II, 88:18) is in effect turned against him.

There is a strong conceptual connection between this difference between Anselm and Luther and the difference between them in their understanding of the means whereby faith advances. Since Luther sees Anselm's conception of sin as being "too weak," it should not surprise us to see that Anselm is found also to have a more optimistic view than Luther of the capabilities of reasoned argument, even argument by reason alone (*sola ratione*). It becomes evident, upon examining both realms of difference, that there is at the roots of their methodological differences a decisive difference in harmatology.

On the Means Whereby Faith Advances

Anselm's *Fides Quaerens Intellectum*

In the eleventh century, the eucharistic controversy pitted Berengar of Tours against Lanfranc of Canterbury, who was Anselm's teacher. Berengar was an extreme dialectician whose rationalistic view of the eucharist finally earned his condemnation from Rome. Against his dialectic there were also the extreme anti-dialectics such as Peter Damian, who rejected everything which lay beyond the simplest rational explanation. Such wildly speculative questions were being asked

---

originalis, non cognoscit peccatum."

in that generation as: Could God make the past not to have been? Lanfranc saw the need to oppose Berengar without going to such extremes as had Peter Damian, employing a restrained and circumspect use of reason, held within the limitations of the Church's official teaching. This was the course Anselm would also take.

Sir Richard Southern contends that "it was his [Anselm's] fixed and universal principle to go to the fountain-head for all his arguments and rules of life" (Southern 1983, 19).[9] On reflection upon Anselm's method, however, I must suggest that that this is not quite right. While it is true that Anselm speaks comfortably and fluently the vocabulary of Scripture, which certainly demonstrates his familiarity with it, and while further it is apparent that the Bible was for Anselm the final authority for all of faith and life, and that he considered his own use of reason to be confined within the limits set for it by Scripture, nonetheless it is not entirely true that Anselm held to its guidance as exclusively as Southern contends. Southern has evidently failed to take into account a major factor in the primary works of Anselm, namely his method. It was his expressed method in the *Monologion*, in the *Cur Deus Homo*, and arguably also in the *Proslogion*, as well as his implicit method elsewhere, to lay Scripture aside altogether in the pursuit of understanding of the truths of Scripture by logical reasoning. This is the essence of the *sola ratione* method of Anselm.

---

[9]Southern attempts in this article to defend the apparent inconsistency in Anselm's willingness to accept his promotion to the archbishopric at Canterbury (9). Since there was, as Southern notes, some sentiment in Rome holding that King William II was a schismatic, the question is raised whether Anselm's consent to his own promotion was inconsistent for one so given to the necessity of propriety and good order. Southern defends Anselm by pointing out his allegiance to Scripture above all other forms of authority. "In the absence of any scriptural prohibition," he then contends, "I doubt whether Anselm would have thought any higher sanction necessary or admissible" (17f). To demonstrate his point all the more forcibly, Southern continues by attempting to show Anselm as one for whom Scripture was the one guiding light in all of his theological thought.

To be sure, it is clear that Anselm's use of reason, though pronounced, was intended to stay within the bounds of what may be called a subordinate or ministerial use, which is to say that reason was for him meant to stay within the limits of subservience to the authority of Scripture. That is, Anselm never gave the impression that reason could establish anything *contrary* to Scripture. This limitation on the use of reason is made clear in the *Cur Deus Homo*, where Anselm declares, "For I am certain that if I say anything which without a doubt contradicts Sacred Scripture, it is because it is false" (CDH I, 18; S II, 82:8-10).[10] This is in keeping with what Southern (1983, 19) notes: "The Bible was the source beyond which it was impossible to go for all the rules of life and conduct: in the memorable phrase of his consecration, 'God was its only author'." Even in the *De Concordia*, written near the close of Anselm's life, Anselm provides evidence that it was not his intention to establish new doctrine by his exercise of reason. Here we find also an expression of Anselm's concept of the relationship between Scripture and reason:

> Moreover, if our understanding clearly opposes that [which is believed], no matter how invincible our reason should seem to us, we should not believe that it is supported by any truth. Thus, in this way, Sacred Scripture contains [i.e., confers] the authority of any truth which reason gathers, as Sacred Scripture either openly affirms it [the truth] or in no way denies it (DC III, 6; S II, 272:4-7).[11]

---

[10]"Certus enim sum, si quid dico quod sacrae scripturae absque dubio contradicat, quia falsum est."

[11]"At si ipsa nostro sensui indubitanter repugnat: quamvis nobis ratio nostra videatur inexpugnabilis, nulla tamen veritate fulciri credenda est. Sic itaque sacra scriptura omnis veritatis quam ratio colligit auctoritatem continet, cum illam aut aperte affirmat aut nullatenus negat."

The influence of Augustine is seen in Anselm's position, comparing the words of the former, in *Epist.* CXLIII, 7: "Si enim ratio contra divinarum Scripturarum auctoritatem redditur, quamlibet acuta sit, fallit veri similitudine; nam vera esse non potest—If our reason is offered as contrary to the authority of divine Scripture, no matter how acute it is, it is but a deceiving resemblance of truth, for it cannot be true." Migne 33, 589 (St. Augustine, vol. 2).

Here Anselm provides a simple explanation of the purpose he sees for reason, and an interpretation of his *fides quaerens intellectum*. Reason may gather any truth (*omnis veritatis quam ratio colligit*), provided that reason's 'truth' is not negated by Scripture. We may therefore conclude that Anselm's *fides quaerens intellectum* was not meant to establish articles of doctrine apart from or at odds with what Scripture has established.[12]   As Southern (1983, 19) notes, the *Proslogion*'s ontological argument itself begins with a reference to Scripture ("The fool hath said in his heart, 'There is no God' ").

But once Anselm has begun with Scripture, as in the case of the ontological argument, or with truth understood as having derived from Scripture, he goes on from there primarily by applying logic, not Scripture, as a demonstration of the scriptural truth.   Although Anselm's *fides quaerens intellectum* was certainly not meant to provide for anything resembling a nineteenth-century concept of development of Christian truth, nor to introduce new doctrine, it was nonetheless deemed by Anselm to be an exercise by which Scripture was generally laid aside while its truths are re-examined from a logical basis. Southern has noted, and rightly so, I believe, that for Anselm Scripture alone was meant to be the *norma absoluta*, the *norma normans*, of all truth. But what Southern has missed is the main highlight of Anselm's method, which is as it were to bracket Scripture off, to lay it aside, in an attempt to show the reasonableness of the faith from reason alone. Thus the purpose of Scripture in this method is to provide the *nihil obstat* for the consecrated musings of reason.

It is in his method that Anselm waxes very unlike Luther, and for this reason a closer look at this method is warranted, requisite to a clearer comparison to Luther on the question of the atonement's necessity.

---

[12]A discussion of this at greater length can be seen in Hopkins 1972, 28.

In the *Monologion*

On the one hand, it is clear that Anselm's method went through some significant alterations over the years, as Evans has demonstrated convincingly enough. It became increasingly necessary for him to incorporate and respond to objections, and partly as a result of this, his later works make their point with perhaps more attention to clarity, but with less attention to the beauty of expression found in the earlier ones.[13]

On the other hand, there is a remarkable consistency seen in Anselm's application of his *sola ratione* principle. Karl Barth, as we observed above, considered the simplicity of this rational method of proving theological truths to be the key to Anselm. "Anselm is not in a position to treat Christian knowledge as an esoteric mystery, as a phenomenon that would have to shun the cold light of secular thinking" (Barth 1960, 68). In Barth's view, this can be said of Anselm in general, and no regard is held for the changes during Anselm's career which Evans has documented. In my view there is indeed reason to suppose that for all Anselm's maturation and the reasons for it, at the roots his method remained pretty much intact throughout the course of his career.

Southern (1983) has noted that Anselm quotes Scripture frequently in all his writings (19), and his vocabulary coalesces well with that of Scripture—a point on which he will compare favorably to Luther—but this is not to be confused with his methodological principle at work in the exercise of faith seeking understanding. It has been said (Phelan 1960, 6) that Anselm's wisdom was contained in that phrase (*fides quaerens intellectum*), which Anselm had employed as the original title for the *Proslogion* (P, Prooemium; S I, 94: 6-13).

---

[13]This is a major contention in Evans 1978.

The expression certainly summarizes his purpose in writing; yet both the phrase and Anselm's purpose can be seen more clearly upon examination of the expressed intentions and method in the *Monologion*, of which the *Proslogion* was the sequel.

In preface to the *Monologion* Anselm lays out very clearly both his method and his reason for the writing.

> Certain brethren have often and eagerly asked me to commit to writing, as a meditation, some of the thoughts I had offered in informal conversation, regarding meditation on the divine essence and certain other related topics. The form they have prescribed for the writing of this meditation, which is offered more in accordance with their wishes than with my expertise or capability, requires that nothing in Scripture be argued from its internal authority, but that any conclusion be asserted from independent investigation, in order that in this way it may in a clear style, with common arguments and a simple contention, and by the compulsion of reason, be briefly considered and clearly shown in the light of truth (S I, 7:2-11).[14]

We can derive from Anselm's words the apparent reason behind the perceived need for this work, whether perceived so by his friends or by himself,[15] in his

---

[14]"Quidam fratres saepe me studioseque precati sunt, ut quaedam, quae illis de meditanda divinitatis essentia et quibusdam aliis huiusmodi meditationi cohaerentibus usitato sermone colloquendo protuleram, sub quodam eis meditationis exemplo describerem. Cuius scilicet scribendae meditationis magis secundum suam voluntatem quam secundum rei facilitatem aut meam possibilitatem hanc mihi formam praestituerunt: quatenus auctoritate scripturae penitus nihil in ea persuaderetur, sed quidquid per singulas investigationes finis assereret, id ita esse plano stilo et vulgaribus argumentis simplicique disputatione et rationis necessitas breviter cogeret et veritatis claritas patenter ostenderet."

[15]Anselm here declares that informal conversation (*usitato sermone colloquendo*) with some friends gave rise to their encouragement to Anselm that he commit his words to writing. The self-deprecating style of Anselm suggests that he did not invent the idea that others had urged him to this task. Others evidently considered his oral wisdom worthy of writing, and he at length appears to have succumbed to their wishes. He continues further on in the preface, "Tandem tamen victus cum precum modesta importunitate tum studii eorum non contemnenda honestate, invitus quidem propter rei difficultatem et ingenii mei imbecillitatem quod precabantur incepi, sed libenter propter eorum caritatem quantum potui secundum ipsorum definitionem effeci—Overcome at length, however, both by their entreaties of modest importunity and by their admirably sincere zeal, and although unwilling because of the difficulty of the task and the feebleness of my capability, I undertook to do that for which they asked; but glady, on account of their love, as well as I was

declared purpose: "that nothing in Scripture be argued from its internal authority." Here the reason for writing is manifest: he wished to demonstrate on a ground of authority other than that of Scripture the truth of Scripture. This is a clear statement of Anselm's method. It calls for "independent investigation", precluding the appeal to Scripture for establishment of a point of truth. Although he considers Scripture the authoritative tradition, he wishes to take a different point of departure, namely reason, and ultimately to arrive at the truths known to be those of the Christian faith without recourse to the authority of Scripture. Anselm's aim is as it were to reconstruct the faith from the ground up, using only reason as his tool. Christian doctrine is not thereby to be called into question, but rather to be ratified from a perspective independent of the written source (i.e., Scripture) of that doctrine.

Evans (1978) takes exception to the criticism Anselm has received over the years on his method. She says that Anselm's appeal to reason

> has little to do with the question of the relationship between faith and reason which has so often preoccupied modern scholars . . . To object that he makes a greater claim for the powers of rigorous reasoning than it will stand, is both to misunderstand Anselm's own awareness of what he was trying to do, and to underestimate the degree of his insight into the workings of other men's minds (167f).

Evans has correctly defended Anselm against a misreading of him which would see in him a prototype of eighteenth-century rationalists. Anselm has no pre-Kantian illusions about the results of inquiry by unfettered reason; his use of reason was quite fettered, by his tacit understanding of the bounds set by Scripture and the Fathers.

> St. Anselm conceives of the process of *fides quaerens intellectum* as one in which faith endeavours to see for itself why the propositions which it affirms are true. The use of the phrase "sees for itself" has to be

---

able, according to the prescription they had set" (S I, 7: 16-19).

understood in a manner which precludes the suggestion that faith does so without the assistance of Divine Grace (McIntyre 1954, 42).

Yet the reason behind this method must be probed, for Anselm's expressed use of reason does appear to give to it a precedence over the Word of God and faith, notwithstanding Evans' attempt to defend him. Anselm's statement of method still begs the question. *Why*, we must ask Anselm, must a ground of authority be established alongside that of Scripture? A return to Anselm's *fides quaerens intellectum* provides his answer: evidently faith seeks understanding by this method. Returning to the *Monologion* quotation given above, we see that Anselm's method is put forward "in order that in this way it [i. e., any conclusion] may in a clear style, with common proofs and a simple argument, and by the compulsion of reason, be briefly considered and clearly shown in the light of truth." The implication is that the light of truth (*veritatis claritas*) is a reference to that which springs from reason. Common arguments and a simple contention (*vulgaribus argumentis simplicique disputatione*) are enlisted to produce the compulsion or necessary conclusions of reason (*rationis necessitas*), and this is called *veritatis claritas*.   This belies a heavily charged optimism about the results of rational inquiry. Anselm assumes that rational, dialectical inquiry will produce that understanding which faith seeks. It is for Anselm an a priori assumption, for which he offers no defense or explanation. It is explained further in the first chapter of the work.

> If anyone, whether from not having heard or from unbelief, is ignorant of the one Nature, which is the highest of all things that are . . . I hold that, even if his capability is mediocre, to a great extent he is able at least to persuade himself of these truths by reason alone.[16]

---

[16]"Si quis unam naturam, summam omnium quae sunt . . . aut non audiendo aut non credendo ignorat: puto quia ea ipsa ex magna parte, si vel mediocris ingenii est, potest ipse sibi saltem sola ratione persuadere" (S I 13: 5-11).

Anselm proceeds then to provide "by reason alone (*sola ratione*)" the means he believes most appropriate (*promptissimum*) for such a person to come to the knowledge of God.[17] One might assume that Anselm's purpose in this exercise is not actually to provide assistance to one who is in such a position, but rather, merely to provide a scenario or format for his engagement in speculative thought. That scenario is the mind of a person with no prior knowledge of God. Given such a setting of mind, Anselm believes that reason alone provides the most appropriate means of coming to the knowledge of God. Does this make reason more appropriate for Anselm in such a case than the Word of God? Would Anselm have stretched the argument this far? This could be an indication that for Anselm reason precedes faith in importance, even if only by suggested inference.

In the *Monologion*, the prevalence of speculative discourse is not seen primarily in the asking of speculative questions; these do not appear as a prominent element of form until the *Cur Deus Homo*. Speculative discourse is seen in the *Monologion* under the form of logical progression of thought—a chain-of-arguments—led purely by reason. The seventy-nine chapters of the Monologion appear to have an unstated linkage, each to its preceding chapter, springing from the meditative musings of philosophical thought. Both from the expressed admission of it in the preface, and from a consideration of the chapters' contents themselves is this seen. Moreover, there is an abundance of linkage between parts. Chapters are short, and regularly linked by such connectives as *igitur*, *at*, *autem*, *denique*, and the like. Even paragraphs within chapters are so linked to their antecedents, in keeping with Anselm's stated purpose of spinning the entire manuscript, in each of its parts, purely out of reason. Stock (1983, 332f) summarizes Anselm's method in the *Monologion* thus:

---

[17]"Quod cum multis modis facere possit, unum ponam, quem illi aestimo esse promptissimum" (S I, 13: 11-12).

In writing out his thoughts Anselm was to bring together in a single treatise and to bind by a unified chain of reasoning whatever had been revealed by his separate investigations. In other words, the final product was to be a logically coherent whole. The correctness of his position was to be established through a plain style, commonplace arguments, and straightforward debate (*plano stilo et vulgaribus argumentis simplicique disputatione*). Above all, it was to be corroborated by necessary reason (*rationis necessitas*), that is, by the logical interrelationship of words in sentences.

Anselm's method can perhaps best be demonstrated by an analysis of the structure of the *Monologion*. Its progression of thought can be garnered from a consideration of its table of contents alone (see Appendix 1). An analysis of the progression of thought demonstrates Anselm's method, by charting his construction of the doctrine of the Trinity from reason alone. Beginning with six chapters covering ontological argumentation for the existence of God (which is developed more fully in the *Proslogion*), Anselm proceeds to the conception of God as Creator of all other beings, and the relation of His being to created beings, in the following eight chapters (7-14). Every point is made on the basis of its reasonableness alone. The logical progression of thought to this point is seen in the movement from God as God to God as Creator; i.e., from God as he is to God as he acts, a plausible step of thought development.

Next, the substance and mode of God's existence are considered (chapters 15-28), expanding on a preliminary notion of God established in preceding chapters, especially 13 and 14, namely the being of God in relation to the being of his creatures. Consideration of God's being as related to the being of his creatures gives rise to questions about the parameters by which the being of God may or may not be considered. Thus again the subject-matter of chapters 15 and following is ordered by the logical progression of thought building upon previous thought.

Beginning with chapter 29, once the considerations of God's mode of being have been exhausted, Anselm moves to the concept of God's self-expression (*locutio*) which had been raised briefly in chapter 12. Thus the expanded discussion of God's mode of existence has given rise finally to a consideration of God as he *expresses* himself. This progression of thought is not explained, but rather assumed to be the reasonable unravelling of thought which had begun from reason. Having painstakingly arrived by reasonable argument at the self-expression of God, he is now prepared to begin discussing plurality in the unity of the Godhead. Every level of what we might call his scaffolding of thought is erected on the foundation of the previous level.

Beginning in chapter 30, God's self-expression is called the Word (*verbum*), a rationally fitting title, and after several manners of consideration of God as the Supreme Spirit (*summus spiritus*, chapter 32) in connection with God as his self-expression or Word, the two are finally given names, again by recourse to what reasonable names would be, and referred to as Father and Son (chapter 42-48). Thus through a careful and "purely" rational exercise, Anselm has now at length arrived at two persons of the Trinity and their names.

Next he proceeds along the same lines to produce the third person. He does this by considering the mutual love (*amor*) of the Father and the Son (from chapter 49), which with logical reasons is finally called the Spirit (*spiritus*, chapter 53), and the Spirit of the Father and the Son (*spiritus patris et filii*, chapter 57). Abstract discussion of the so named Trinity continues to the end of the *Monologion*, coupled beginning with chapter 64 with considerations of the relation of the rational creature to this God, and faith. The scaffolding is thus complete, having been erected alongside the Scriptures but without recourse to them, to arrive at last at the same heights of truth. Stock (1983, 336) lays out the stages in Anselm's process as being three:

> First, he sets up a system of comparison based on the acceptance of abstractions as the highest order of reality. Then he generalizes from such concepts to the existence of a superior nature through which they derive their being or essence. Finally, he argues that the manner in which the

summa natura creates from within itself is analogous to logically informed discourse.

Scripture is indeed the guide of this,[18] but Scripture is the guide only in the sense that the same ends as Scripture has established must be met. The task is to construct truth by recourse to reason alone, yet without deviation from what Scripture has first established. Clearly the work is a masterpiece of brilliant reasoning. Anselm comes across as having constructed by reason alone the same Holy Trinity as the Creeds derive from the font of the Sacred Scriptures.

We pause to note, however, that in so doing Anselm actually appears after all to have provided something which the Scriptures have not provided, though not in so many words. Though he makes it clear elsewhere that the establishment of anything contrary to Scripture is to be rejected, he has provided by means of reason a compelling explanation of *why* God is Triune. This Scripture does not do; Anselm appears to have spun it from reason alone.[19] It was of course inevitable that something new would be provided, in spite of all of Anselm's insistence that Scripture is the ultimate authority, for were this not the case, then the exercise might be seen as entirely perfunctory and without purpose. Faith seeks understanding, Anselm admits; the understanding would have to be new, else why would it have to be sought? Scripture alone has for Anselm given the truths of the faith, but reason alone now gives reasons for the truths of the faith.

Anselm's manner of looking at the Trinity was really nothing new to him, being also patristic, and particularly Augustinian. The Father as God expresses

---

[18]We might more correctly say Scripture and the Creeds, though in Anselm's mind the creedal formulations, while not found in Scripture, are what the Lutheran dogmaticians would have called *norma secundaria or norma normata*, that is, "normed" by Scripture. In Anselm we find, on the one hand, the clear statements that indicate that Sacred Scripture is the absolute norm, and on the other, citations of creedal formulations in normative support of his position.

[19]One could argue that the Creeds do the same, for example, in providing the doctrine of the Trinity. In the case of the Trinity, however, what is new is merely the trinitarian formulation, whereas in the case of Anselm's reasoning, what is new is an explanation for the ontological, shall we say, structure? of God.

himself; this self-expression is the Word, i.e., the Son. The Father and the Son love each other, and their mutual love is the Holy Spirit.[20] What is unique about Anselm's treatment of these ideas is that his manner of presentation purports to have gleaned these thoughts out of contemplation alone. Even the names *"Pater"*, *"Filius"*, and *"Spiritus Sanctus"* are not presented as having derived from Scripture, but from reason alone.[21] Every element of doctrine traditionally understood as having been given by the Word of God is now arrived at by means of rational speculation and inquiry alone, even as if there were no Word of God to verify it. As one reads the *Monologion*, one is confronted with arguments which stand alone, not purporting to require verification or even derivation from Scripture. This is Anselm's way of seeking understanding for faith. The exercise is intended for the enablement of faith's pursuit.

It is clear to me that Anselm's liking for this rational exercise is indicative of a bold confidence in the capacity of human reason, a confidence which appears even higher than that with which he asserts the veracity of Scripture. Reason is to Anselm what Scripture will be to Luther, as the former sees reason to be in fact the only proper approach to God. Indeed, Anselm makes bold to claim as

---

[20]In St. Augustine, *De Trinitate*, Book 6, chapter 5, we read, "Spiritus ergo sanctus commune aliquid est Patris et Filii, quidquid est. At ipsa communio, consubstantialis et coaeterna; quae si amicitia convenienter dici potest, dicatur; sed aptius dicitur caritas. Et haec quoque substantia, quia Deus substantia, et Deus charitas, sicut scriptum est. Sicut autem substantia simul cum Patre et Filio, ita simul magna, et simul bona, et simul sancta—Therefore the Holy Spirit is something common to the Father and the Son, whatever it is. But the communion itself is consubstantial and co-eternal; and if it is fitting to call it friendship, let it so be called, but it is more aptly called love. And this is also a substance, since God is a substance, and God is love, as it is written. But as he is a substance at the same time as the Father and the Son, so also is he at the same time great, at the same time good, and at the same time holy." Migne 42, 928 (St. Augustine, vol. 8).

[21]Anselm discusses the terms *pater* and *filius*, which arise rationally from begetting and being begotten, and explains from reason alone even why the masculine terms are preferable to *mater* and *filia* (S I, 58-59).

He later discusses the term *spiritus* applied to the third person, explaining first by reason why it cannot be another son (S I, 67), and then arguing for the term *spiritus* via the consideration that the Father and the Son breathe (*spirant*) their love (S I, 68).

much, in chapter 66 of the *Monologion*, titled, "How the nearest approach to the knowledge of the highest essence is through the rational mind":

> Since therefore it is patent that nothing of this Nature can be gathered through its own properties, but through something else, it is certain that a nearer approach to the knowledge of it is made by that which approaches nearer to it in likeness. For whatever among creatures stands nearer to its essence is itself necessarily more excellent in essence by nature. Therefore this being, also by greater likeness, is of more help to the investigating mind in approaching the highest Truth, and through its more excellent created essense it is better able to teach what of the Creator the mind ought to regard. Therefore without doubt the Creator is known the more essentially, the more the investigating creature resembles it. For every being, even as much as it exists, is in so much like the highest Being, as indeed reasons considered above do not permit us to doubt. It is patent, then, that as the rational mind alone among all creatures is so equipped to rise to the investigation of that Being, so it is no less that same mind alone through which the greatest advancement toward the discovery is enabled. For it is already known that this approaches it most nearly, through likeness of natural essence. What is therefore more apparent than that as much as the natural mind is earnestly devoted to studying itself, so efficiently does it ascend to the cognition of that Being; and that as much as the same is negligent in contemplating itself, so far does it descend from speculation on that Being? (M 66; S I, 77:4-24)[22]

---

[22]"Capitulum LXVI. *Quod per rationalem mentem maxime accedatur ad cognoscendum summam essentiam.*

"Cum igitur pateat quia nihil de hac natura possit percipi per suam proprietatem sed per aliud, certum est quia per illud magis ad eius cognitionem acceditur, quod illi magis per similitudinem propinquat. Quidquid enim inter creata constat illi esse similius, id necesse est esse natura praestantius. Quapropter id et per maiorem similitudinem plus iuvat mentem indagantem summae veritati propinquare, et per excellentiorem creatam essentiam plus docet, quid de creante mens ipsa debeat aestimare. Procul dubio itaque tanto altius creatrix essentia cognoscitur, quanto per propinquiorem sibi creaturam indagatur. Nam quod omnis essentia, in quantum est, in tantum sit summae similis essentiae, ratio iam supra considerata dubitare non permittit. Patet itaque quia, sicut sola est mens rationalis inter omnes creaturas, quae ad eius investigationem assurgere valeat, ita nihilominus eadem sola est, per quam maxime ipsamet ad eiusdem inventionem proficere queat. Nam iam cognitum est, quia haec illi maxime per naturalis essentiae propinquat similitudinem. Quid igitur apertius quam quia mens rationalis quanto studiosius ad se discendum intendit, tanto efficacius ad illius cognitionem ascendit; et quanto seipsam intueri negligit, tanto ab eius speculatione descendit?"

Here Anselm has gone to great lengths attempting logically to demonstrate the likeness of the rational mind to God. The rational mind is so much like God that by contemplating *itself* it ascends to the knowledge of God. This, as we shall see, is diametrically opposed to the position of Luther, and contributes heavily to the glaring differences in method between the two.

In the *Proslogion*

The *Proslogion*, Anselm's well-known ontological argument for the existence of God, follows the very same method as its companion treatise, the *Monologion*, and provides a further indication of his penchant for this *sola ratione* approach to theology. Like the *Monologion*, the *Proslogion* prefers the use of rational arguments to support theological truth, even though Anselm allows himself to refer to Scripture in this treatise. Still, following the lead of the *Monologion*, the *Proslogion* bases its arguments on reason, consistent with the expressed aim of Anselm in the preface of the latter. "In the person of one who undertaking to lift his mind to the contemplation of God, and seeking to understand what he believes, I have written the following little work" (S I, 93:21-94:2).[23] It becomes evident early on that what Anselm means by the contemplation of God is not that derived primarily from a consideration of the Sacred Scriptures. In order to contemplate God, Anselm's instructions here are to "enter into the chamber of your mind, exclude everything except God and that which aids you in seeking him, and close the door, to seek him" (P I; S I, 97:7-9).[24] This

---

[23]"Sub persona conantis erigere mentem suam ad contemplandum deum et quaerentis intelligere quod credit, subditum scripsi opusculum."

[24]"Intra in cubiculum mentis tuae, exclude omnia praeter deum et quae te iuvent ad quaerendum eum, et clauso ostio quaere eum."

draws on Matthew 6.6, Jesus' prescription of the alternative to the Pharisaical practice of praying on street corners for the purpose of being seen. Drawn now out of this context, Anselm employs the text here to encourage the monastic discipline of solitary meditation. It is significant that, although Anselm's frequent use of the vocabulary of Scripture might seem to suggest a constant adherence to the text of Scripture, his advice actually remains less than specific at a point at which we would expect him to have made his encouragement more precise on the importance of following Scripture in his seeking of God. He might have said, for example, "exclude everything except God *and the Sacred Scriptures,* which aid you in seeking him." But Anselm's method, which is carried through to the *Proslogion*, indicates that it is reason which is to be employed in the service of seeking God. It is to be remembered that the *Proslogion* and the *Monologion* were meant by their author to be companion treatises. The *Proslogion* thus carries on this exercise in the same manner as the *Monologion*. Unlike the *Monologion*, the *Proslogion* is not unwilling to employ Scriptural references throughout, yet it remains clear that the major thrust of the piece is not to apply or give an exposition of Scripture, but rather to carry out the intentions listed in the preface by rational speculation, in full continuation of the exercise introduced in the *Monologion*.

In the *Proslogion* as elsewhere, Anselm's use of reason was meant to be thoroughly subservient to Scripture, even in spite of his method; or rather, as an intended ingredient of his method. Reason was not to run wild, but instead, following only logical rationale as its apparent and explicit authority, to repeat along every step of the way truths which could also be found in Scripture. Anselm provided a safeguard on this method, whether intentional or not, in his use of Biblical phrases and wording.

The central argument of the *Proslogion* is a purely rational one. True to his established method, Anselm deduces the existence of God without the aid of

Scripture. His deduction about the existence of God, which forms the central point of the treatise, is made on the basis of the concept of perfection in God, and of existence being germane to perfection. The argument springs purely from logic.

> Certainly that than which a greater cannot be conceived, cannot exist in the understanding alone. For if one takes it to exist in the understanding alone, then it is able to exist in reality, which is greater. Therefore, if that, than which nothing greater is possible, exists in the understanding alone, the being itself, than which nothing greater is possible, is one than which a greater is possible. But this is certainly not possible. Hence, there is no doubt that there exists a being, than which nothing greater can be conceived, and it exists both in the understanding and in reality (P 2; S I, 101:15-102:3).[25]

As was the case in the *Monologion*, Anselm's method here is to provide a purely rational basis for the Christian faith, specifically here the simple belief that God exists. Here it appears that though reason follows upon faith, nonetheless it plays a key role in the life of faith, and we see again that this is what is meant by faith's seeking of understanding. When Anselm sets forth this ontological argument in the *Proslogion*, he explains his purpose in doing so. This explanation also serves well as a clarification of the *fides quaerens intellectum* principle. He declares, "I do not seek to understand in order that I might believe, but I believe in order that I might understand; for I also believe this: unless I believed, I would not understand."(P 1; S I, 100:18-19).[26] Thus

---

[25]"Certe id quo maius cogitari nequit, non potest esse in solo intellectu. Si enim vel in solo intellectu est, potest cogitari esse et in re, quod maius est. Si ergo id quo maius cogitari non potest, est in solo intellectu: id ipsum quo maius cogitari non potest, est quo maius cogitari potest. Sed certe hoc esse non potest. Existit ergo procul dubio aliquid quo maius cogitari non valet, et in intellectu et in re."

[26]"Neque enim quaero intelligere ut credam, sed credo ut intelligam. Nam et hoc credo: quia nisi credidero, non intelligam."

Anselm is referring to Isaiah 7.9, and may also be borrowing from a sermon of Augustine's on the same text: "Intelligam inquis, ut credam: Crede, inquam, ut intelligas. Respondeat propheta: *Nisi credideritis, non intelligetis*—Let me understand, you say, in order to believe.

although Anselm here denies that reason, which for him is proximate to "understanding", actually leads to faith, it is nonetheless clear that reason plays a key role in the life of faith. Faith seeks understanding, by which Anselm means that it pushes toward rational speculation about that which it believes. It is for Anselm the task of faith to seek *by rational speculation* to understand itself.

It should be noted that the *Proslogion* appears in places to detract from this method. Unlike the *Monologion* and the *Cur Deus Homo*, the *Proslogion* is comfortable with specific and openly intentional references to Scriptural passages in places, and is seen to gain direction from them at times. Perhaps because it is more meditative and devotional in nature, this piece tends on occasion to blend rational discussions quite naturally with Scripture, as if to show an implicit harmony. The very principle of faith seeking understanding is cast in the first chapter as having derived from a consideration of Psalm 27 (26).8 (*"Tibi dixit cor meum; exquisivit te facies mea; Faciem tuam, Domine, requiram*—My heart said to you, when you said, Seek my face, Your face, Lord, will I seek"), as Anselm says, *"Dic nunc, totum cor meum, dic nunc deo: Quaero vultum tuum, vultum tuum, domine, requiro*—Speak now, my whole heart, speak now to God: I will seek your countenance, your countenance, Lord, will I seek" (S I, 97:9-10; see also 114:9-10). Next, the reference in Psalm 14.1 (S I, 101:6-7). to the fool's atheism provides material in chapter two from which Anselm springs into his ontological argument. The bulk of the material throughout the rest of the work is based on reason alone, until the final two chapters, in which Scriptural references abound and are even used to bring into consideration matters considered to be true purely because of their being in Scripture.[27] Anselm asks

---

Believe, I say, in order to understand. Let the prophet respond: Unless you believe, you shall not understand." Augustine, Sermon XLIV; Migne 38, 257 (St. Augustine, vol. 5).

[27]P 26-27; S I, 118-122.

God for an abundance of joy, wondering aloud whether this can be claimed on
the basis of Jesus' words in John 16.24.

> My God and my Lord, my hope and the joy of my heart, speak to my
> soul; if this is the joy of which you speak by your Son: "Ask and you
> shall receive, that your joy may be full" (P 27; S I, 120:23-121:1).[28]

This petition is informative of Anselm's view of the relation between Scripture
and the *intellectus* to be gained from the seeking of faith. Anselm must in his
meditative moment ask God for an additional revelation, presumably *extra
scripturam*, in order to gain an understanding of the meaning of Jesus' words.
Thus even where Anselm employs Scripture, there is evidence of a belief that
Scripture does not in itself enable faith to gain understanding. This is consistent
with Anselm's overall purpose in his choice of method. From his prolegomenal
statements in the *Monologion* and the *Proslogion*, we saw that he wishes to
employ reason alone in the search for a deeper understanding of the Biblical
truths, and now from this statement we see that when a Biblical declaration is
directly before him he must ask God for additional, presumably extra-Biblical,
help to understand it. Anselm is asking God to guide his *reason*, as he considers
the text, that understanding may be achieved. The apparent piety of this prayer
notwithstanding, it provides further evidence that for Anselm Scripture cannot do
what reason can. Even allowing for the sanctification of reason by divine
guidance does not alter the indication that reason is considered that through which
the understanding is to come.

Here in the *Proslogion* we see what appears to be a detraction from the
method of Anselm established in its earlier companion, the *Monologion*, which
is to set the authority of Scripture completely aside while rebuilding the Christian
truths from reason alone. In the earlier work, Anselm appears to have perceived

---

[28]"Deus meus et dominus meus, spes mea et gaudium cordis mei, dic animae meae, si hoc
est gaudiam de quo nobis dicis per filium tuum: petite et accipietis, ut gaudium vestrum sit
plenum."

his theological task to be the seeking of understanding of what is already believed, according to his chosen method of employing only reason to rebuild it from a basis entirely devoid of the authoritative tradition given in Scripture. But here, his reference to Scripture is free and open. Nonetheless, there is a marked use of the same kind of method, in spite of the references to Scripture. For even here in the *Proslogion*, these references are not used in a way which mitigates against his *sola ratione* method of making points. He does not cite Scripture in order to prove the points which he wishes to establish *sola ratione*; rather, he appears to be employing it precisely to justify his own seeking and asking, his own *quaerens intellectum*; and that by his *sola ratione* principle.

In the *Cur Deus Homo*

The *Cur Deus Homo*, which is the primary treatise from which Anselm's understanding of the necessity for the atonement can be gleaned,[29] exhibits the same method as we saw to be first delineated in the *Monologion* and employed also in the *Proslogion*. The significance of our preliminary consideration of those two former works is best seen upon discovering that it is precisely the method established therein which is at work here.[30] Anselm's view on the necessity for the atonement can only be understood once his method of approach to the question is established (so McIntyre 1954:3f). *Fides quaerens intellectum*, with

---

[29] Although Gerald Phelan (1960, 6) calls the *Proslogion* Anselm's most famous work, Evans (1978, 171) calls the *Cur Deus Homo* "in every way a work of Anselm's maturity."

[30] Evans (1978, 134) notes, however, the major difference between the style of the *Cur Deus Homo* and the *Proslogion*, pointing out that the *Cur Deus Homo* lacks the excitement and inspiration of the *Proslogion*. She suggests that the reason is that in the *Proslogion*, Anselm's purpose was to share his illumination and excitement over his discovery of the ontological argument, whereas in the *Cur Deus Homo* "he wants them to experience his own calmer certainties."

that *quaerens*, that seeking, being *sola ratione*, is his method established in the *Monologion* and the *Proslogion*. This method is briefly reiterated in the preface of the *Cur Deus Homo*.

> In accordance with the material published herein, I have named it *Cur Deus Homo* and divided it into two short books. The prior contains the objections of infidels to the Christian faith, that they believe it contrary to reason, and the responses of the faithful. And by removing Christ (*remoto Christo*), as if nothing were known of him, I demonstrate the necessary reasons why it is impossible for humanity to be saved without him. But in the second book, similarly as if nothing were known of Christ, it is shown no less by apparent reasoning and truth that human nature was ordained for this reason, namely that the whole man should enjoy a blessed immortality, that is, in body and in soul; and that it was necessary that this purpose for which humanity was made should be accomplished; but not except by the man-God; moreover that it was necessary that all things which we believe of Christ were to occur (S II, 42:8-43:3).[31]

Here both Anselm's purpose and his method are clearly set forth again. His purpose is to "demonstrate" (*probat*) the faith "by absolute reasons"; his method is to "remove Christ (*remoto Christo*), as if nothing were known of him." Although the method in the *Cur Deus Homo* is more appropriately labelled *remoto Christo*, it is evident that the term is really identical with *sola ratione*, the term derived from the *Monologion*. Again we see an implicit optimism about the capabilities of reason. Reason is here assumed to have the ability to set forth the preeminence of the Christain faith, and, in view of the finality of Anselm's use here of "*necessarius*", as in "I demonstrate the necessary reasons" (*probat*

---

[31]"Quod secundum materiam de qua editum est, *Cur deus homo* nominavi et in duos libellos distinxi. Quorum prior quidem infidelium Christianam fidem, quia rationi putant illam repugnare, respuentium continet obiectiones et fidelium responsiones. Ac tandem remoto Christo, quasi numquam aliquid fuerit de illo, probat rationibus necessariis esse impossibile ullum hominem salvari sine illo. In secundo autem libro similiter quasi nihil sciatur de Christo, monstratur non minus aperta ratione et veritate naturam humanam ad hoc institutam esse, ut aliquando immortalitate beata totus homo, id est in corpore et anima, frueretur; ac necesse esse ut hoc fiat de homine propter quod factus est, sed non nisi per hominem-deum; atque ex necessitate omnia quae de Christo credimus fieri oportere."

rationibus necessariis), to do so at least as well as any other means. Perhaps it did not occur to Anselm that this sets reason on at least an even keel with the Scriptures, if not to place it above them. Anselm sets forth to demonstrate "the necessary reasons why it is impossible for humanity to be saved without him [Christ]." By this he does not mean to say that Scripture's word is the last, that where Scripture has spoken, the last word has been said, and thus acceptance of its declaration is necessary. Though he does not deny that here, what he does is place reason into the place of Scripture, and, in effect, declare that reason's word is the last, for reason provides the necessary reasons for the faith. Faith's reasons are for Anselm reason's reasons.

Evans (1978, 167) contends that "Anselm's appeal to reason in the *Cur Deus Homo* has little to do with the question of the relation between faith and reason which has so often preoccupied modern scholars." Her argument is based on her demonstration that Anselm's method here is to employ "whatever technique of analysis appears to be convenient," being much more flexible in his carrying out of his method than the *remoto Christo* method would at first have had us believe (161). The point is well taken, for we must recall that Anselm's overall aim is not simply to make his point *sola ratione*, but *pulcherrima*, in the most beautiful or fitting way he is able. Still, Anselm's appeal to reason in itself must be called into question, even if it is only the penultimate purpose of his method.

In the *Cur Deus Homo*, the form takes on a new element. Anselm employs an interlocutor, creating his treatise out of a conversation he has with the student Boso. The form is rather like that of a play, in which the characters' lines are given following their names and a colon. Anselm does most of the talking, and Boso asks the questions under consideration, making brief statements of agreement or interjecting an occasional point in need of clarification.[32] Anselm's rationale for this format is given in the first chapter.

> Since it is by interrogation and answer that investigations are made more clear to many, especially to those of slower intelligence, and are therefore the more pleasing, I have chosen to argue with me one of those who inquire on this matter, who among others agitates me with more perseverence. So Boso asks and Anselm answers in this way (CDH I.1; S II, 48:11-15).[33]

It is therefore Anselm's conviction that interrogation and answer make investigations more plain. This change in form, whose explanation can be seen to serve as a plausible explanation for the form of the later scholastic *summae*, which are filled with *quaestiones*,[34] is worthy of note only because we may wonder whether it contributes to or detracts from the beauty of Anselm's discourse. In one respect it may be said to detract, since it makes the treatise somewhat more pedantic; yet in another respect it may be seen as more attractive, since, as Evans (1978, 163) has pointed out, Boso the interlocutor has the effect of suggesting to the reader a preferred response, one which leads the reader to give more attention to the discussion.[35] Boso's contribution does not exactly serve the purpose of the questions we find in Luther's catechetical style, since

---

[32]Actually, the first treatises of Anselm's to employ this form are the *De Grammatico*, the *De Libertate Arbitrii*, and the *De Veritate*, all written between 1080 and 1085. In those works, the interlocutor is an impersonal unnamed "student", whereas here in the *Cur Deus Homo* it is Boso, a real and not a fictional disciple.

[33]"Et quoniam ea quae per interrogationem et responsionem investigantur, multis et maxime tardioribus ingeniis magis patent et ideo plus placent, unum ex illis qui hoc flagitant, qui inter alios instantius ad hoc me sollicitat, accipiam mecum disputantem, ut BOSO quaerat et ANSELMUS respondeat hoc modo."

[34]Anselm appears to have been a pioneer not only of this method of employing reason, but also, in a very primitive sense, of scholastic form, as manifested in the later *summae*.

[35]Stock (1983, 361) contributes the insight that "what has been called 'the Anselmic method' is really a type of 'proof' utilizing logic in which the human interlocutors have in part the status of means of communication."

there is more of an exchange taking place here than is seen in simple catechetical questioning.   The exchange does not appear to be designed as a simple catechetical device, but rather as another means of drawing the reader to the topic because of the pleasure gained from the reading (see Evans 1978, 143). Anselm's efforts at achieving beauty in his writing were evidently not only due to the fittingness of speaking of divine matters in beautiful terms, but also for a more pragmatical reason: he evidently felt the need to convince his opponents— McIntyre (1954, 4f et passim) says there is "no doubt" of this in the *Cur Deus Homo*—by attempting to make the truths of Scripture attractive to reason.   His efforts were thus offered in the naive assumption that reason can accommodate these truths at all.

It must be remembered that it was the early twelfth-century which saw the first rounds of the realist-nominalist battles that would endure throughout the scholastic era.   To be sure, these were the battles of philosophers, yet they left an indelible impression on theological thought, which in so many minds of the era was practically indistinguishable from philosophical thought.   The dialectician Roscelin, who was an opponent of Anselm, held in accordance with his extreme nominalism what to Anselm the realist appeared clearly to be a tritheist position.[36]   It may be, therefore, that Roscelin was at least partly responsible

---

[36]"The origins of the medieval debate on universals are still uncertain, but it seems clear that Roscelin of Compiègne (1050-1125), who taught at Soissons, Paris and Rheims, was, though probably not the founder of Nominalism, at least its first influential advocate. His only surviving writing is an unattractive letter on the Trinity to Abelard, and much of the scanty information we have of him comes from references by Anselm . . . Recent scholarship has tended to credit Roscelin with opinions less superficial than sheer Nominalism. He was reacting, we are told, against the current extreme realism which found subsistent reality in qualities and accidents of every kind, so that the individual existing being was merely a chance collection of characteristics, while reality lay in a world of multitudinous ideas. Roscelin, wishing to assert the reality of the existent individual, could only do so by asserting that any analysis or classification of the individual beings of our experience was a matter of words, not of things, in the well known Boethian dichotomy. This may be so, but undoubtedly many of those who attacked him, or who subsequently wrote of him, understood his nominalism in a less subtle, more radical sense" (Knowles 1962: 111).

for Anselm's efforts to make greater appeal to reason by the method chosen for the *Cur Deus Homo*, the latter perceiving the necessity laid upon him of defending the faith against the likes of Roscelin. Anselm indeed speaks of this necessity in the preface to the *Cur Deus Homo*, where he explains that the first of its two books "contains the objections of infidels to the Christian faith, that they believe it contrary to reason, and the responses of the faithful" (CDH Praefatio; S II, 42:10-11).[37] But Anselm was already given to arguing *sola ratione*, due to his desire for fittingness and beauty, and therefore it is really quite in keeping with his established method to undertake this new form, since he was all the more moved, now that he was archbishop of Canterbury, to perfect his efforts at appealing to reason. Now he had been thrust, albeit against his will, into the first realist-nominalist debates which had so shaken the philosophical world (Knowles 1962:107-113).[38] This called for a reasoned approach, in order that the gainsayers may not only be refuted, but if possible convinced.

Anselm spoke in the *Cur Deus Homo* the language of the dialectician, however dressed it was in the terms of Scripture. Moreover, in Anselm's discourse here, as was particularly the case in his discourse on the being of God in the *Monologion*, his treatment still bears more the character of abstract, detached philosophical thought than of polemics or confessional defense, in spite of his having had the infidels at least partly in mind. Although his use of reason may still be called subordinate to the authority of Scripture, meaning that reason must not venture *beyond* what is revealed, nonetheless for Anselm reason itself appears with regularity as the authority to which his arguments appeal, due to his regularly expressed purpose. Barth (1960) correctly understood that what Anselm

---

[37]See n. 31, above, p. 135.

[38]There is to the contrary Evans' (1978:127) indication that Anselm's work on the *Cur Deus Homo* was finished during his first exile in England, from Eadmer's description of Anselm's pleasure when he found a remote mountaintop in Capua to work in peace. This could suggest that Anselm was not forced into this style but may have preferred it.

believes could also be achieved *nulla ratione*. "Faith is independent of the validity of these human propositions" (16). But this does not alter the fact that Anselm never does seek to establish his position *nulla ratione*, and this is clearly indicative of the emphasis he wishes to lay upon reason in the establishment of his position. Even if the authority of reason is understood by Anselm as being penultimate, and even though Biblical language is employed at will, it is nonetheless reason alone to which his method dictates that he appeal. This is the chief characteristic of his method. Anselm's purpose is to demonstrate that the revealed truths are agreeable to reason, and his method is to show this from reason alone.

We have now seen that this purpose and chosen method are explicitly stated in the *Cur Deus Homo* and in the *Monologion* whose companion work, the *Proslogion*, applies the same principle to a narrower scope, the ontological proof of God's existence. We therefore begin to see a consistency in purpose, which is to facilitate faith's seeking of understanding. To achieve his purpose, Anselm's method employs reason alone and, starting from scratch, arrives a second time at the accepted truths of the faith which had first been received from the Sacred Scriptures. Anselm's method does not intend to establish what he does not understand Scripture to have previously established; he appears to be entirely consistent in his application of the *sola ratione/remoto Christo* principle, and this, as far as I can see, is no less so in the case of the vicarious satisfaction than in the case of the existence of God (contra McIntyre 1954, 37). Anselm's exercise of reason, disciplined explicitly by his expressions of firm refusal to venture beyond the revelation of Scripture, and disciplined implicitly by the language of Scripture, but given as purely rational in itself, is held to provide the understanding faith seeks.

This brings us at last to a reconsideration of Anselm's expression of the vicarious satisfaction in the *Cur Deus Homo*. Inasmuch as Anselm was as intent in the *Cur Deus Homo* as he was in the *Monologion* on demonstrating the truths of the faith by reason alone, as though there were nothing but reason on which to rely (i.e., *remoto Christo*), we may draw some clear inferences with regard to his expression of the vicarious satisfaction and in particular the necessity for it. Anselm is speaking of necessity in logical terms, employing only rational explanations, because he must be true to the aims of his method. This gives his position the ring of irrefutability, since any attempt at refuting this argument would tend to attempt also to be reasoned. As Anselm's method is one of demonstrating truth by reason alone, the style of Anselm is one which bolsters arguments with a penchant for a glowing confidence of expression. It is rational and reasonable, and it is in the beauty of this reasonableness that it makes its appeal to reason. One must take his method fully into account, in order to understand why he speaks in such absolute-sounding a priori terms on the subject. Otherwise one will make the same error as Forde (1984, 20) and Aulén (1969, 82) have made, misreading Anselm as nothing more than a rigid systematician. When Anselm's method is understood, the relation in Anselm between a truth as fitting and a truth as necessary is understood most clearly. When a truth's rational acceptability is shown, i.e., that it is fitting, then its necessity becomes a given, inasmuch as for Anselm logic is itself the determining factor in the formation of an argument.

In the *De Processione Spiritus Sancti*

This document provides some additional opportunities to show Anselm's use of reason. Anselm's *sola ratione* means of argument is heavily employed here, and yet his willingness to remain subservient to the Chalcedonian tradition is apparent. Again we see in this document the limits beyond which his reason refuses to venture, as he declares, for a prime example, that although the Persons of the Trinity number three, making the logical consequence more than one God, nonetheless such a conclusion is forbidden because of the inviolable simplicity of the deity, "which we believe to be only one God" (DPSS 1; S II, 181:10-14).[39] Anselm admits the logic in predicating three Gods from the three Persons, but strikes it down by a simple reference to the faith, which presents an instance of his awareness that reason cannot penetrate this mystery of the Trinity.

Yet Anselm's use of his *sola ratione* principle is quite evident, providing the lynchpin in his argument for the *filioque* against the Greeks: *est aut filius de spiritu sancto, aut spiritus sanctus de filio*—either the Son is of the Holy Spirit or the Holy Spirit of the Son (183:18-19). This deduction is based on carefully laid reasons, demonstrating *sola ratione* that the same alternatives necessarily exist between any two of the three Persons, namely that one must be of the other. Anselm's conclusion is that one who denies his point—*est aut filius de spiritu sancto, aut spiritus sanctus de filio*—must also deny either that that there is only one God, or that the Son is God or that the Holy Spirit is God or that God exists of God (183:19-21).[40] Having established his point, therefore, he proceeds to rule out the first alternative (*filius de spiritu sancto*) by a simple reference to the catholic faith (185:19),[41] leaving only the second (*spiritus sanctus de filio*). Continuing in this manner he eventually establishes the error of the Greeks and the propriety of confessing the *filioque*.

---

[39]"At pater est deus et filius et spiritus sanctus deus. Quid itaque consequentius—si praedicta personarum pluralitas suam servat proprietatem—, quam patrem et filium et spiritum sanctum plures deos esse et alios ab invincem? Sed hoc nullatenus admittit inviolabilis simplicitas deitatis, quam unum solum deum esse credimus."

[40]"Quod qui negat, neget etiam necesse est unum solum deum esse aut filium esse deum aut spiritum sanctum esse deum aut deum esse de deo, quia ex his sequitur quod dico."

[41]Anselm's term *catholica fides* is evidently a reference, in this instance at least, to the *Quicunque vult*, the Athanasian Creed.

The purpose of this study, however, is not to enter Anselm's debate, but only to demonstrate his use of reason. It is evident here that Anselm's idea of what is meant by *sola ratione* is not necessarily to exclude Scripture or the "givens" of faith from all sides of his arguments, but only to exclude Scripture as a means of arguing from his premises to the conclutions at which he arrives (so McIntyre 1954, 39). What Anselm concludes about the procession of the Holy Spirit is clearly a *sola ratione* conclusion; yet he says it is a conclusion which is reached by a completely impregnable necessity (*omnimoda igitur et inexpugnabili necessitate*, S II, 185:16), and he repeats, his reasoning is impregnable (*inexpugnabili ratione*, 185:27). The consistency in Anselm's method is really quite remarkable, even if the premises of his arguments may in one case be from reason alone and in other cases, as here, not so. His conclusions are reached *sola ratione*, by reason alone, and since this reason is neither (as far as Anselm can see) flawed in logic, nor contradictory to the faith, the conclusions are therefore pronounced impregnable, that is, absolute and irrefutable.

Luther's Adherence to the Word of God

Sola Scriptura; Luther's Mistrust of Reason

Unlike Anselm, Luther was never wont to embark on topics of abstract thought. This difference is easy to consider insignificant, until one appreciates the intentions with which Luther undertakes the theological task. Luther confessed to being compelled to speak and write, even against his will, as one driven by the exigency of his vocation. One does not get this impression upon reading Anselm, nor, for that matter, upon reading any of the scholastics after

him. This striking contrast between the medieval schoolmen and Luther in itself
suggests something more significant than stylistic preference. Anselm introduced
to the theological world a method of inquiry from reason alone into theological
truths, and this method of probing theological questions was employed for
centuries after him.   It was a method by which scholasticism itself can be
marked, and from which the schoolmen were not to depart throughout the
medieval period. Seen from Luther's perspective, which was ever suspicious of
reason, this exercise is bound to produce spoiled fruits, whether at once or upon
centuries of growth.

Most attempts to contrast Luther sharply against Anselm on specific
doctrinal issues, as, for example, the question of the meaning of the incarnation,
are bound to be fraught with misunderstanding of one or the other, the major
exception to this being the question of original sin. On the other hand, on the
question of method, it is far easier to see a difference between them. For Luther,
reason cannot be expected to provide the understanding faith seeks, regardless of
whether one can successfully harmonize the answers of reason with the articles
of faith. For Luther, the *imago Dei* is totally destroyed by sin; for Anselm, the
image, though corrupted, remains. Thus for Anselm, reason, and not the Sacred
Page, is called upon to provide the method of approach to theology. Anselm's
introduction of this method set the standard for the manner of inquiry into the
Christian faith seen in the *summae* of the medieval period.

It was Anselm who first began to employ the method of inquiry which,
ironically, would ultimately lead to positions directly contrary to his own, with
regard to the necessity for the atonement. The late medieval nominalists, though
Anselm's heirs in terms of method, were at the opposite pole from him on the
question of the necessity for the atonement. For Luther, the *remoto Christo* or
sola ratione method cannot be expected to bear pure fruits, for the simple reason
that the treatment of issues of theology in such form has the effect of directing

one's theological thought toward one's reason. This is doubly dangerous, since it not only fails to recognize the fallenness of reason, but also directs theology away from the Scriptures. That Christ is our salvation is "the thing over which all reason and wisdom stumbles" (WA, DB 7, 83:14-16; AE 35, 380).[42] For Luther, the Sacred Page must itself provide what Anselm expected reason to provide, namely *intellectum*.

Besides this, Luther's conception of the task of the theologian mitigates in principle against Anselm's *remoto Christo*. The theologian's task is to bring the message of the Scriptures into the public realm, where it belongs. So clearly does Luther see the matter thus that he even goes so far as to declare that the Gospel should not even be understood at all as something written, but rather proclaimed (WA 10/I,1, 17; AE 35, 123).[43] Kenneth Hagen, whose research deals with Luther's approach to Scripture, has provided convincing evidence to support the view that for Luther, the theology of Scripture must be "enarrated."

> The term that Luther uses throughout his work and throughout his life to describe his publications on Galatians is "enarrare" or "enarratio."
> . . .
> To "enarrate" Pauline theology means to set forth in detail Paul's theology in the public arena. "Narrate" means to tell the story. "Enarrate" means to take out the message and to apply it and tell the story in public. The story is the "one true faith in Christ alone." In the Preface [to the Galatians commentary] of 1535 to "enarrate the Epistle" means to go public against the Devil (Hagen 1989, 13).

---

[42]"Das Christus unser heil ist . . . An welchem sich alle vernunfft und weisheit stösset."

[43]"Das gantz allte testament . . . doch alleyn den namen hatt, das es heylige schrifft heyst, Und Euangeli eygentlich nitt schrifft, ssondern mundlich wort seyn solt, das die schrifft erfur truge, wie Christus und die Apostel than haben; Darumb auch Christus selbs nichts geschrieben, ssondern nur geredt hatt, und seyn lere nit schrifft, sonder Euangeli, das ist eyn gutt botschafft odder vorkundigung genennet hatt, das nitt mit der feddernn, sondern mit dem mund soll getrieben werden—The entire Old Testament . . . alone has the name Holy Scripture. And the gospel should really not be something written, but a spoken word which brought forth the Scriptures, as Christ and the apostles have done. This is why Christ himself did not write anything but only spoke. He called his teaching not Scripture but gospel, meaning good news or a proclamation that is spread not by pen but by word of mouth."

Luther's understanding of theology therefore not only requires on the one hand that he mistrust reason, but on the other that he make the message of the Scriptures public. Both of these requirements set him against the method of Anselm.

Luther's conception of the theological task drove him to undertake it even in spite of his expressed desire not to do so. His awareness of the pains involved with bringing the Gospel into the public realm could not dissuade him from his task, as he makes clear both early and late in his career. In his 1519 Galatians commentary, he confesses,

> I wish for nothing more ardently than to lie hidden in a corner; but since I am altogether obligated to deal publicly with Holy Writ, I want to render as pure a service as I can to my Lord Jesus Christ. For if Divine Scriptures are treated in such a way as to be understood only with regard to the past and not to be applied also to our own manner of life, of what benefit will they be? Then they are cold, dead, and not even divine (AE 27, 386; WA 2, 600f).

Luther's aversion to his own task as preacher is also found in his 1530 "Exhortation to all Clergy . . . ":

> Not that we take such great delight in preaching, because, speaking for myself, I would rather hear no other news than that I had been deposed from the preaching office. I am so very tired of it, as a result of the great ingratitude of the people, but much more because of the unbearable hardships which the devil and the world deal out to me (AE 34, 50; WA 30/II, 340:29-33).[44]

In a sermon preached on January 1st of the same year, Luther is actually reported to have stopped preaching, and did not finish the sermon, due to the ingratitude

---

[44]"Nicht das wir so grosse lust hetten zu predigen, Denn, für mich zu reden, wolt ich kein lieber botschafft hören, denn die, so mich vom predigt ampt absetzt, Ich bins wol so müde, der grossen undanckbarkeit haben jm volck, aber viel mehr der untreglichen beschwerung halben, so mir der Teuffel und die welt zu messen." Cf. Ebeling 1970, 45.

and disobedience of the people.[45]   Thus Luther was not driven to his task because of personal enjoyment or satisfaction he derived from it; he was driven, rather, by a sense of responsibility to his vocation under God.

Because of Luther's compulsion to preach the Gospel into the public realm, he was no Anselm, and the Anselmian method is nowhere found in him. Luther's approach, much like that of Augustine, is more appropriately labelled rhetorical where Anselm's is dialectical. The difference between the two means of communication should not be underestimated, especially when detected in the study of theology. "One will commit a serious error if one tries to reduce his [Luther's] position to a dialectic of Scholastic syllogisms" (McDonough 1963, 146). Marjorie O'Rourke Boyle (1989) has recently provided an important distinction between the two. "Dialectic seeks an act of the intellect, judgment, and secures its religious end in contemplation. Rhetoric seeks an act of the will, assent, and secures its religious end in conversion" (30). According to Boyle, Augustine's works are often misunderstood and unfairly criticized as being intellectually simple, due to a failure to notice the distinction between dialectic and rhetoric. "The criterion of epideictic rhetoric," she explains, "is not the intellectuality of truth and falsehood, but the affectivity of good and evil, as promoting a decision of praise or blame" (27).

In like manner as Boyle defends Augustine from unjust criticism, Siggins speaks on Luther's behalf. As Boyle's defense is to point to a misunderstanding of the rhetorical method, which method was for Augustine necessitated by what he considered his theological task to be, so Siggins speaks on Luther's behalf against a similar reproach of his style. Luther's unsystematic approach is a deliberate choice, he maintains, "part of his conception of the theological task"

---

[45]The Nürenberg Codex Solger appends a note at the place where the text of Luther's sermon breaks off: "Hic D. D. Lutherus suspendit organa suarum concionum propter populi ingratitudinem et inobedienciam" (WA 32, 4:16-17; AE 34, 50n).

(Siggins 1970, 267). The reason neither Luther nor Augustine ever wrote a comprehensive text containing a systematic outline of the Christian faith may well be that they, unlike the scholastics, could not force what they perceived their task to be into the constraints of systematization.

Augustine, like Luther, declared himself first a preacher of the Gospel, notwithstanding his expressed fears of his own shortcomings in this regard (Fabrizius 1988, 3-6).[46] Luther, like Augustine and unlike Anselm and the scholastics after him, considered himself first not a dialectician nor a systematician, but a preacher of the Gospel. So Luther's approach could not be that of a dialectician, because that was not in keeping with his vocation. Luther could not superimpose philosophical or reason-based agendas on Scripture; this would in fact be an abuse of Scripture.

This provides a way of seeing why Luther could not live with scholastic method. His task was not merely that of the dry philosopher or theologian who pursues the explanation of truths as if only for personal entertainment. Indeed, such a criticism could easily be considered appropriate for the peripatetic schoolmen who enjoyed debate over such topics as whether God can make things not to have been, or whether something can be true in such a way that it can never have been true.[47] Such exercises do not benefit the Church or her subjects, and for this reason Luther was not only loathe to partake, but quick to condemn. McDonough (1963, 33f) contends that Luther was not intimately

---

[46]In support, Fabrizius cites Augustine's Letter 21 in Augustine of Hippo, *Letters*, transl., Sister Wilfrid Parsons (Washington: Catholic University of America, 1951-56), 49.

[47]On the question of whether the past can be made not to have been, Aristotle and Ockham answered in the negative (Adams 1969, 36), while the affirmative was given by William of Auvergne and Gilbert of Poitiers in the 1200s, and by Thomas Buckingham in the 1300s (28f). William of Ockham similarly mused over the question of whether something is true in such a way that it can never have been true (11). His refutation of two theories on this may parallel that of Peter Damian (see Knowles 1962, 90-105).

acquainted with the great scholastic systems of the thirteenth-century. The reason this appears to be so may well be simply that Luther had no use for them.

Luther gives clear evidence, early on in his career, of being irritated at the dialecticians who seem to confuse their discipline with theology. Following Luther's publication of the Ninety-Five Theses, which Luther had intended as a catalyst for debate with the theologians of his day, he received a response from the Dominican Silvester Prierias, official theological adviser to Pope Leo X. Prierias gave reply by way of a hastily-written *Streitschrift*, entitled, "Dialogue Concerning the Powers of the Pope." This document simply rejected Luther's position out of hand, without explanation, without debating Luther's points, and with no comments other than "in error," "false," and the like. The result was a summons to Luther to appear in Rome within sixty days of receipt of notice (see Schwiebert 1950, 338f). Luther's hurried reply suggested an awareness on his part that the reason his adversaries did not agree to debate him on his theological points was that their discipline as philosophers was not the same as his.

> And I wish your profession would restrain you, in order that, as often as you adduce to me your divine Thomas without Scripture, without the Fathers, without the Church, without reason, so might you be mindful that you are a dialectic, not playing the theologian (WA 1, 664:39 - 665:2).[48]

Far from putting himself above the authority of Scripture in his hermeneutics, Luther will allow in no way for his treatment of Scripture to be other than that intended by Scripture. Thus he is not found creating chains-of-arguments constructed *sola ratione*.

---

[48]"Et hac tua professione obstrictum te volo, ut, quoties mihi divum Thomam adducis sine scriptura, sine patribus, sine ecclesia, sine ratione loquentem, memor sis te dialecticum, non theologum agere."

Luther's most direct renunciation of Anselm's method is made in his commentary on the First Epistle of St. Peter, in his exposition of 3.15: "Always be prepared to make a defense to anyone who calls you to account (*rationem reddere*) for the hope that is in you." He does not refer here to Anselm by name, though his grasp of Anselm in general, seen in his marginal notes of circa 1513 indicating that he studied Anselm's works rather extensively, leads to the supposition that he is likely to have been aware that it was Anselm who, more so than anyone, was responsible for the medieval genesis of the *sola ratione* method. That Luther rejects the method is clear from his comment on this text—I Peter 3.15—to which Anselm specifically refers in the opening chapter of the *Cur Deus Homo* (S II, 47:10-11). Almost as if in direct rebuttal of Anselm's usage of the text in support of his method, Luther declares,

> The sophists have also perverted this text. They say that one must vanquish the heretics with reason and on the basis of the natural light of Aristotle, since the Latin expression *rationem reddere* is used here, as though St. Peter meant that this should be done by means of human reason. Therefore they say that Scripture is far too weak to overthrow heretics. This, they say, must be done by reason and must come from the brain, which must be the source of the proof that faith is right, even though our faith transcends all reason and is solely a power of God (AE 30:107; WA 12, 362:10-17).[49]

Anselm nowhere admits that Scripture is too weak to overthrow heretics, but Luther's charge here is the inference he draws from the use by the "sophists" of the term *rationem reddere*.

Luther's approach was *sola scriptura* where Anselm's had been *sola ratione*. Not only is this so in his message itself, but in the manner in which his

---

[49]"Aber den text haben die Sophisten auch verkeret, das man soll mit der vernunfft und aus naturlichem liecht Aristotele die ketzer ubirwinden, darumb das hie ym latinischen stehet '*Rationem reddere*', als meynet S. Peter, man soll es mit menschlicher vernunfft thun. Drumb sagen sie, die schrifft were viel zu schwach, das sie sollt ketzer umb stossen, Es müsse mit der vernunfft zů gehen und auss dem gehyrn komen, daraus müsse mans beweysen, das der glawb recht sey, so doch unser glawb ubir alle vernunfft und alleyn Gottis krafft ist."

message is constructed and put forward. His preface to the New Testament opens with an apology of sorts, a recognition that the Word of God, i.e., the Scriptures, ideally should have no preface, and that the only reason for his preface is to counter the many unfounded interpretations and prefaces in publication. "It would be right and proper," Luther contends, "for this book to go forth without any preface or foreign names, and speak by its own name and for itself" (WA, DB 6, 2:2-7; AE 35, 357).[50] For Luther it is very clear that the Word of God needs no help from the theologian's creativity or personal input.

Luther's opposition to the *sola ratione* method is perhaps most especially evident in his sermons. It is clear from examination of Luther's *postilla* that his purpose there is to be consistently expository, to bring the words of the text into the public realm by way of preaching; moreover he demonstrates consistently how it is the texts on which he preaches which say what he is preaching. While Luther can make reference to current affairs in connection with the text, he employs the text itself frequently in making his point; he wishes the hearers to know that the point being made is not his own, but that of the text.

Luther does not superimpose a "preaching outline" upon the text in order to preach it, but rather follows the order of the text, out of respect for that order. His sermon on the Gospel for the First Sunday in Advent, for example, contains an exposition, in order, on each word or phrase of the words of Isaiah contained within the lesson: "Tell ye the daughter of Zion, Behold thy King cometh unto thee, Meek, and riding upon an ass, and upon a colt the foal of an ass." Luther devotes at least a paragraph each to the first seven phrases or words of this sentence, considered separately: Tell ye / the daughter of Zion, / Behold, / thy

---

[50]"Es were wol recht und billich, das dis buch on alle vorrhede unnd frembden namen aussgieng, unnd nur seyn selbs eygen namen und rede furete, Aber die weyl durch manche wilde deuttung und vorrhede, der Christen synn da hyn vertrieben ist, das man schier nit mer weys, was Euangeli oder gesetz, new oder alt testament—. . .But at the same time there have been many wild interpretations and prefaces in which the Christian sense is lost, with the result that one can scarcely know what is gospel or law, New or Old testament."

king / cometh / unto thee, / Meek. He does not superimpose another order, but follows here the order of the lesson, and his intent is to explain what each of the words means (AP 1, 20-29; StL 11, 2-10). Generally his sermons do not break sentences into such small segments, but they do tend, by and large, to follow the order of the text, much like a commentary.[51] As a rule, the ordering of textual interpretation within the sermon is not violated. Nor does Luther generally depart from the Biblical order in his application of the text. The application to current affairs, even when this makes up the bulk of the sermon, still tends to follow the same order.

Luther's use of extra-Biblical sermon illustrations, moreover, is generally limited to short phrases, employing similies or metaphors, and these are generally not used to illustrate a major point.[52] Luther certainly would have had no use for a preaching manual filled with ideas for sermon illustrations; he generally found his illustrations amply provided by the Sacred Scriptures. Here too, as in the case his choice of order, Luther prefers to employ the text. This is particularly so, of course, when treating the Gospels. For instance, the Gospel for the Second Sunday after Epiphany, on the wedding at Cana, becomes for Luther fertile ground for illustrating the confidence of faith, using the requests of Jesus' mother as an example. First, she feels the need for wine at the wedding, and comes to him "in a humble and polite request," not demanding that he answer in her way, but merely expressing the need.

> Thus she merely touches his kindness, of which she is fully assured. As though she would say: He is so good and gracious, there is no need of my

---

[51]The difference is that Luther's understanding of the purpose of the Scriptures leads him to make even his own "commentaries" actually something other than commentaries in the modern sense of the word, or, for that matter, in the medieval sense of the word. See Hagen 1989, 6.

[52]For an example, from a 1523 sermon for Easter Sunday: "Just as a pig's bladder [Schweinsblase] must be rubbed with salt and thoroughly worked to distend it, so this old hide [alte Haut] of ours must be well salted and plagued until we call for help and cry aloud, and so stretch and expand ourselves" (AP 2, 253; StL 11, 636).

asking, I will only tell him what is lacking, and he will of his own accord do more than one could ask (AP 2, 61f; StL 11, 469f).[53]

Then Jesus responds in what appears a most unkindly manner, which Luther sees as an opportunity for faith's testing. "Now observe the nature of faith. What has it to rely on? Absolutely nothing, all is darkness." Thus Luther turns the story to the hearers and declares that this was not only so on this occasion at the wedding of Cana (John 2.1-11), but in the case of every Christian: "This is where faith stands in the heat of battle." So he continues, employing the response of Jesus' mother as an example, who

> here becomes our teacher. However harsh his words sound, however unkind he appears, she does not in her heart interpret this as anger, or as the opposite of kindness, but adheres firmly to the conviction that he is kind, refusing to give up this opinion because of the thrust she received, and unwilling to dishonor him in her heart by thinking him to be otherwise than kind and gracious (AP 2, 62; StL 11, 470).[54]

Luther's sermon on the Gospel for the Second Sunday in Lent, on the Canaanite woman (Matthew 15.21-28) similarly takes the response of the woman to Jesus' rough treatment of her as an example for Christian faith, and the woman herself becomes an illustration. After her pleas are repeatedly spurned by Jesus, she, rather than despairing, becomes more earnest.

---

[53]"Das siehe hier in seiner Mutter: die fühlt und klagt ihm den Mangel, begehrt auch Hülfe und Rath von ihm mit demüthigem und sittigem antragen. Denn sie spricht nicht: Lieber Sohn, schaffe uns Wein; sondern: 'Sie haben nicht Wein.' Damit rühret sie nur seine Güte, der sie sich gänzlich zu ihm versieht. Als sollte sie sagen: Er ist so gut und gnädig, dass nicht Bittens darf; ich will ihm nur anzeigen, woran es fehlt, so wird er von sich selbst thun, mehr denn man bittet."

[54]"Da siehe, wie der Glaube gestaltet sei; was hat er nun vor sich? Eitel Nichts und Finsterniss . . .

"Hier steht nun der Glaube im rechten Kampf; da siehe, wie seine Mutter thut, und uns hier lehrt. Wie hart seine Worte lauten, wie unfreundlich er sich stellt; so deutet sie dennoch das alles in ihrem Herzen nicht auf Zorn oder wider seine Güte, sondern bleibt fest auf dem Sinn, er sei gütig, und lässt sich solchen Wahn nicht nehmen durch den Puff, dass sie ihm sollte darum auch im Herzen die Schande aufthun und ihn nicht gütig noch gnädig halten."

Now, what does the poor woman do? She turns her eyes from all
this unfriendly treatment of Christ; all this does not lead her astray,
neither does she take it to heart, but she continues immediately and firmly
to cling in her confidence to the good news she had heard and embraced
concerning him, and never gives up. We must also do the same and learn
firmly to cling to the Word, even though God with all his creatures
appears different than his Word teaches. But, oh, how painful it is to
nature and reason, that this woman should strip herself of self and forsake
all that she experienced, and cling alone to God's bare Word, until she
experienced the contrary. May God help us in time of need and of death
to possess like courage and faith! (AP 2, 150; StL 11, 547)[55]

Thus Luther employs the example of the woman's faith to exhort his hearers to
a like faith.

Luther's sermon on the Gospel for the Sixteenth Sunday after Trinity, on
the widow of Nain (Luke 7.11-17), similarly makes the text into his illustration
of faith. The widow loses her son and is left with nothing; then Jesus comes and
raises him, returning to her more than she ever had. This, then, becomes the
point of departure for faith.

As now this wife was fully convinced that there was no hope for her son,
that it was impossible for her to receive him back alive again . . .
Behold, here comes God before she looks around, and does what she
never dared to ask of him, as it is impossible, and he restores her son
alive to her again.
    . But why does God do this? He permits man to fall so deeply into
danger and anxiety, until no help or advice is within reach, and still he
desires that we should not doubt, but trust in him who out of an

---

[55]"Nun, was thut das Weiblein hiezu? Sie thut solch unfreundliche Geberde Christi aus den
Augen, lässt sich das alles nicht irren, nimmts auch nicht zu Sinn, sondern bleibt stracks und fest
in ihrere Zuversicht hangen an dem guten Gerücht, das sie von ihm gehört und gefasst hatte, und
lässt nicht ab. Also müssen wir auch thun und lernen allein am Wort fest hangen, obgleich Gott
mit allen Creaturen sich anders stellt, denn das Wort von im sagt. Aber, o wie wehe thut das der
Natur und Vernunft, das sie sich soll so nackt ausziehen, und lassen alles, was sie fühlt, und allein
am blossen Wort hangen, dass sie auch das Widerspiel fühlt. Gott helfe uns in Nöthen und
Sterben zu solchem Muth und Glauben!''

impossible thing can make something possible, and make something out of nothing (AP 5, 132f; StL 11, 1651).[56]

So it is that Luther's illustrations for his sermonic message are taken from the text, and the story thus becomes a sermon.

The samples of sermonic material I have employed all treat Gospels in which is the story of a woman and the response of her faith. But it is no coincidence that Luther's use of the women of the texts is generally to illustrate their faith. Luther's exposition of the "spiritual" or allegorical meanings of the texts on which he preaches is internally very consistent. One example of this internal consistency is his allegorical interpretation of men and women in his texts. Allegorically, the men are often preachers, or representative of God, and the women are often the faithful, or representative of the church. Mary is the Christian church, Joseph, the servants of the church (StL 11, 152; AP 1, 169); Simeon is one speaking with "all the prophets (StL 11, 250; AP 1, 274), but Anna is "the holy Synagogue, the people of Israel, whose life and history are recorded in the Bible (StL 11, 259; AP 1, 283); Herod is a false Christ (StL 11, 341; AP 1, 368); at the feeding of the five thousand (John 6), Philip's and Andrew's doubtings signify, respectively, the teachers with confused consciences or who confuse God's grace and his laws (StL 11, 565f; AP 2, 171); the soldiers who crucified Christ are bishops and teachers who suppress the Gospel (StL 11, 134; AP 1, 150). Although this application of allegorical meaning is not entirely consistent—one exception would be the shepherds in the Christmas Gospel, whom we would expect to be preachers, but whom Luther depicts as examples for

---

[56]"Da dies Weib darauf stund, es wäre nun verloren mit ihrem Sohn, es wäre unmöglich, dass sie ihn wieder lebendig überkommen sollte . . . sehet, da kommt Gott, ehe sie sich umsiehet, und thut, das sie nimmermehr als ein unmöglich Ding hätte von ihm dürfen bitten, und macht ihr den Sohn wieder lebendig. Warum thut doch Gott das? Darum, er lässt den Menschen in solche Fährlichkeit und Angst so tief fallen, dass gar kein Rath noch Hilfe mehr da ist; und will doch, dass wir nicht verzweifeln sollen, sondern dem vertrauen, der da aus einem unmöglichen Ding ein mögliches und aus nichts etwas machen kann."

Christian life (StL 11, 137; AP 1, 154); another possible exception would be the wise men who are implicitly taken to depict the Christians (StL 11, 417; AP 1, 444)—it provides a further indication of Luther's sense of being bound to the text, even in his allegorical use.

The study of Luther's sermons is fascinating in itself, and it would require far more than what I have briefly shown here; my intent is merely to demonstrate Luther's own sense of being bound to and led by the texts he treats. There is no room in Luther's works for a *remoto Christo* exercise, which would be contrary to his principles.

Reason for Luther cannot assist faith, which is to say the whole realm of nature is entirely out of sync with the realm of grace. Luther's aversion to a magisterial use of reason is well known and can be supported by an abundance of references. He referred to reason as a whore, a prostitute, '*Frau Hulda*', 'Madam Reason', 'the greatest whore that the Devil has', '*Frau Putze*'.[57] He contended that "philosophy is a practical wisdom of the flesh which is hostile to God" (AE 34, 144; WA 39/I, 180),[58] and warned against making "your own ideas into articles of faith" (WA 7,455; AE 32,98).[59] In a sermon on the Gospel for Epiphany, Luther explains his distaste for reason.

> Reason and nature never proceed any farther than they can see and feel. When they cease to feel they at once deny God's existence and say as Ps. 14, 1 says. "There is no God," therefore the devil must be here. This is the light of the universities which is to lead men to God, but rather leads to the abyss of hell. The light of nature and the light of grace cannot be friends. Nature wants to feel and be certain before she believes, grace believes before she perceives. For this reason, nature does

---

[57]WA 10/I/1, 326; 18, 164, 182; AE 40, 174, 192; WA 51, 126; AE 51, 374; WA, TR 6, 689; WA 18, 674, 729; AE 33, 122, 206, AP1, 363; StL 11, 335. See Althaus, 70.

[58]For additional references see Althaus 1966, 70-1.

[59]"Mach nit Artickell des glawbensz ausz deinen gedanckenn, wie der grewel zu Rom thut, das nit villeicht ausz deinem glawben ein trawm werde."

not go further than her own light. Grace joyfully steps out into the
darkness, follows the mere word of Scripture, no matter how it appears.
Whether nature holds it true or false, she clings to the Word (AP 1, 362;
StL 11, 334).[60]

Having made Luther's position clear, I should state on the contrary that
Luther's invective against reason does not make him a nominalist. The
nominalists of the *via moderna*, William of Ockham's fifteenth-century heirs,[61]
in a vein similar to that of the nominalists of Anselm's day, were intent on
demonstrating the division between reason and faith to the extent which required
a conception of the *potentia absoluta Dei* where God may be considered
according to his absolute power and not in connection with what he has ordained,
or according to this *potentia ordinata Dei*. But Luther's professed rejection of
reason in the establishment of faith did not lead him to the same result. Luther
did not hold to the *credo quia absurdum* version of faith; he nowhere considers
the truths of faith to be incommunicable in rational terms. To the contrary,
Luther expressly rejected the suppositions which the nominalists had put forward
in connection with the *potentia absoluta*. Luther directly confronted these ideas
in his 1517 "Disputation against Scholastic Theology," which takes scholastic
thought itself to task. Though the chief point of attack in these theses is the
scholastic use of reason, and the main thrust is a negative reaction to the
professions of scholastic employment of Greek philosophy to demonstrate
Christian theology, the nominalists are also directly attacked for their own use of

---

[60]"Siehe, also thut die Vernunft und Natur allezeit, dass sie nicht weiter folgt, denn sie fühlt;
wenn sie nimmer fühlt, so darf sie alsbald Gott leugnen und sagen, wie Ps. 14,1 von ihr gesagt
hat: 'Hier ist Gott nicht,' der Teufel muss hier sein. Das ist das Licht der Hohen Schulen, das
sie zu Gott führen soll; ja, in Abgrund der Hölle. Es mag nicht Naturlicht und Gnadenlicht
Freund sein. Natur will fühlen und gewiss sein, ehe sie glaubt: Gnade will glauben, ehe sie fühlt.
Darum geht die Natur nicht weiter denn in ihr Licht. Gnade tritt heraus fröhlich in die
Finsterniss, folgt dem blossen Wort und Schrift, es scheine sonst oder so; es dünke die Natur wahr
oder falsch, so hält sie am Wort fest.''

[61]Especially D'Ailly and Biel.

syllogisms. On the question of whether Luther agreed with the nominalist
distinctions in what is possible for God, Luther's simple answer is to reject the
question altogether. "No syllogistic form is valid when applied to divine terms"
(AE 31, 12; WA 1, 226:21).[62] But Luther does go on to answer the
illegitimate question specifically, asserting that not even the so-called *potentia
absoluta Dei* can cause certain things to happen.[63]

Considerations of the *potentia absoluta* lead inevitably to the question
whether divine *acceptatio* of sinners without atonement is conceivable in another
order. That is, could God in another, absolute order simply receive and forgive
sinners without an act of atonement availing on their behalf? Luther's answer is
to reject the question; he sticks adamantly to the order which is in existence,
refusing to consider another, and insisting that God is bound. "It is not true that
God can accept man without his justifying grace."[64] This declaration is of key
importance to the present study, for it provides clear evidence from Luther for
a basic presupposition entertained herein that Luther, in general agreement with
Anselm on this point, was diametrically opposed to the concept of divine
acceptatio. For Luther God cannot accept man without the fulfillment of a certain
precondition, viz., God's "justifying grace." That Luther considers this grace
to be bound only to the merit of Christ is clear from his insistence that "the law
. . . will not be overcome except by the 'child, who has been born to us'" (AE

---

[62]Thesis 47: "Nulla forma syllogistica tenet in terminis divinis."

[63]Thesis 55: "Gratia dei nunquam sic coexistit ut ociosa, Sed est vivus, mobilis et operosus
spiritus, Nec per Dei absolutam potenciam fieri potest, ut actus amiciciae sit et gratia Dei praesens
non sit. Contra Gab.—The grace of God is never present in such a way that it is inactive, but it
is a living, active, and operative spirit; nor can it happen that through the absolute power of God
an act of friendship may be present without the presence of the grace of God. Against Gabriel
[Biel]" (WA 1, 227:1-3; AE 31, 13).

[64]Thesis 56: "Non potest deus acceptare hominem sine gratia dei iustificante. Contra
Occam." WA 1, 227:4-5; AE 31, 13.

31, 14; WA 1, 227:29).[65] "I have often said that faith alone is not enough before God, but the price of redemption must also be there. The Turk and Jew, too, believe in God, but without the mediator and price." (StL 11, 1085; AP 3, 342).[66]

Yet Luther's agreement with Anselm against the notion of *acceptatio* is not from the same perspective. For Luther, reason cannot be synthesized with theology to arrive at the truths of revelation, and faith in what has been revealed is necessary. This sounds similar to the nominalist approach, but the latter was largely apologetic, meant to destroy the synthesis between faith and reason which had been created by the Thomist and Scotist parties. Ockham's "razor" served to demonstrate the artificial, tautological nature of the underlying assumptions providing the basis for the great thirteenth-century systems of thought. Thus its effect was primarily negative; its purpose was to destroy and remove what was in place. Luther, on the other hand, had no such ultimate motive; his emphasis on *fidem solam* was not a position to which he was driven by a prior elimination of any philosophical systems to which he might have had recourse, but rather by a concurrent emphasis on *Christum solum*. The *sola scriptura* maxim to which Luther adhered was of another breed than that which the nominalists had employed. While their theological expressions tended to be supported by a more positivistic recourse to faith alone, Luther was unwilling to dispense altogether with the use of reason in the expression of Christian doctrine. Accordingly, we may conclude that Luther was no nominalist bent on demonstrating the dubious credibility of any theological use of reason, his admission of 1520 notwithstanding, that philosophically he was still a nominalist. He in fact gave

---

[65]Thesis 73: "Lex est exactor voluntatis, qui non superatur nisi per 'parvulum, qui natus est nobis'." We note again Luther's weaving of the Biblical phrasing of Is. 9.6.

[66]"Denn ich habe zuvor oft gesagt, dass der Glaube nicht allein genug sei zu Gott, sondern die Köste muss auch da sein. Der Türke und Juden glauben auch an Gott, aber ohne Mittel und ohne Köste."

evidence together with this admission, made in his response to his condemnation by the faculties of Louvain and Cologne, that his particular philosophical orientation could be sacrificed if necessary.

> They accomplished little by speaking against me with bare words, which served only to show their displeasure and to charge me with errors. I already knew their position and in fact have suffered much grief over it. Neither did I ask them to refer me to their own authors, as if I am unaware of what they say. What I have asked is that they would convince me either by recourse to the authority of Scripture or by acceptable reason, that they are right and I am wrong. This is therefore my main request, and I do not care if my position is condemned by Aristotle himself; my request is that they respond to the matter itself which I attack. But this they have not examined, heard, addressed, or even perceived; they prefer instead simply to build on their own support. To put it another way, why would even I consider opposing my own philosophical orientation, which is Occamist or Modernist, and which I resolutely hold, if I all I wanted to do was to restrain myself from considering a particular way of thinking? (WA 6, 194:36-195:5)[67]

Although for Luther reason could not be allowed a place in the authoritative establishment of theological truth, at which point his rejoinders against it are apropos, yet a sanctified reason could be permitted limited service in the explanation and synthesis of doctrine, for without it, no form of argument ever could be allowed at all. This is not to say that he occasionally used reason authoritatively; his use was consistently in service of his explanations and

---

[67]"Non erat necesse ut dicerent nudis verbis, mea sibi displicere et erronea videri: sciebam id fore et in hoc ipsum passus sum edi. Nec hoc quaesivi, ut me ad suos autores remitterent quasi mihi incognitos, sed ut scripturae autoritate aut ratione probabili sua vera et mea falsa esse convincerent. Quae est enim ista (etiam suo Aristotele prohibita) petitio principii, mihi responderi per haec ipsa, quae impugno. Non est quaestio, quid didicerint, audierint, legerint, senserint unquam, Sed quibus firmamentis ea muniant. Alioqui, cur et meae sectae resisterem, scilicet Occanicae seu Modernorum, quam penitus imbibitam teneo, si verbis voluissem aut vi compesci?"

Another 1520 admission occurs in his "Adversus Execrabilem Antichristi Bullam Martin Lutherus," where he simply declares, more in demonstration of the absurdity of his condemnation than anything else, "Sum enim Occanicae factionis, qui respectus contemnunt, omnia autem absoluta habent, ut sic iocer in istam Moriam—In fact I am of the Occamists, which they despise, although they have acquitted them of all things, and so this 'Death-kiss' of theirs is a joke" (WA 6, 600:11-12). See also WA, TR 2, 516:6; WA 30/II, 300:9; WA, TR 9, 600:10.

arguments. But Luther's use of reason in the service of arguing a point was nothing like Anselm's *sola ratione* method. Rather, it only went as far as to permit Luther to accept the order of reality and language as reasonable. Reason was never given the status of ultimate authority reserved for Scripture alone, and Luther is never found to argue *sola ratione*. Luther's consistency on this matter is seen in this willingness to set his own philosophical orientation aside in the face of Scripture's authority. He made a clear distinction between the authority of Scripture and all other forms of authority.

Still, his apparent willingness to allow on at least two occasions for the authority of evident or acceptable reason (*ratione evidente aut probabili*) may raise in the minds of some the question whether his professed adherence to the Scriptures alone is compromised. The first occasion is that seen in the quotation above, wherein appears the tandem phrase *scripturae autoritate aut ratione probabili*. The second is seen in Luther's challenge to his adversaries, to show him his errors from Scripture or evident reason, which is passionately repeated in his famous profession at the Diet of Worms:

> Unless I am convinced by the testimony of Scripture or evident reason (for neither in the Pope nor in Councils alone do I believe, since it has been established that they have erred often and have contradicted themselves), I am captive to the Scriptures adduced by me and my conscience siezed by the words of God, neither able nor willing to recant, since to act against conscience is neither safe nor right to do (WA 7, 838, 4-8).[68]

---

[68]"Nisi convictus fuero testimoniis scripturarum aut ratione evidente (nam neque Papae neque conciliis solis credo, cum constet eos et errasse sepius et sibiipsis contradixisse), victus sum scripturis a me adductis et capta conscientia in verbis dei, revocare neque possum nec volo quicquam, cum contra conscientiam agere neque tutum neque integrum sit." (1521)

Here he allows the same inclusion of reason to pass (*scripturarum aut ratione evidente*), yet with a strong profession of allegiance to Scripture alone.[69] But a consideration of the context into which this assertion was made should indicate the cause of these allowances. The refusal of Luther's opponents even to consider the issues he raised was for him a cause of great disappointment, in view of his own eagerness to debate. His reference here to reason can well be seen to demonstrate in him nothing more than a sense of consternation over his opponents' refusal to face the issues he raised. He makes allowance for his adversaries, if they will, to use *ratione evidente* in their arguments, if this will at least elicit from them a discussion of substance. Further, that he makes this allowance in no way suggests that he himself will argue in this way. That is, in allowing *ratione evidente* here he is merely saying that he will refute his adversaries' arguments against him on these terms if they choose them, but making no implications about his own choice of argument otherwise.

All this means, therefore, is that Luther is no follower of the *credo quia absurdam* tradition, in spite of its longevity,[70] and his willingness to allow *ratione evidente* in theological arguments sets him at odds with the nominalist school. The nominalist approach to reason was to Luther no better than that of its historical victims.

---

[69]The position of Tavard, that Luther failed to recognize the place of the church in the establishment of authority, is misguided. To suggest, as Tavard has, that the authority of the Church was so intimately bound together with the authority of Scripture in the first six centuries as to make the two a single authority, is to fail to recognize the supreme place reserved in the early church for apostolic authority. He asserts that what was later to be called tradition and contradistinguished from Scripture was at first identified with Holy Writ. The novelty of this idea is partly demonstrated by Tavard himself, as he provides a lengthy catena of the names of those who do not share it; and thus it appears to be a peculiar theologoumenon on his part. See Tavard 1959.

[70]The term has been used to assess Tertullian's thought.

Luther's *Theologia Crucis*, Correlative to His Adherence to Scripture

Luther's *theologia crucis* is fully consistent with a rejection of natural reason in the establishment of divine truth. For Luther, faith and natural reason are necessarily opposed to each other; if they were not, faith would be unnecessary.

> Faith has to do do with things not seen. Hence in order that there may be room for faith, it is necessary that everything which is believed should be hidden. It cannot, however, be more deeply hidden than under an object, perception, or experience which is contrary to it. . . .
> Thus God hides his eternal goodness and mercy under eternal wrath, his righteousness under iniquity. This is the highest degree of faith, to believe him merciful when he saves so few and damns so many, and to believe him righteous when by his own will he makes us necessarily damnable, so that he seems, according to Erasmus, to delight in the torments of the wretched and to be worthy of hatred rather than of love. If, then, I could by any means comprehend how this God can be merciful and just who displays so much wrath and iniquity, there would be no need of faith. (AE 33, 62f; WA 18, 633:14-21).[71]

Faith dwells in darkness (DBD, 240; WA 40/I, 229:15-17; AE 26, 129f).[72] It "closes its eyes and simply and joyfully leaves everything in the hands of God" (WA 10/II, 323; DBD 237).[73] Siggins (1980) rightly declares, "It is beyond dispute that Luther's theology was from first to last a theology of the cross, set explicitly against any vain attempt at a theology of glory, *theologia*

---

[71]*De Servo Arbitrio* (1525): "Sic aeternam suam clementiam et misericordiam abscondit sub aeterna ira, Iustitiam sub iniquitate. Hic est fidei summus gradus, credere illum esse clementem, qui tam paucos salvat, tam multos damnat, credere iustum, qui sua voluntate nos necessario damnabilies facit, ut videatur, referente Erasmo, delectari cruciatibus miserorum et odio potius quam amore dignus. Si igitur possem ulla ratione comprehendere, quomodo is Deus sit misericors et iustus, qui tantam iram et iniquitatem ostendit, non esset opus fide."

[72]Galatians commentary (1535): "Fides ergo est cognitio quaedam vel tenebra quae nihil videt, Et tamen in istis tenebris Christus fide apprehensus sedet—Faith is such a knowledge that, though it is completely and utterly dark, and nothing is visible, it is yet sure and sees, in such utter darkness, that it really holds Christ."

[73]Letter to Hans v. Rechenberg, 1522.

maiestatis" (7).[74]   Being so encompassing for Luther, the mention of the theology of the cross cannot be avoided in any serious discussion of his thought. Much has been said about it since the 1933 publication of Walther von Loewenich's famous *Luthers Theologia Crucis*. Von Loewenich's book, which demonstrates a sound grasp on the centrality of this perspective in Luther (contra Green 1980, 43), served well as a catalyst in the Luther renaissance of the twentieth century.[75]   Althaus (1966), whose section on *theologia crucis* is based primarily on von Loewenich's work, points out that the theology of the cross and God's being God are most intimately connected (25). God will not allow himself to be found by the imagining of human reason, but rather hides himself under his opposite. This is most manifestly the case at the cross of Jesus, where the monstrosity of the event hides its glorious significance for faith. "So it is that a wretched figure is presented to us for faith" (WA 47, 71:16).

From the cross, this theology extends itself to the life of the Christian, which thus becomes cruciform; we find that God's presence is not experienced as a glorious theophany, but rather that the experience of the faithful is of necessity one veiled by the crosses, the *Anfechtungen*, of Christian life. In this way Christian anxiety is interpreted otherwise than as a sign of an errant faith; rather, it is seen as a

---

[74]Siggins continues: "Yet serious question needs to be raised about the common assumption that Luther's *theologia crucis* means the same thing throughout his career — the assumption that the form of this theme in the Heidelberg Disputation, for instance, remains normative for the knowledge of God in the later theology. Again, close comparison reveals that he never abandoned his insistence that God will be known only as the crucified God; but that the doctrine of the knowledge of God is dramatically recast by a later insistence that faith's knowledge of God in Christ is a knowledge of God fully as He is, with sweeping implications for Christology and for faith" (7f).

[75]General statements at the outset of *Luthers Theologia Crucis* indicate the weight placed on the principle by von Loewenich: "The theology of the cross is a principle of Luther's entire theology" (12f). "It is the aim of our investigation to trace the significance of this principle of knowledge in Luther's thought" (13f). "In the cross of Christ we have redemption, here and nowhere else . . . [the] shibboleth of all genuine Lutherans" (17). The cross opens scripture (23).

necessary element of a true faith. Pesch (1972, 20) is essentially correct in commenting that for Luther, "in principle faith is never without anxiety about God."

Luther's understanding of Christian experience must be understood from this perspective. Bernard's emphasis on humility found a sympathetic ear in Luther not because the latter in his earlier years had not developed to the point of rejecting merits in it (contra Green 1980, 35), but because he recognized, aside from all questions of merit, that trials are precisely that which produce the kind of humility which is prerequisite to faith. "In trial the existential aspect of faith comes to its full expression. The same must be said of prayer" (von Loewenich 1976, 139). This is not to say that faith depends upon humility as upon a *meritum de condigno*, but rather that as contrition of heart logically precedes faith, so a humility imposed by trials is continually of benefit for faith, in that pride, which is contrary to faith, is thus extracted.

Luther's explanation of the Magnificat, which von Loewenich sees as his most beautiful piece (94f), declares that the Holy Spirit instructs us through experience (WA 7, 546-548; AE 21, 299-301). This must not be seen as a remnant of the mysticism Luther encountered in Biel and the Brethren of the Common Life, however. By experience Luther means something altogether different than they. Experience is helpful in a twofold sense, first, that it drives faith to the Gospel promise and finally, that it verifies that promise. In the first sense it is seen as a negative influence on the Christian: the Christian must suffer harsh treatment at the hands of God; Christ here appears under his opposite, and faith must trust as it were in the darkness (so von Loewenich 1976, 86). In this first sense experience is seen as suffering, which makes faith assert itself (119). God here pretends to be the devil (WA 41, 675:8; 24, 632:31; 17/II, 13:16).[76]

---

[76]Pesch (1972, 17n) remarks that Luther "dares to say" this.

Here, faith believes, nor questions how (Siggins 1970, 211). It will not give up, being the creation of the Holy Ghost. Therefore true faith will not merely endure suffering, but will actually welcome and demand it, since suffering is what at length forces faith's self assertion. On this point Luther appears even to assert a *resignatio ad infernum* (WA 56, 388ff; 56, 391:12; 18, 708:8. See Pesch 1972, 25; Althaus 1966, 286; Holl 1977, 65f). Von Loewenich (1976) sees that faith demands a hidden God, calling it a paradox implicit in Luther's thought. On the one side, the hidden God is a logical consequence of faith; on the other side, there is a sharp disjunction between the hidden and the revealed God. The hidden God in the first view is not the same as the hidden God in the second; the intersection is in faith (39-42).[77] The *theologia crucis* becomes thus for Luther the extreme paradox of faith (so Siggins 1970, 181).

This theology not only opposes but in a sense precludes the kind of speculation which had been prevalent in the medieval schools. "For Luther all religious speculation is a theology of glory" (von Loewenich 1976, 27). The theologian under the cross can see no need to speculate, for the experience of his own cross leaves faith demanding the cross of the Crucified too insistently. The suffering Christian, that is, receives comfort amid suffering not from speculation but from the Gospel, the revelation of God in Christ. In the suffering Christ one sees the proof of God's love, notwithstanding the present experience of its opposite. Thus the comfort of the Christian does not derive from this experience but from the message, the Gospel of the cross of Christ. The experience is contrary to faith, thus pushing faith back to its source, namely the word of the cross, for sustenance.

---

[77]Luther: "They will pass over [the revealed God in Christ] and take only those that deal with the hidden God." WA 48, 463; AE 5, 50. See also WA 44, 429:24f; AE 7, 175; WA 47, 599:29ff; AE 3, 71; WA 47, 460:26ff; AE 5, 46; WA 31, 2:38; AE 16, 54ff; WA 40/I, 77:11ff; AE 26, 29; WA 45/I, 79:20, cf. 93:23ff and 602:20ff; AE 26, 30, cf. 39 and 396.

On Theological Approach

Mark Edwards (1983) has done much to vindicate Luther against the charge that the polemics of Luther were the product of a psychologically as well as physically sick man.[78] Edwards contends that Luther's keen apocalyptic vision was at the heart of his sometimes harsh and abusive treatment of his opponents. Seeing these as enemies of God, while at the same time convinced that the End Time was near at hand, Luther felt himself to be under obligation as a servant of God to attack them with fierce invective. Moreover,

> he was well equipped for the battle. He possessed extraordinary rhetorical skills, and he had always had the ability to generate a towering anger against his opponents and to express this anger to good rhetorical effect (204).

Edwards has thus pointed us to two determining factors in Luther's approach, namely his sense of vocation and his consequent style of expression. These factors are related, which is to say that his own understanding of his sense of vocation worked mightily to determine his style of expression.

Luther was a pastor and preacher of the Gospel before he was anything else. He refers often to his vocation as the reason for his outspokenness. For Luther, the role of the pastor is the same as that of Christ. Not surprisingly, therefore, Luther's normal word for Christ's ministry is *Predigtamt*.[79] Christ's

---

[78] So Heinrich Denifle, *Luther und Luthertum in der ersten Entwicklung* (Mainz, 1904); Albert Maria Weiss, *Lutherpsychologie als Schlüssel zur Lutherlegende: Ergänzungen zu Denifles Luther und Lutherthum* (Mainz, 1906); Hartmann Grisar, *Luther*, 3 vols. (Freiburg, 1911-12); Paul J. Reiter, *Martin Luthers Umwelt, Character und Psychose*, vol. 2 (Copenhagen, 1941); and Erik Erikson, *Young Man Luther* (New York, 1958). All cited in Edwards 1983, 214.

[79] According to Siggins (1970, 51), "The office of Christ . . . for Luther almost always means His role as preacher or teacher. . . . There are some exceptions, but they are very few in number. By contrast, there are more references to Christ as preacher and teacher than under any

office is for Luther his role as preacher or teacher. And the *Predigtamt*, the office of the ministry, is therefore as critical as is Christ himself to the church. The pastor must speak out, for this is as essential as Christ's own speaking, being in essence the very same thing.

Luther's convictions about his vocation are strengthened by his confidence in the power of the Word of God which is entrusted to him for preaching. Luther demonstrated clearly his belief that the only power by which to advance the kingdom of God is that of the Gospel. This belief is fully congruent with his use of the Sacred Page for *enarratio*. The message of Scripture must be communicated, and cannot be thought to need the aid of reasoned argument for its reception. Reason and the Gospel are antithetical. Thus Luther had by necessity to see himself as a herald of a message which he fully expected to be treated harshly and often rejected.

This being the case, Luther sees the necessity also of being as it were armed for battle when bearing the Gospel into the world. In the familiar line from *Ein feste Burg*, Luther employs this battle imagery, declaring, "He's by our side upon the plain." But Luther was never inclined to interpret his militancy in physical terms. Unlike the knights and the peasants who revolted with force, Luther was firm on the point that all battles must be engaged using only the Word of God, i.e., the Sacred Scriptures. This requires faith, rather than work. The use of force betrays a lack of faith (see, e.g., WA 18, 310:24-28).[80] Thus

---

titles except savior and lord. 'The office of Christ is very clearly described: He will not bear the sword or found a new state, but He will be a teacher, to instruct men about an unheard of but eternal decree of God' [WA 40/II, 242:29]. To have seen Christ and His office is to have heard His preaching and seen His miracles [WA 10/I/2, 357:29]. Luther's normal word for Christ's ministry is *Predigtampt*—'preaching office.' Christ's mission and ministry was 'to preach truth and to apply it to us'; proclaiming the gospel was 'the highest function of His office' [WA 12, 191:12, 285:29].''

[80]"An Admonition to Peace: A Reply to the Twelve Articles of the Peasants in Swabia" (1525): "Denn an diesen sprüchen greyfft ein kind wol, das Christlich recht sey, nicht sich strewben widder unrecht, nicht zum schwerd greiffen, nicht sich weren, nicht sich rechen, sondern

faith arms the preacher with only the Word of God in whose hidden power he trusts.

If we understand Luther to have seen himself thus as a soldier, it is not surprising to see Luther's robust and sometimes rough language. But this is none other, to his way of thinking, than the robust and sometimes rough language of Scripture. Did not Jesus speak harshly to his enemies? Did not Jesus attack them with vigorous words? Luther's invective against his enemies arises from his convictions about the vocation of the pastor as spokesman for Christ, who routinely assailed his opponents.

Anselm, on the other hand, was ever the man of peace, whose heart, so-to-speak, stayed behind at Bec when he was uprooted and thrust into the archbishopric at Canterbury. His laments over this change appear clearly to be more than homages to some convention dictating to those of high estate a superficially humble manner of referring to their own dignified standing. On the contrary, Anselm longed for the sylvan and peaceful idyll that Bec was.[81]

Anselm was not captive, as was Luther, to the conviction that the Gospel must be proclaimed relentlessly and forcefully by those to whom its proclamation has been entrusted, and here we see the heart of the most glaring difference between these two men. For Anselm, to be sure, all that was impiously taught in opposition to the faith of the Church was to be rejected; in spite of his general aversion to conflict, Anselm was dutiful to what he perceived his task to be. An epitomal example of this is seen in his contentions against Roscelin's tritheistic

---

dahyn geben leyb und gut, das es raube, wer da raubet, wyr haben doch gnug an unserm HERRN, der uns nicht lassen wird, wie er verheissen hat—For this lesson a child grasps well, that rightly to be Christian is not to strew discord about, not to grab for a sword, not to bear it, not to use it, but in its place to give love and good, so that the one who in that place would rob may thus be robbed. We have quite enough in our Lord, who will not leave us, as he has promised."

[81]Eadmer reports, "When Anselm began new to think of all the peace he had lost and all the labour he had found, his spirit was torn and tormented with bitter anguish." Eadmer 1962, 69.

dialectics. Yet Anselm's dislike for the task can be read between the lines of his discourse as well as from his expressed preference for the monastic life. Anselm never saw, as did Luther, that the Gospel came as a complete foreigner into the world with all its natural reason. Anselm preferred to think that if one could reason well with the infidel, there was always cause for optimism that unbelief might give way to faith. Not so for Luther, who recognized natural reason as an enemy of the Gospel. Therefore the only hope of advancing the Gospel into the heart of the infidel was by preaching the Gospel, *nulla ratione*, which is to say, without recourse to the use of reason. Thus Luther knew his preaching must be militant, an unwelcome guest in a fallen world, yet one which, if faithful in communicating the message of the Sacred Page, would create its own adherents. At the root, then, of the difference between Anselm and Luther is an implicit disagreement over the power and purpose of that message.

Chapter V

Was the Atonement "Necessary"?: Toward an Appreciation of Anselm and Luther

"Necessary" for Anselm:
Perfectly Appealing to Reason

Anselm's reckoning of the question of the atonement's necessity is made from reason's point of view. The *Cur Deus Homo* asks reason to answer precisely this question. This is in fact the impetus for the entire treatise: reason is asked why God became man. So the great difference between Anselm and Luther on Anselm's question of the incarnation is seen in the fact that Anselm does not ask Scripture to answer this question, and this makes it a purely speculative question. The method established in the *Monologion* persists in the *Cur Deus Homo*. Anselm is still asking reason his questions in order to provide by means of reason answers which harmonize with the answers given by the Christian tradition. He is therefore employing a methodology which is not seen in Luther, who was more inclined when questioning simply to allow Scripture to speak. The articles of the faith being established by Scripture, Luther examines the articles catechetically, by asking, "What does this mean?" and turning back to Scripture for the answers. Anselm's *fides quaerens intellectum* is faith seeking *elsewhere* than Scripture to obtain knowledge of what it believes, as though Scripture were unable to provide this, or at least unable to provide the higher levels of *intellectum* sought by faith. For Anselm, faith seeks understanding by employing the rational mind to explore what is known by logic and reason without the direct aid of Scripture.

But Anselm's argument for the purpose of the incarnation, being constructed out of reason alone, arrives at a position which not only explains the incarnation's purpose, but provides something further, as was also case with the rational exercise employed in the *Monologion*. The fruit of that work *was* after all something new, namely a rational reason for the Trinity's being what it is, an attempt to make discursive sense, *extra Scripturam*, of what Scripture teaches. In consideration of the *Cur Deus Homo*, we likewise find something new, for this work goes beyond the explanation of the incarnation, but has Anselm also contending for its absolute rational necessity.

> Does not the reason seem sufficiently necessary, why God ought to do that of which we speak? Because the human race, so utterly precious a work of his, was utterly ruined, nor was it fitting (*decebat*) that what God had designed concerning man should be thoroughly annihilated; nor, moreover, could that design be put into effect, unless the human race were liberated by the Creator himself? (CDH I,4; S II, 52:7-11).[1]

While Luther will agree with a position which regards the indispensability of the incarnation, he nowhere states it in the terms set forth as a result purely of logical deduction and reasoning.

---

[1] "Nonne satis necessaria ratio videtur, cur deus ea quae dicimus facere debuerit: quia genus humanum, tam scilicet pretiosum opus eius, omnino perierat, nec decebat ut, quod deus de homine proposuerat, penitus annihilaretur, nec idem eius propositum ad effectum duci poterat, nisi genus hominum ab ipso creatore suo liberaretur?"

The same kind of reasoning extends also to the *Cur Deus Homo*'s explanation of the doctrine of atonement as *satisfactio vicaria*. As Aulén (1969, 1) has pointed out, Anselm has given the first "real beginnings of a thought-out doctrine of the atonement." Yet what Aulén fails to point out is that Anselm's chosen method of putting his view forward under the guise of entirely rational persuasion gives it an ingredient it would not otherwise have had. Forde (1984, 21f) has also noticed this, pointing out that "Anselm was the first to pose the question about the necessity for the actual event of the cross. . . . not the a posteriori necessity of previous pictures, but a rationally deduced *a priori* necessity."[2] Hopkins too (1972, 3) recognizes that "the immediate occasion of the *Cur Deus Homo* is to demonstrate why man's salvation rationally necessitates the incarnation." Anselm's position reads as one of logical necessity, by Anselm's own design: in order for God to accomplish salvation, it was absolutely necessary, which is to say, necessary by the absolute dictates of logical reasoning, and therefore necessary a priori, that it be done in this way, by this indispensable and sufficient satisfaction in the blood of Christ.

Aulén's assessment of Anselm credits him with stressing the atonement as a legal, substitutionary action, a *satisfactio vicaria* (1969, 82). But this stress is due to Anselm's method. Anselm's expression of the incarnation in terms of absolute divine necessity, which he gave perhaps more forcefully than any other theologian in the history of the Church, was now for the first time being argued from the standpoint of rational deduction. Though we find much the same contentions as Anselm as early as Irenaeus,[3] we do not find them expressed in

---

[2] Evans (1980, 163f) notes that Abelard also asked *qua necessitate* God became man, but that he answers differently, saying that God could simply have remitted the debt. Abelard's contentions may be said to constitute the earliest response to Anselm's claim.

[3] Irenaeus declared, though more or less in passing, that "it was not possible that the man who had once for all been conquered . . . could reform himself . . . and as it was also impossible that he could attain to salvation who had fallen under the power of sin,—the Son effected both these

the same dialectical or rational terms. Thus while Aulén has noticed a rational orientation behind Anselm's reasons for determining this atonement was necessary, he has fallen short of understanding Anselm's unique method and the purpose behind it.

When Anselm claims that man "owed . . . this obedience to God the Father, and humanity to Deity; and this the Father exacted from him" (CDH I,9; S II, 61:18-19),[4] and then points out the necessity for a sufficient satisfaction in view of this need for justice, he is doing so by way of purely logical response to anticipated objections to his purely logical position on necessity. When Anselm asks "why God was not able to save man in some other way, and if he was able, why he willed to do it in this way" (CDH I,10; S II, 66:21-22),[5] it must be seen as a question asked of reason, not Scripture. Anselm makes a bold delineation not only of the answer to the question of necessity in the atonement, but also of the rational question itself, embodied even in the very title of this his most prominent work: *cur deus homo*. Anselm steadfastly insists, from reason alone, that God had to become incarnate because our salvation could not have been achieved in another way.

There is more than one sense in which the atonement can be called necessary, and it is not clear whether Anselm was aware of this. He speaks of necessity without making clear distinctions between the different nuances of necessity as Thomas Aquinas would later do. There is no distinction made, for

---

things." Irenaeus, *Against Heresies*, 3.18.2; in Roberts and Donaldson 1987, 446. Aulén (1969, 44f) points out too that the Greek fathers frequently discussed whether God could not have saved men by some other way than that the Incarnation and Redemption, as by almighty fiat. Debate is entered by Athanasius and John of Damascus.

[4]"Hanc igitur oboedientiam debebat homo ille deo patri, et humanitas divinitati, et hanc ab illo exigebat pater."

[5]"Quaeritur enim cur deus aliter hominem salvare non potuit; aut si potuit, cur hoc modo voluit." Hopkins (1972, 192) calls this question "urgently central."

example, between necessity of consequent and necessity of consequence, nor is the relationship between 'necessary' and 'fitting' clearly delineated.[6] As I see it, this is also due to Anselm's method. It is because he is arguing from the standpoint of logical demonstration that he makes no great distinction between what is fitting or appropriate for God and what is deemed necessary. If it is fitting, it is necessary, since this is a primary criterion serving as a basis for logical proof. There is a clear link in Anselm to the fittingness of God's action and its necessity. That which Anselm recognizes as beautiful in God's plan is argued, generally on that basis, to be appropriate for God. When seen to be appropriate for God, the logical deduction is to call it necessary, since the idea that God would act inappropriately would be inconceivable to Anselm.

Anselm's references in the *Cur Deus Homo* to the fitting character of God's action are abundant.

> It was fitting (*oportebat*) that as by human disobedience death came upon the human race, so by human obedience [i.e., of Christ] life should be restored. And inasmuch as sin, which was the cause of our damnation, had its initiation in a woman, so the author our righteousness and salvation should have been born (*nasceretur*) of a woman. And thus the devil, who conquered man by the eating of the tree to which he had tempted him, should be conquered (*vinceretur*) by the passion of the tree which was borne by man. There are also many other things which when studiously considered, show in our redemption by this mode in which it was procured an ineffable beauty (CDH I,3; S II, 51:5-12).[7]

---

[6]Dr. Ronald Feenstra of Marquette University has been of great assistance to me in pointing out Anselm's lack of distinctions of nuance in 'necessity'. For a discussion on the variations in understanding 'necessary' in connection with Anselm, see Hartshorne 1965, 10.

[7]"Oportebat namque ut, sicut per hominis inoboedientiam mors in humanum genus intraverat, ita per hominis oboedientiam vita restitueretur. Et quemadmodum peccatum quod fuit causa nostrae damnationis, initium habuit a femina, sic nostrae iustitiae et salutis auctor nasceretur de femina. Et ut diabolus, qui per gustum ligni quem persuasit hominem vicerat, per passionem ligni quam intulit ab homine vinceretur. Sunt quoque multa alia quae studiose considerata, inenarrabilem quandam nostrae redemptionis hoc modo procuratae pulchritudinem ostendunt."

This is Anselm's manner of procedure. He proceeds to give the beauty of the incarnation and redemption as a demonstration of its fittingness, and then, even in the following chapter, blends this concept with that of logical necessity. When Anselm has shown an article of faith to make perfect sense to reason, he has already accomplished his task, and it is in this sense, I believe, that he understands the idea of necessity shown to be absolute.

So for Anselm, the incarnation and its resultant atonement are absolutely necessary—that is, perfectly appealing to a prudent use of reason—in order for a just God to receive sinners into his kingdom. Any analysis of the *Cur Deus Homo* which fails to bear in mind the expressed method of Anselm cannot help but miss the gist of Anselm's thought on the necessity for the work of Christ. Even a cursory glance at the chapter headings (see Appendix 2) will show that Anselm's appeal is exclusively to reason. Thus when Anselm declares that "it was impossible to save the world" except by Christ's atonement (CDH I, 10; S II, 66:2-3),[8] what he means is that it has been shown by clear and reasonable argument.

> Without satisfaction, that is, without voluntary payment of the debt, God can neither pass by the sin unpunished, nor can the sinner attain that happiness, or happiness like that, which he had before he sinned; for man cannot in this way be restored, or become such as he was before he sinned (CDH I, 19; S II, 85:28-32).

Because Anselm is making his case from reason alone, there are for Anselm some things not even God can do, since they would be unreasonable. God cannot do without atonement if he desires to save his people, and his desire to save his people is necessarily part of his essence, since he is love.[9] Anselm's reasons

---

[8]"mundum erat aliter impossibile salvari."

[9]Tavard's (1983, 32) claim, that Anselm's doctrine was handicapped because of his quantitative measuring of grace, seems to me a caricature of Anselm's legal orientation, and furthermore it does not follow that this stress lessens the infinite compassion of God, as Tavard contends. One could just as easily argue to the contrary that it more greatly demonstrates God's

for his position are just as clear as his stance itself. For Anselm God cannot remit sin without sufficient payment for sin. Atonement is absolutely necessary for salvation to be accomplished because "remission of sin is necessary" (CDH I, 10; S II, 67:18) and "it does not belong to [God's] liberty or compassion or will to let the sinner go unpunished" (CDH I, 12; S II, 70:28-30). Further, "the honor taken away must be repaid, or punishment must follow; otherwise, either God will not be just to himself, or he will be weak in respect to both parties; and this it is impious even to think of" (CDH I, 13; S II, 71:24-26). Necessity, as Anselm sees it, has to do with what is fitting, and God cannot—*will* not, would never—act otherwise than in a fitting way. We might say that "necessity" for Anselm means stylistic consistency, that it is in God's style as an artist to use this medium of salvation, and not another. God cannot be inconsistent with his own *pulchritudo* and still be God.

Therefore Anselm's position, which posits thus an absolute, i.e., perfectly reasonable, necessity for a legal satisfaction of divine justice in redemption, has been set forth in precisely the same way as his position in the *Monologion*. Reason's purpose for Anselm is to re-process every article of faith which has been previously established, for reason is quite evidently the means by which faith seeks understanding.

---

love. See above, pp. 57-59.

"Necessary" for Luther:
Unalterable, and Necessary to Proclaim

Luther's Rejection of the Anselmian Type of Question

The fact that Luther rejected scholasticism is widely recognized, but a surprising few have suggested Luther's aversion to scholastic method in itself as a major contributor to the difference in Luther's thought. Most of the research tends to bring out differences in content or direction of theological stress (von Loewenich, Oberman, Ebeling, Althaus, Holl, et al.). Only some of these have addressed the opposition of Luther's method to that of all scholastics dating to Anselm. Siggins (1970, 267) has noted, but only briefly, that Luther's choice of an unsystematic approach is part of his conception of the theological task. Denis Janz refers to Luther's "fundamentally different approach to theology" over against Thomas, attributing it primarily to differing points of departure for the theological task (Janz 1989, 16).[10] Janz attributes the difference largely to Luther's rejection of Aristotle, but with the admission that something more is at stake, as he notices that Luther at times explicitly includes Bonaventure in his criticism of Thomas, though the former opposed the use of Aristotle in theology. Moreover, according to Janz, Luther criticizes the Lombard, who did not use Aristotle. Janz's conclusion is that "while some scholastic errors are attributable to the methodological mistake of using Aristotle, many others are not." He

---

[10]"Experience is central to Luther's theology precisely because theology is done from within the experience of faith and has this experience as its theme. On the other hand, experience is to some extent programmatically excluded in Thomas because the central task of theology is not reflection on faith but the description of reality from God's point of view. In his critique of the absence of an experiential dimension in Thomas' theology, Luther was criticizing in fact a fundamentally different approach to theology. Luther's critique thus represents an awareness of their diverging.theological methods."

further contends that "in the final analysis, it is the teachings produced by the method which either distort or faithfully represent the gospel"(23). But he does not come up with a unified suggestion of a fundamental difference in method between Luther and the scholastics. In general, though scholars notice the fundamental difference in approach between Luther and scholasticism in general, little is said about it. [11]

I have attempted to show herein that if one gains an appreciation for their differences in approach to theology, one can more clearly see an underlying cause for the true differences, as well as the similarities, between Luther and Anselm in general. When one approaches the comparison between these figures from the standpoint of method, a more unified analysis is possible. Luther's approach is to start with the Sacred Page, and to hold all Christian thought captive to it. In principle, Anselm's *sola ratione* is anathema to Luther.

When Luther approaches many matters which to any medieval theologian would be considered speculative, he does not handle them speculatively but on the basis of the Gospel. [12] So Luther can declare that "nothing is so small but God is still smaller; nothing is so large but God is still larger" (WA 26,339; AE 37, 228). But this is no speculation; its assertive nature is due to Luther's conviction that God is God. *Gottes Gottheit* is such that one ought not speculate about how things might be were God to be otherwise than he is or to act otherwise than he has. Thus Luther can come across sounding rather like Anselm on the question of necessity. Both oppose the excesses of nominalism.

---

[11]Others who have commented include Yves Marie Congar (1983), who in a brief article draws attention to Luther's refusal of admitting philosophical concepts in theology and a constant determination to remain within the tenets of and the language of God's Word. David Dockery (1983) has also written briefly on the connection between Luther's Christology and his hermeneutics.

[12]Hagen's work on Luther's Galatians commentary takes issue with Melanchthon's assessment of Luther on this score. Melanchthon, says Hagen, failed to note the difference between Luther's approach and that of the humanists (Hagen 1989, 20-27).

But Luther does not handle the question whether God is able to do things differently in a different order (*de potentia absoluta*) as Anselm had handled similar questions. Anselm's reply had been to argue on the basis of reason, and thus to refute the radical dialecticians on their own grounds. For Anselm, "abstraction is fundamental" (Stock 1983, 336). Luther, on the other hand, prefers simply to dismiss the speculative ideas by returning at once to what is known about God. Says Luther, for example, "God could easily give you grain and fruit without your plowing and planting, but he does not want to do so. . . . He could give children without man and woman. But he does not want to do this" (WA 31/I, 435; AE 14, 114).[13] To steer the question thus, to return to what God wills to do, is to return to God's being God, and hence to his self-revelation by the Sacred Scriptures.

Therefore I agree with Althaus' (1966) understanding of Luther on this point. He refers with approval to Holl's contention that for Luther, it is "not the infinite capacity for possibilities freely available to God but that infinite power which is active in the formulation of the existing world" (110).[14] Put simply, abstract discussions about the absolute power of God are fruitless. For Luther, God's omnipotence is not "the potentiality by which he could do many things which he does not, but the active power by which he potently works all in all" (AE 33, 189; WA 18, 718).[15] Althaus goes on to note that Luther's first answer to the question of why God let Adam fall is to reject the question (Althaus 1966, 159). God is God, and ultimately, man deals only with God (167). This must be so, because "*deus solus verax, omnis homo mendax*—God alone is true,

---

[13]Commentary on Psalm 147 (1531).

[14]The work to which Althaus refers is Karl Holl, *Gesammelte Aufsätze zur Kirchengeschichte* (3 vols.; Tübingen: Mohr, 1932), I, 45. See also WA 5, 168.

[15]*De servo arbitrio* (1525).

and every man a liar" (WA 2, 453:35-36; AE 27, 165).[16] Althaus points out that Psalm 116:11 (". . . All men are liars") was a favorite passage of Luther's, and that its truth is implicit in Luther's theology at every point; Luther's intention is to let God be God, and the doctrine of justification is the most sublime example of this (Althaus 1966, 128f). When Luther's thought is viewed from this vantage point its internal consistency becomes striking. God is God, and this is why Luther cannot allow himself to speculate with the nominalists on other created orders (105); thoughts of another order would suggest a condition in which God is not God (337). Albrecht Ritschl's attempt to liken Luther's doctrine of God to the nominalists' idea of a god who is unlimited in arbitrariness is therefore quite wrong, according to Althaus (283). And in his conception of Luther's understanding of such questions of necessity, I contend, Althaus is quite right. An insistence on letting God be God is entirely incompatible with the nominalist discussions about the *potentia absoluta Dei*. Here as clearly as anywhere Luther's break with the movement of scholasticism toward speculation can be seen. God is the God who *is*. Therefore no theological discussions about what *is not* can be allowed.

Nor, in view of the *theologia crucis*, is one free to brood over God's being in itself. Luther's contention that God is God is not in itself to be taken as an a priori philosophical principle about God. Unlike the Anselmian question, this is not based on a priori considerations about God. Rather, it springs from the divine revelation to which Luther is held captive. "True theology must understand clearly that it has to be a theology of revelation" (von Loewenich 1976, 19). For Luther, this conviction derives from Scripture. It could also be said to derive from Luther's understanding of the Person of Christ, who could not

---

[16]Galatians commentary (1519).

be known at all apart from Scripture. For Luther, God's Word is exactly like God (WA 10/I/1, 187:9; cited in Siggins 1970, 15).[17]

Luther's Rejection of the Acceptational View

The story of Luther's monastic struggle is well-known. The focus of this research leads to the suggestion that it may have been the Scotist and nominalist developments on the power of God which led the pre-Reformational Luther, honest young nominalist that he was, to despair. Perhaps he could not bring himself to terms with a God about whom unbounded speculation is permitted, a God who, *de potentia absoluta*, could do anything even including the undoing of what had been done. McDonough (1963, 41) agrees, saying that Luther "instead of questioning the reasonableness of Ockhamist 'voluntarism', seeks rather to escape the incertitude of God's whimsical decrees." So when at length the objectivity and Christocentricity of the Gospel were made plain to him, the conviction would also have arisen not only that the system of ascending merits must go, but that the whole scholastic system and patterns of thought about God must go as well.

The nominalist idea of divine acceptance of the atonement by sheer divine will is related to the scholastic stress on divine acceptance of the sinner's merit, likewise by sheer divine will, which Luther also rejected altogether. Indeed, Luther's wholesale rejection of divine acceptance of merits can be better understood when one gains an appreciation for Luther's fierce aversion to any kind of divine acceptation based ultimately on the will of God alone. God's being God means that God's way of achieving atonement is the only way.

---

[17]Luther's use of the term "God's Word" is not identical to that of Anselm, the former using it to refer to the Sacred Scriptures and the latter using it to refer to Christ. I will discuss this below, pp. 186-187.

What this means in comparison with the faith of the nominalists, is that in spite of all of Luther's insistence on faith alone for justification, no sympathy can be found in his perspective for the nominalist conception of divine *acceptatio* of merits by sheer will. Faith does not justify by itself, and faith is not sufficient alone, because faith must have an object (so Althaus 1966, 232; Siggins 1970, 149; Green 1980, 239f; McDonough 1963, 146). The mere act of believing is not what makes God gracious, but rather the Christ in whom one believes. Christ is always the heart of Luther's thought, and whenever he speaks of the paramountcy of faith, he does not mean faith exclusive of its object.

In "The Freedom of a Christian" (1520), Luther does use the term *propter fidem*, declaring that "God . . . does us that great honor of considering us truthful and righteous by this faith—*propter hanc fidem,*" namely, on account of the fact that "we consider him truthful," and that "faith works truth and righteousness by giving God what belongs to him" (WA 7, 54:21-25; AE 31, 351).[18] But this is not an application of the nominalist understanding of divine *acceptatio* to the act of believing.   Edmund Schlink (1961) provides an explanation of apparent confusion over the occurance of the same term in the Augsburg Confession. He contends that there "Christ and faith are so intimately united that *propter fidem* may be said for *propter Christum*, and *per Christum* for *per fidem*" (99f).

Luther's rejection of the distinction between divine *potentia absoluta* and *potentia ordinata*, which was fully congruent with his negative view of reason's ability, was due to his convictions on the revelation of God in Christ. Unlike Ockham, however, he did not accept this revelation in a positivistic sense, a sense which in Ockham sounds rather like blind faith, but rather as what the word itself

---

[18]"Ubi autem deus videt, veritatem sibi tribui et fide cordis nostri se honorari tanto honore, quo ipse dignus est, Rursus et ipse nos honorat, tribuens et nobis veritatem et iustitiam propter hanc fidem. Fides enim facit veritatem et iustitiam, reddens deo suum, ideo rursus reddit deus iustitiae nostrae gloriam."

imports: revelation. One must be careful to remember that Biel and Ockham, while employing the Scotist distinction between the absolute and the ordained power of God, were arguing against a fusion of philosophy and theology. Luther's rejection of these nominalist distinctions might therefore be said to imply a like rejection of their theological positivism. Luther's theology was not positivistic any more than it was rationalistic. While he spoke negatively of reason (as *Frau Hulda*, etc.), he never intended to reject its use altogether; to the contrary, he demonstrated a willingness on occasion to argue from evident or acceptable reason (see above, pp. 160-162). Yet for Luther even such reason must always be employed within the bounds authoritatively set for it by the Gospel. Nor did he embark upon the types of ventures Anselm preferred, *remoto Christo*.   Luther's *theologia crucis* leaves no alternative to the cross for salvation. Thus when Luther speaks of a necessity for a theology of the cross, his rejection of the nominalist distinction between the absolute and ordained power of God is implicit. If a *theologia crucis* is a perspective without which the Christian theologian cannot do, then certainly the *crux ipsa* can no less be set aside. As Luther sees God revealed in the Man Jesus Christ and nowhere else, we may learn of the necessity for the atonement from Christ himself. Luther's thought is straightforward: in Christ, God has become visible; he does not remain invisible, despite the continued hiddenness of his glory in the humility of this revelation. For Luther there is no place for the mincing of words on this point: Christ *is* God, fully and bodily; there is no other God than this Man. Thus also in Christ we see that the atonement is not merely one possibility among many, but rather the only acceptable way of looking at the matter. As Christ is God, so his work is necessarily God's work, and so too may we conclude its value to be intrinsically infinite. Luther's discovery of the Gospel was bound together intimately with an insistence upon a necessity for real, not merely accepted, value adhering to the God's chosen method of human salvation.

Luther makes this point most emphatically and unmistakably, setting himself ostensibly against the nominalists, whom he refers to as "the new teachers," with their concept of divine *acceptatio*, in a sermon on New Year's Day, in 1522.

> There are found among the new teachers those who say that the forgiveness of sins and justification by grace lie completely in divine imputation; in other words, that all depends on the reckoning of God, and that it is enough, whether God reckons sin or does not reckon it, that a man is justified or not justified from his sin solely on that account . . . If this were true, then the whole New Testament would be nothing and all in vain. Then Christ would have worked foolishly and vainly when he suffered for sin. Then also God would have carried on purely a shadow-fight or party-tricks without any need thereof. For surely without the need of Christ's suffering he could have forgiven and not imputed sin, or faith other than that in Christ might have justified and brought salvation. Such are they who confide in a type of gracious divine mercy by which they think that their sins are not taken into account. Against this abominable, frightful interpretation, this error, the holy apostle used to bind justifying faith upon Jesus Christ (StL 12, 261; translation from Green, 240).[19]

---

[19]"Es sind etliche, zuvor unter den neuen hohen Schullehrern, die da sagen: Es liege die Vergebung der Sünden und Rechtfertigung der Gnaden ganz und gar in der göttlichen *imputatio*, das ist, an Gottes Zurechnen, dass es genug sei, welchen Gott die Sünde zurechne oder nicht zurechne, derselbige sei dadurch gerechtfertigt oder nicht gerechtfertigt von seinen Sünden, [wie der 32. Psalm v.2 und Röm 4,78. Sie dünket lauten, da er sagt: 'Selig ist der Mensch, dem Gott nicht zurechnet seine Sünde.'] Wo dies wahr wäre, so ist das ganze Neue Testament schon nichts und vergebens, und Christus hat närrisch und unnützlich gearbeitet, dass er für die Sünde gelitten hat; auch Gott selbst hätte damit ein lauter Spiegelfechten und Gaukelspiel ohne alle Noth getrieben; sintemal er wohl ohne Christi Leiden hätte mögen vergeben und nicht zurechnen die Sünde, und also möchte auch wohl en andrer Glaube denn an Christum gerecht und selig machen, nämlich, der auf solche gnädige Gottes Barmherzigkeit sich verliesse, dass ihm seine Sünden nicht würden gerechnet.

"Wider diesen greulichen, schrecklichen Verstand und Irrthum hat der heilige Apostel den Brauch, das er immer den Glauben auf Jesum Christum zieht."

The *Crux* of the Matter

It is somewhat ironic that Luther's use of the expression "Word of God" is not identical to Anselm's use. Anselm, in good patristic fashion, regularly employed the term "the Word" to refer to Christ, i.e., the Second Person of the Trinity. Luther deviates from this tradition with his preference for using the term to refer to the contents of the Sacred Scriptures. When Luther speaks of the Word of God, he generally means the Scriptures, particularly the Scriptures in the public realm. In this shift in Luther's usage from the patristic, Johannine references to the *Logos*, we see what appears at first to be a deviation in Luther from patristic thought, and a greater likeness to it in Anselm.[20] What is ironic about this is that while we may be inclined therefore to call Anselm's use the "higher" use, Luther's is in fact more consistent with a high christology "from below". We recall the fact that Luther's ascription of divinity to Christ means more than Anselm's, as his christology tends to be "from below" (see above, p. 50, 97). Anselm's Word is the eternal *Logos*; but for Luther, the Word of God, the Word which is Sacred Scripture, is necessarily a fully human word. Though he does not generally use the term to refer to Christ himself, Luther's use is illustrative of his incarnational theology, for the message of the Sacred Page is Christ, the eternal though incarnate *Logos*, a message of a fully human Person, appropriately "clothed" in fully human language. The human Person is fully God, and the human language is fully God's; in both cases, the finite houses the infinite, *finitum est capax infiniti*, to reverse the Zwinglian phrase.

---

[20]Luther does on occasion refer to the Word in the Johannine sense, not only when commenting on John's Gospel, but also, for instance, in his Genesis commentary, where he declares that the Word is God and yet is a Person distinct from the Father (WA 42, 13; AE 1,17). Such references are relatively rare, however.

Interestingly, Anselm's Word is the Person of the *Logos*, who stands behind the veneer of created nature or the "book" of nature, making possible in Anselm's mind the access to *intellectum* via reason; but for Luther the Person of the *Logos* is behind every word of Scripture, through which alone he may be approached. For Luther, the Word is the Bible, the manger which holds Christ (StL 11, 135; AP 1, 152), whereas for Anselm, the Word is the Christ whom the manger holds. Thus in this comparison of usage in terms, Anselm's usage becomes indicative of what Luther would see as a *theologia gloriae*. For Anselm, the Person of the Word is the exemplar of beauty, whereas for Luther the Person of the Word *incarnate* is both the substance of the message of the Scriptures and the key to understanding the Scriptures, which he calls the Word of God. Because of the fallenness of human nature, and because God's response to that fallenness is seen in his incarnation, Christian theology must be for Luther a *theologia crucis*. Combining the imagery of both, we might say first that the "Word" (Scripture) is therefore the access to the "Word" (Christ) and second that the "Word" (Christ) is the access to the Father. Both men agree on the latter point, but Anselm essentially fails to see the former point. Herein then is a crude summary of their agreement and disagreement.

I say crude, because there of course is much more to it than this. Where Luther was a man of *angst*, of argument, of the heat of battle, of the theology of the cross, and of the church militant, Anselm is seen to be a man of beauty, of serenity, of repose, and of the church at peace. So appropriate to each was his preferred setting: for Anselm there was the quietude of the monastery and its pastoral simplicity, whereas for the Reformer there was the turmoil of the University at Wittenberg set in the midst of a turbulent Germany. We might therefore point simply to these as differences in outlook or (to open a can of worms) in personality, and attribute any variance between these figures to these roots. But that would be to beg the question. What was it that made Luther the man of war and Anselm the man of peace? Can we not say that the roots of difference run deeper than this?

Early on I suggested that there was something fundamentally at stake in recognizing that certain articles of doctrine are easier to treat by examining Anselm first and then comparing Luther, while others are best treated vice-versa. The universality of sin, the justice of God, and the vicarious satisfaction were, in my estimation, easiest to treat from the Anselm-to-Luther angle, while Christology, the love of God, and faith appeared best to examine looking from Luther-to-Anselm. These, I pointed out at the outset, would correlate with some more significant differences.

Having now discussed the more significant differences, this correlation can be made. We have seen that the major areas of difference can be found primarily in two places, of which the first is the question of the essence of sin, and the second is in the realm of method and purpose. Now let us consider the relationship of these two. I have shown that method and purpose are not insignificant points of difference, inasmuch as Anselm's *sola ratione* is fundamentally at odds with Luther's *sola scriptura*, at least in terms of how one's faith moves forward. For Anselm, faith is moving forward, i.e., *quaerens intellectum*, when it is investigating the *ratione* for itself. Karl Barth (1960, 20f) held that for Anselm the essence of faith is essentially to seek *intellectum*, noting that *credo ut intelligam* is not a storming of the gates of heaven, since only revelation can do this. And this, Barth contends, is the reason for the absence of crisis in Anselm's theologizing (26). But the real reason the exercise of faith's seeking is devoid of crisis for Anselm (and for Barth!), is that in it Christ is not removed existentially, but merely intellectually. For Luther, the crisis (*Anfechtung*) of faith is a real challenge to faith itself, and not merely to the *intellectus*. The *Anfechtungen* of faith are not merely exercises of the mind which can as it were be turned on or off at will, as in Anselm's *sola ratione* exercises.

They are, rather, forced upon the Christian by way of trials and a theology of the cross.

For Anselm, it is the character of faith to understand itself; for Luther, faith seeks not so much the *intellectus* but the *certitudo* which only the Gospel can give. Where in Anselm the seeking of faith is for its *ratio*, which is desirable because of its *pulchritudo*, in Luther, faith is ever learning to trust precisely where there is no *pulchritudo* to be found either in experience or in the understanding. Luther can speak in more than one sense of faith's trusting where it cannot see. On one hand faith trusts where it cannot experience the help of God; on the other it trusts also where it cannot comprehend the goodness of God in what the intellect receives: for Luther the ultimate in faith is to believe God merciful when he damns so many and saves so few (WA 18, 633; AE 33, 62). But it is precisely here, where faith cannot obtain further *intellectus*, and the *quaerens* of Anselm is at an end, that Luther finds opportunity for faith to wax strongest. So the areas which are most clearly Anselm's points of stress are primarily areas fit for rational estimation: universal sin, divine justice, and vicarious satisfaction. These three, when factored together, result in a rational, pulchritudinal balance. But the areas of Luther's high stress, Christology, divine lovingkindness, and faith, are those areas which the Christian whose experience is existentially devoid of these things must learn to know. Luther must stress what Sacred Scripture stresses as the needed Gospel for a sinner who is troubled about his status before God.

It is at this point that it becomes evident that for Luther faith's advancement can only come about by means of the power of the Word of God. Luther's employment of that Word at every turn contrasts him sharply against Anselm and his *sola ratione* methodology, and at the root of this contrast are fundamental differences in view on the nature of faith, the nature of sin, and on the nature of grace. Anselm's conception of sin as privation has him attempting

by means of faith's seeking to replace what has been lost; Luther's conception of
sin as an inbred and comprehensive wickedness leaves him no alternative but to
turn away from any *ratione* to which he may have access by nature; for all is
soiled with sin. But Luther turns to the word of the Gospel for grace.

Anselm's *sola ratione* method betrays a failure to grasp the power and
fullness of the word of the Gospel; perhaps this is due to what Luther calls his
weak definition of sin, and with it a tendency to make the Gospel into something
it is not already deemed to be, because in itself it is not seen to be potent enough
for the purpose of faith's growth. Anselm's desire was to analyze the Word with
reason so that by reason *pulchritudo* may be attained. So Anselm added the
method which reason provides. But for Luther, there is no *pulchritudo*
recognizable to faith other than that of the Gospel itself. The Gospel, therefore,
is for Luther the only end and goal of faith.

Was the atonement "necessary"? For Anselm, the very question is
speculative, and he ventures to answer speculatively. His answer to the question,
then, is to declare, by reason alone, that matters could not have been otherwise,
lest inconsistency arise within God. Anselm sees this as an exercise of faith's
seeking, and therefore as a salutary venture of the mind. Luther, on the contrary,
understands necessity differently, in accordance with what God has revealed.
Yes, the atonement was necessary, then, because this is what happened, and God
is God. So while Luther and Anselm both answer the question of necessity
similarly, their answers are in fact voiced from quite different perspectives.
Anselm employs reason where Luther employs Scripture.

But the difference does not stop here. For Luther, necessity does not stop
with the atonement in itself. As necessary as the atonement is, so is the
preaching of the atonement necessary, and Luther, understanding himself as
having been appointed by God himself to the *Predigtamt*, the preaching office,
must therefore of necessity preach. Not only was the atonement necessary;

preaching is necessary too. This is not to say that the preaching of the Gospel is in itself part of the act of redemption (contra Forde 1984, 68). Luther is clear on this: The Word is not a means of redemption but a means of grace (WA 26, 40; cited in Siggins 1970, 74). As God's appointed means of grace, however, the necessity for its preaching is just as great as the necessity for the atonement; Luther cannot speak of the atonement without the realization that his speaking of it is his task as a preacher: he is to bring it before the people. Thus Luther is not free to speculate, and to engage in *sola ratione* exercises would in fact be contrary to his vocation.

This, then, is how Anselm and Luther truly differ. The notion of incompatibility in their views on the meaning of the atonement has been alive long enough. It was born in the nineteenth-century attack on Theodosius Harnack by Albrecht Ritschl, awakened in Gustaf Aulén's *Christus Victor*, and fed by Gerhard Forde's recent dogmatics text. But it is wrong. These analyses have missed the true differences between them, not having been careful to examine each on his own terms. Both Luther and Anselm speak in terms of payment for sin, of substitution, and of redemption by the blood of Christ. This is not where they differ, and if we fail to see this, we will not be able to appreciate the remaining similarities and differences, the discussion of which is far more fruitful.

What Anselm and Luther shared, besides a traditional, essentially Chalcedonian theology, was a fluent and abundant use of the Sacred Scriptures in their discourse. Both tended, in this sense, to have a more or less patristic form of writing. Though for differing reasons, both tended to prefer the terms, phrases, and grammar of Scripture to their own, and both were so familiar with Scripture that they were able to use it at will in their own speech. This, in my estimation, is one of the most refreshing elements to be found both in Anselm and in Luther. In some respects it is in Anselm, with his derivation of pulchritude from the language of the Scriptures, that the greater satisfaction in reading is gained. It is unfortunate that he lost this penchant for capitalizing on the beauty of the Scriptural vocabulary after some years at Canterbury. In my estimation it is from his earlier years—extending just as far as the writing of the *Cur Deus Homo*—that his more compelling and hence more fruitful writing is found. The most convincing evidence that he lost this writing style is found in the correspondence between him and Bishop Walram, coming near the end of Anselm's life; might we not have expected Walram's weaving of Scriptural quotations into his letter to Anselm to have rekindled in the latter at least some flourish of his own former manner of writing? But evidently Anselm had lost this touch. Perhaps Anselm came to the point, after all, of recognizing for himself the apparent inconsistency of employing this Biblical design in speech together with the *sola ratione/remoto Christo* methodology, and he resolved the inconsistency in favor of the method. Whatever the reason, it is most clearly in his Biblical language—until this was lost on him—and not in his method that Anselm's works are found to bear a certain likeness in appearance to Luther's.

But even here, the similarity stops with the appearance, for Anselm's aim in his employment of the vocabulary of Scripture was pulchritude, while Luther's, on the other hand, was power. Luther's profuse employment of Scripture in his writing was compatible with his convictions about the poverty of his own reason and strength and about the strength of God in, with, and under the words and meaning of the Gospel. Since these words are the words of Scripture, Luther employs Scripture in abundance, in order that his proclamation may be rife with the power of God.

Anselm was at heart a speculator, the first in a long line of them which continues to the present day. For him, and for them, the atonement is fit to probe, to ponder, and to analyze in abstraction. But for Luther, the atonement by itself, while complete in itself, is not helpful until it is preached; and Luther was at heart a preacher of that Gospel of Christ whose blood of atonement takes away the sin of the world.   These matters are not so much for peripatetic schoolman to muse over in the idyllic confines of the universities or monasteries, far from the danger of opposition and violence against them; they are meant rather for a militant Church, for the preachers to bring to the highways and hedges, whatever the cost personally, and whatever the consequences.   For Luther these matters, which are the sum and substance of the Word of God, are not meant for abstract discussion, but at every turn for proclamation.   For it is only by proclamation that the necessity adhering to the atonement is fully realized.

Appendix 1

THE *MONOLOGION*

TABLE OF CONTENTS[1]

Chapter

---

[1]S I, 9-12.

10.   That that thought is a kind of expression of things, even as an artist forms first in his mind what he makes.

11.   That however many similarities there are in that analogy, it is deficient.

12.   That this expression of the Highest Essence is the Highest Essence.

13.   That, as all beings are made through the Highest Essence, so they live through it.

14.   That this being is in all things and through all, and all things are from it and through it and in it.

15.   What it is possible or not possible to say concerning that being substantially.

16.   That it is the same for this being to be just as it is to be justice; and that mode of expression is the same with regard to attributes that can be spoken of similarly; and that nothing of these shows what sort or how great it is, but what it is.

17.   That it is likewise simple that all things which can be said of its essence, are one and the same in it, and nothing can be said of it substantially except in terms of that which is.

18.   That it is without beginning and without end.

19.   How it is that nothing existed before nor will exist after this being.

20.   That that being exists in every place and time.

21.   That it exists in no place or time.

22.   How it is in every and in no place and time.

23.   How it is better understood as being able to be everywhere than in every place.

24.   How it is better understood as being able to exist always than at every time.

25.   That it never changes by accidents.

26.   How that nature is called and is substance, and that it is beyond all substances, and uniquely is what it is.

27.   That it is not included among commonly treated substances, yet is a substance and an indivisible Spirit.

28.   That the same Spirit exists simply, and created beings are not comparable to it.

29.   That his expression is not the same as himself, yet neither are there two, but one Spirit.

30.   That the same expression is not comprised of many words, but is one Word.

31.   That the same Word is not like created beings, but their true essence, created beings being a kind of imitation of his true essence; and which natures are greater than others and preferable to them.

32.   That the Highest Spirit expresses himself by the coeternal Word.

33.   That by the one Word he expresses himself and what he makes.

the Father and the Son the same essence and wisdom, etc.

59.   That the Father and the Son and their Spirit exist equally in each other.
60.   That none of them needs another for memory or intelligence or love, because each is singularly memory and intelligence and love and whatever is necessary to the Highest Essence.
61.   That nonetheless there are not three, but one Father and Son and Spirit of both.
62.   How it seems that of these many sons are born.
63.   How it is that there is not other than one [Son] of one [Father].
64.   How this, though inexplicable, is nonetheless to be believed.
65.   How by this there can be true discussion of an ineffable thing.
66.   How the nearest approach to the knowledge of the Highest Essence is through the rational mind.
67.   That the mind itself is the mirror and the image of that being.
68.   How the rational creature was made to love that being.
69.   That the soul always loving that Being at the same time truly lives in blessedness.
70.   That that being gives himself in return to that soul that loves him.
71.   That the one who contemns that Being is eternally in misery.
72.   That every human soul is immortal.
73.   That it is ever miserable or at some time is truly blessed.
74.   That no soul is unjustly deprived of the supreme good; and that every effort is to be made toward it.
75.   That the Highest Essence is to be hoped for.
76.   That we must believe in that Essence.
77.   That we must believe in the Father and the Son and their Spirit equally and singularly, and at the same time in all three.
78.   What is living and what dead faith.
79.   Why it is possible to say that the Highest Essence is in some way three.
80.   That the same, lord of all and ruler of all, is alone God.

Appendix 2

---

[2]S II, 44-46.

Book Two

Reference List

PRIMARY WORKS

Anselm of Canterbury (1033-1109):

Critical edition:

1946   *Sancti Anselmi Opera Omnia*. Edited by Franciscus
            Schmitt. Five volumes plus a volume of indices.
            Edinburgh: Thomas Nelson & Sons.

Translations:

1956   *A Scholastic Miscellany: Anselm to Ockham*. Edited and
            translated by Eugene Fairweather. The Library of
            Christian Classics, Ichthus Edition. Philadelphia:
            Westminster.

1973   *The Prayers and Meditations of St. Anselm*. Translated
            with an introduction by Benedicta Ward. Middlesex,
            England: Penguin Books.

1974-76   *Anselm of Canterbury.* Edited and translated by Jasper
                 Hopkins and Herbert W. Richardson. Three volumes, plus
                 companion volume. SCM, London, and Edwin Mellen,
                 Toronto and New York.

Martin Luther (1483-1546):

German/Latin editions:

1880-1910   *Martin Luthers sämmtliche Schriften.* Edited by Johan
                 Georg Walch. Second edition, in modern German. 23
                 volumes. St. Louis: Concordia.

1883-   *D. Martin Luthers Werke.* Kritische Gesamtausgabe. 58
                 volumes. Weimar.

1903-1948   *D. Martin Luthers Werke.* Briefwechsel. Weimar.

1906-   *D. Martin Luthers Werke.* Deutsche Bibel. Weimar.

1912-1921   *D. Martin Luthers Werke.* Tischreden. Weimar.

1921   *Concordia Triglotta: Die symbolischen Bücher der
                 evangelisch-lutherischen Kirche.* German, Latin, English.
                 Translated by Gerhard Friedrich Bente and William H. T.
                 Dau. Introduction by Gerhard Friedrich Bente. St. Louis:
                 Concordia.

Translations:

1955-   *Luther's Works.* American Edition. Edited by J. Pelikan
                 and H. T. Lehman. 55 volumes, plus companion volume.
                 St. Louis: Concordia and Philadelphia: Fortress.

1982   *Day by Day We Magnify Thee: Daily Readings for the
                 Church Year Selected from the writings of Martin Luther.*
                 Edited and translated by Margarete Steiner and Percy Scott.
                 London: Epworth Press, n.d.; reprint, Philadelphia:
                 Fortress (page references are to reprint edition).

1988   *Sermons of Martin Luther*. Translated by John Nicholas
                Lenker et al. Minneapolis: Lutherans in All Lands, 1905,
                under the title *The Precious and Sacred Writings of Martin
                Luther*. Reprint, Grand Rapids, Michigan: Baker Book
                House (page references are to reprint edition).

Other Primary sources:

Eadmer (c1060–c1130):

1962   *The Life of St. Anselm, Archbishop of Canterbury*. Edited
                with introduction, notes, and translation on pages facing the
                Latin text, by R. W. Southern. Oxford: Clarendon Press.

Irenaeus, (d. c200):

1987   "Against Heresies." In *The Ante-Nicene Fathers:
                Translations of the Writings of the Fathers down to A.D.
                325*, ed., Alexander Roberts and James Donaldson, 309–
                567. Edinburgh, n.d.; reprint, Grand Rapids, Michigan:
                Eerdmans (page references are to reprint edition).

Augustine of Hippo (354-430):

1857-1912   *Patrologia, cursus completus, series latina*. Edited by J.
                P. Migne.   221 vols., of which vols. 32-46 contain
                Augustine's works. Paris.

SECONDARY WORKS

Adams, Marilyn McCord
    1969   Introduction to *Predestination, God's Foreknowledge, and
                        Future Contingents*, by William of Ockham, transl.,
                        Marilyn McCord Adams and Norman Kretzmann. New
                        York: Appleton-Century-Crofts.

Althaus, Paul
    1966   *The Theology of Martin Luther*. Translated by Robert C.
                        Schulz.   German original, 2nd edition, Gütersloh,
                        Germany: Gütersloher Verlaghaus Gerd Mohn, 1963.
                        Philadelphia: Fortress.

Aulén, Gustaf
    1969   *Christus Victor: an Historical Study of the Three Main
                        Types of the Idea of the Atonement*. Translated by A. G.
                        Hebert.   Forward by Jaroslav Pelikan.   New York:
                        Macmillan. First published in 1931.

Barth, Karl
    1960   *Anselm: Fides Quaerens Intellectum*. Translated by Ian W.
                        Robertson.   German original, n.p., 1931; 2nd edition,
                        Zürich: Evangelischer Verlag A. G., 1958; reprint,
                        London: SCM Press.

Bente, Gerhard Friedrich
    1921   "Historical Introductions to the Symbolical Books of the
                        Evangelical Lutheran Church."   In *Concordia Triglotta:
                        Die symbolischen Bücher der evangelisch-lutherischen
                        Kirche*, St. Louis: Concordia, 3-266.

Bertram, Robert W.
    1985   " 'Faith alone Justifies': Luther on *Iustitia Fidei*. Theses."
                        In *Justification by Faith: Lutherans and Catholics in
                        Dialogue VII*, ed. H. George Anderson, T. Austin Murphy
                        and Joseph A. Burgess, 172-184. Minneapolis: Augsburg.

Boyle, Marjorie O'Rourke
1989   "A Likely Story: The Autobiographical as Epideictic,"
               Journal of the American Academy of Religion LVII/1
               (Spring).

Burgess, Joseph
1985   "Rewards, but in a Very Different Sense." In
               *Justification by Faith: Lutherans and Catholics in Dialogue
               VII*, ed., H. George Anderson, T. Austin Murphy and
               Joseph A. Burgess. Minneapolis: Augsburg, 94-110.

Congar, Yves Marie
1983   "'Novo et Miro Vocabulo et Theologico.' Luther,
               Reformateur de la theologie." RHPR, 1983, 63 (1/2):7-
               15.

Dillistone, F. W.
1984   *The Christian Understanding of Atonement.* First published
               1968. London: SCM.

Dockery, David S.
1983   "Martin Luther's christological hermeneutics." Grace Th
               J 4, 189-203.

Ebeling, Gerhard
1970   *Luther: An Introduction to his Thought.* Translated by R.
               A. Wilson from the German *Luther: Einführung in sein
               Denken*, Tübingen: JCB Mohr (Paul Siebeck), 1964.
               London: William Collins Sons, and Philadelphia: Fortress.

Eckardt, Burnell F., Jr.
1985   "Luther and Moltmann: The Theology of the Cross," CTQ
               49: 19-28.

Edwards, Mark U., Jr.
1983   *Luther's Last Battles: Politics and Polemics, 1531-46.*
               Ithaca, NY, and London: Cornell University Press.

Evans, Gillian R.
1978   *Anselm and Talking about God.* Oxford: Clarendon.

_____.

1980   *Anselm and a New Generation.* Oxford: Clarendon.

_____.

1989   *Anselm.* Outstanding Christian Thinkers Series, ed. Brian
                Davies. London: Geoffrey Chapman; Wilton, Connecticut:
                Morehouse-Barlow.

Fabrizius, Karl F.
1988   Augustine and the Pastoral Office. Unpublished graduate
                paper written for Father Joseph Lienhard at Marquette
                University.

Fagerberg, Holsten
1972   *A New Look at the Lutheran Confessions (1529-1537).*
                Translated by Gene J. Lund. St. Louis: Concordia.

Fairweather, Eugene, ed. and transl.
1956   *A Scholastic Miscellany: Anselm to Ockham.* The Library
                of Christian Classics, Ichthus Edition. Philadelphia:
                Westminster.

Forde, Gerhard R.
1969   *The Law-Gospel Debate: An Interpretation of Its Historical
                Development.* Minneapolis: Augsburg.

_____.

1984   "The Work of Christ." In *Christian Dogmatics*, vol. 2,
                ed. Carl E. Braaten and Robert W. Jenson, 5-104.
                Philadelphia: Fortress.

Froelich, Karlfried
1985   "Justification Language in the Middle Ages." In
                *Justification by Faith: Lutherans and Catholics in Dialogue
                VII*, ed. H. George Anderson, T. Austin Murphy and
                Joseph A. Burgess, 143-161. Minneapolis: Augsburg.

Green, Lowell C.
1980   *How Melanchthon Helped Luther Discover the Gospel.*
                Fallbrook, CA: Verdict Publications.

Hagen, Kenneth
    1989   Luther's Approach to Scripture as seen in his
                    'Commentaries' on Galatians 1519-1538. Copyrighted
                    manuscript in preparation.

Harnack, Theodosius (1817-1889)
    1969   *Luthers Theologie mit besonderer Beziehung auf seine
                    Versöhnungs - und Erlösungslehre.* First edition, Erlangen:
                    Andreas Deichert, 1886. Reprint edition, Amsterdam:
                    Rodop.

Hartshorne, Charles
    1965   *Anselm's Discovery: A Re-examination of the Ontological
                    Proof for God's Existence.* La Salle, Illinois: Open Court.

Hoffman, Bengt R.
    1976   *Luther and the Mystics: A re-examination of Luther's
                    spiritual experience and his relationship to the mystics.*
                    Minneapolis: Augsburg.

Hofmann, Johann Christian Konrad von
    1959   *Interpreting the Bible.* Translated from the German by
                    Christian Preus. Minneapolis: Augsburg.

Holl, Karl
    1977   *What Did Luther Understand by Religion?* Edited by
                    James L. Adams and Walter F. Bense. Translated by Fred
                    W. Meuser and Walter R. Wietzke, from the essay "Was
                    verstand Luther unter Religion?" in Karl Holl, *Gesammelte
                    Aufsätze zur Kirchengeschichte*, vol. 1, 1-110, Tübingen:
                    JCB Mohr [Paul Siebeck], 7th ed., 1948. Philadelphia:
                    Fortress.

Hopkins, Jasper
    1972   *A Companion to the Study of St. Anselm.* Minneapolis:
                    University of Minnesota press.

_____.
    1976   *Anselm of Canterbury, Volume Four: Hermeneutical and
                    Textual Problems in the Complete Treatises of St. Anselm.*
                    Toronto and New York: Edwin Mellen.

Janz, Denis R.
1989   *Luther on Thomas Aquinas: the Angelic Doctor in the*
                Thought of the Reformer. Stuttgart: Franz Steiner Verlag
                Wiesbaden GMBH.

Knowles, David
1962   *The Evolution of Medieval Thought.* Baltimore: Helicon.

Loewenich, Walther von
1976   *Luther's Theology of the Cross.* Translated by Herbert J.
                A. Bouman.   German edition first published 1933.
                Minneapolis: Augsburg.

McDonough, Thomas M.
1963   *The Law and the Gospel in Luther: A Study of Martin
                Luther's Confessional Writings.*   London: Oxford
                University Press.

McIntyre, John
1954   *St. Anselm and His Critics.* Edinburgh: Oliver & Boyd.

Moltmann, Jürgen
1974   *The Crucified God: the Cross of Christ as the Foundation
                and Criticism of Christian Theology.* Translated by R. A.
                Wilson and John Bowden.

Pesch, Otto Hermann
1972   *The God Question in Thomas Aquinas and Martin Luther.*
                Translated by Gottfried G. Krodel. Intro. by Charles S.
                Anderson.   Facet Books, Historical Series — 21
                (Reformation), Charles S. Anderson, ed.   Philadelphia:
                Fortress.

Pfürtner, Stephen
1964   *Luther and Aquinas on Salvation.* Translated by Edward
                Quinn, with introduction by Jaroslav Pelikan. New York:
                Sheed and Ward.

Phelan, Gerald. B.
1960   *The Wisdom of Saint Anselm.* Latrobe, Pennsylvania: The
                Archabbey Press.

Pieper, Francis
1951   *Christian Dogmatics*. Vol. II. First published in German, 1917. St. Louis: Concordia.

Ritschl, Albrecht (1822-1889)
1966   *The Christian Doctrine of Justification and Reconciliation*. Translated and edited by H. R. Mackintosh and A. B.Macaulay. Clifton, New Jersey: Reference Book Publishers.

Saarinen, Risto
1990   "The Word of God in Luther's Theology" *Lutheran Quarterly* 4:1, 31-44.

Scaer, David P.
1976   "Theology of Hope." In *Tensions in Contemporary Theology*, ed., Stanley N. Gundry and Alan F. Johnson, 197-236. Chicago: Moody.

Schlink, Edmund
1961   *The Theology of the Lutheran Confessions*. Translated by Paul F. Koehneke and Herbert J. A. Bouman. First published in German, 1948. Philadelphia: Fortress.

Schütte, Heinz
1980   "On the Possibility of a Catholic Recognition of the *Confessio Augustana* as a Legitimate Expression of Christian Truth." In *The Role of the Augsburg Confession: Catholic and Lutheran Views*, ed., Joseph A. Burgess, 47-67. Philadelphia: Fortress.

Schwiebert, Ernest G.
1950   *Luther and His Times: the Reformation from a New Perspective*. St. Louis: Concordia.

Siggins, Ian
1970   *Martin Luther's Doctrine of Christ*. New Haven, Connecticut: Yale University Press.

Southern, Richard W.
1983   "Anselm at Canterbury." In *Anselm Studies: an Occasional Journal*, I, edited by Marjorie Chibnall, Gillian Evans, et. al, 7-22. Millwood, New York: Kraus International Publications.

Stock, Brian.
1983   *The Implications of Literacy: Written Language and Models of Interpretation in the Eleventh and Twelfth Centuries.* Princeton, New Jersey: Princeton University Press.

Tavard, George H.
1959   *Holy Writ or Holy Church.* London: Burns & Oates.

_____.
1983   *Justification: an Ecumenical Study.* New York: Paulist Press.

Ward, Benedicta
1973   *The Prayers and Meditations of St. Anselm*, translated and with an introduction. Middlesex, England: Penguin Books.

General Index

Index of Anselm's Works

Index of Luther's Works

Sermons

Index of Scripture References

DDS